Beyond the Annual Budget

Beyond the Annual Budget

Global Experience with Medium-Term Expenditure Frameworks

THE WORLD BANK
Washington, D.C.

Contents

Figures

Map

Tables

Acknowledgments

This report was closely supervised by Jim Brumby (World Bank) and represents a collaborative effort involving Nataliya Biletska (World Bank), Francesco Grigoli (World Bank, currently International Monetary Fund), Richard Hemming (Duke University), Young Kyu Kang (World Bank), Jong Wook Lee (World Bank, currently with the Ministry of Strategy and Finance of the Republic of Korea), Zachary Mills (World Bank), Saw Young Min (World Bank), Blanca Moreno-Dodson (World Bank), Razvan Vlaicu (University of Maryland), Marijn Verhoeven (World Bank), Ha Vu (World Bank), and Laura Zoratto (World Bank).

The review of global experience with medium-term expenditure frameworks (MTEFs) and publication of this report were greatly assisted by the generous financial support of the Korea Development Institute School of Public Policy and Management and Norwegian Ministry of Foreign Affairs. This support is gratefully acknowledged.

Special thanks are due to the contributors to the case studies: for Albania, Erjon Luci (World Bank); for Armenia, Gohar Gyulumyan (World Bank); for Brazil, Tarsila Velloso (World Bank); for Ghana, Ghada Ahmed and Richard Hemming (Duke University); for Jordan, Manal Fouad (International Monetary Fund); for the Republic of Korea, Young Sun Koh (Korea Development Institute); for Nicaragua, José Eduardo Gutiérrez Ossio (World Bank); for the Russian Federation, Bill Dorotinsky

(World Bank); for South Africa, Ghada Ahmed and Richard Hemming (Duke University); and for Uganda, Tony Verheijen (World Bank).

Data on MTEF status were provided by staff of the World Bank, the International Monetary Fund, and the Organisation for Economic Co-operation and Development (OECD) as well as by the authorities of many countries. The main authors would like to acknowledge the inputs from colleagues within and outside the World Bank.

The authors would also like to thank the peer reviewers, including Richard Allen (World Bank, currently International Monetary Fund), Adrian Fozzard (World Bank), Verena Fritz (World Bank), Malcolm Holmes (formerly World Bank), Philip Keefer (World Bank), Ian Lienert (formerly International Monetary Fund), Rino Schiavo-Campo (formerly World Bank), and Pazhayannur Subramanian (World Bank), for their valuable comments. Ghada Ahmed (Duke University) assisted with the case studies.

The views expressed in this report are entirely those of the authors and do not necessarily reflect the views of the World Bank Group, the institutions with which the authors are affiliated, or the countries they represent. Errors remain our own.

Abbreviations

AAA	analytical and advisory activities
AIDS	acquired immune deficiency syndrome
BII	Budget Institutions Index
BPEMS	Budgeting and Public Expenditure Management System, Ghana
CIDA	Canadian International Development Agency
CPIA	country policy and institutional assessment
CSCW	Centre for the Study of Civil War
DFID	U.K. Department for International Development
DPI	Database of Political Institutions
DPL	development policy loan
DROND	Report on Results and Main Areas of Activity, Russia
EC	European Commission
ESW	economic and sector work
FAD	Fiscal Affairs Department, IMF
FPD	Finance and Private Sector Development (network)
GDP	gross domestic product
GIZ	German Agency for International Cooperation
GMM	generalized method of moments
GPRS	Government Poverty Reduction Strategy, Albania
HDN	Human Development Network

HIPC	Heavily Indebted Poor Country
HIV	human immunodeficiency virus
HP	Hodrick-Prescott
ICR	Implementation Completion Report
IMF	International Monetary Fund
ISR	Implementation Status Report
KAGA	Key Areas of the Government Activities till 2012, Russia
LDO	Budget Guidelines Law, Brazil
MoF	Ministry of Finance
MoFEP	Ministry of Finance and Economic Planning, Ghana
MoFPED	Ministry of Finance, Planning, and Economic Development, Uganda
MoSF	Ministry of Strategy and Finance, Korea
MTBF	medium-term budgetary framework
MTEF	medium-term expenditure framework
MTFF	medium-term fiscal framework
MTPF	medium-term performance framework
NDP	national development plan
NFMP	National Fiscal Management Plan, Korea
NSDI	National Strategies for Development and Integration, Albania
OBI	Open Budget Index
OECD	Organisation for Economic Co-operation and Development
OLS	ordinary least squares
OPCS	Operations Policy and Country Services
PEAP	Poverty Eradication Action Plan, Uganda
PEFA	public expenditure and financial accountability
PER	Public Expenditure Review
PFM	public financial management
PforR	program for results
PIMI	Public Investment Management Index
PIP	public investment plan
PPA	*Plano Plurianual* (for Brazil)
PPP	purchasing power parity
PREM	Poverty Reduction and Economic Management
PRSC	Poverty Reduction Strategy Credit
PRSP	Poverty Reduction Strategy Paper
PUFMARP	Public Financial Management Reform Program, Ghana
ROSC	Report on the Observance of Standards and Codes, IMF
S&P	Standard and Poor's
SAR	Special Administrative Region

SDN	Sustainable Development Network
SIGFA	*Sistema Integrado de Gestión, Administrativa, Financiera, y Auditoría* (information financial management system), Nicaragua
SNIP	*Sistema Nacional de Inversión Pública* (National System for Public Investment), Nicaragua
SWAP	sectorwide approach
TA	technical assistance
UN	United Nations
USAID	U.S. Agency for International Development
WDI	World Development Indicators
WEO	World Economic Outlook
WGI	World Governance Indicators
WHO	World Health Organization

CHAPTER 1

Introduction

By the end of 2008, more than two-thirds of all countries had adopted a medium-term expenditure framework (MTEF). As map 1.1 shows, MTEFs are found in countries all across the world. Even though they have been around since the early 1980s, MTEFs did not gain prominence until the late 1990s. Two trends explain their spread. Low- and middle-income countries adopted MTEFs primarily because donors viewed them as a way to ensure a multiyear commitment of resources to the policies included in poverty reduction strategy papers (PRSPs) and incorporated them into their standard advice on budget reforms. The World Bank has been involved with MTEF reforms in more than half of these countries. High-income countries adopted MTEFs as a way to support budgetary targets, improve expenditure prioritization, and foster improved government performance.

However, successful implementation of MTEFs and their impact on budget management and fiscal performance vary widely across countries. An MTEF requires policy makers to look across sectors, programs, and projects to examine how public spending can best serve national development objectives over the medium term. In doing so, they must weigh the importance attached to short-term goals against that attached to medium-term objectives and set aside the narrow self-interests of spending

Map 1.1 MTEFs Worldwide, 2008

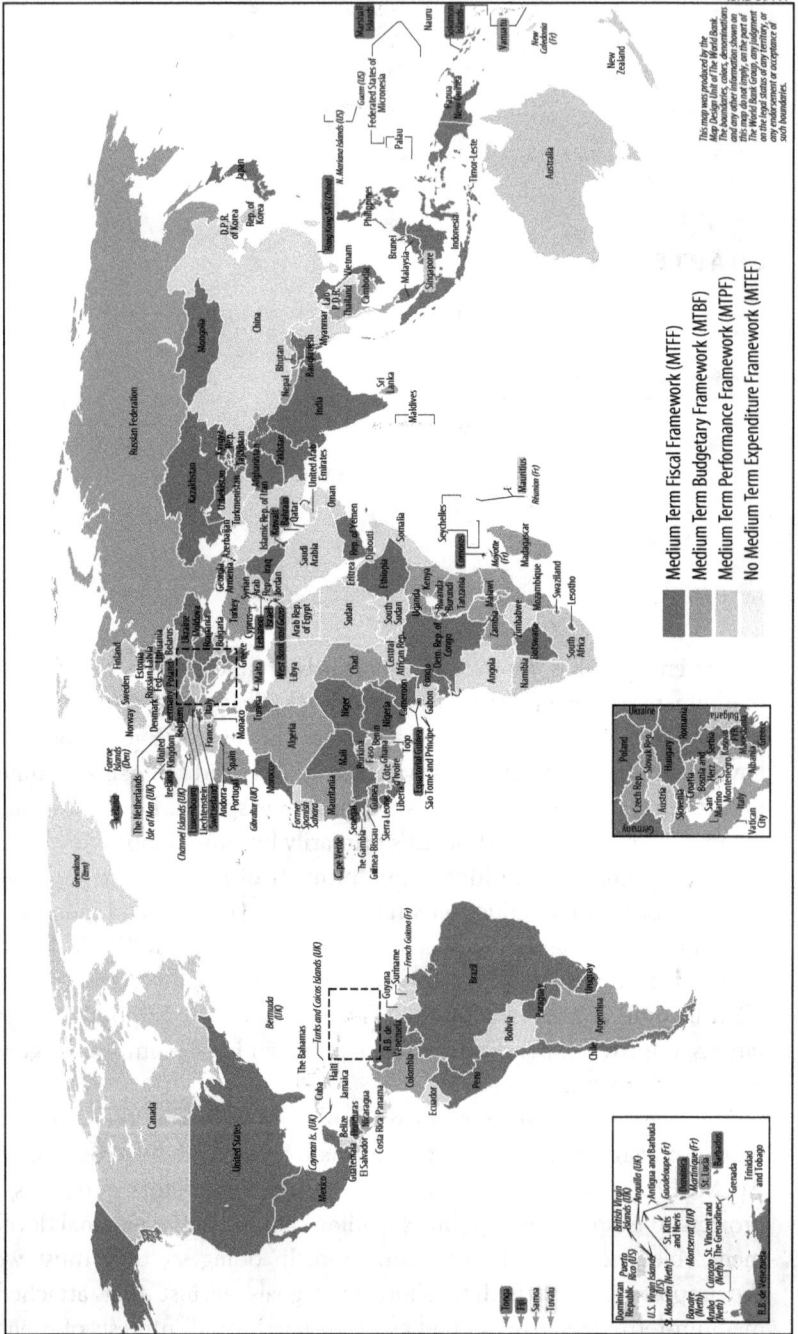

Medium Term Fiscal Framework (MTFF)

Medium Term Budgetary Framework (MTBF)

Medium Term Performance Framework (MTPF)

No Medium Term Expenditure Framework (MTEF)

IBRD 39441

This map was produced by the Map Design Unit of The World Bank. The boundaries, colors, denominations and any other information shown on this map do not imply, on the part of The World Bank Group, any judgment on the legal status of any territory, or any endorsement or acceptance of such boundaries.

JUNE 2012

Source: World Bank.

2

agencies, politicians, and spending beneficiaries. Prioritization subject to resource constraints becomes the guiding principle of budgeting. The general view is that economic, political, and institutional factors have limited the application of this principle, along with the effectiveness of MTEFs.

In this connection, some analytical studies from the early 2000s, by the World Bank and others, identify important shortcomings of planning and implementation of MTEF reforms. These studies, which focus mainly on low-income countries, conclude that reforms have not paid sufficient attention to basic aspects of budget management or adequately addressed the political and institutional realities of budget reform. These weaknesses cast doubt on the feasibility of introducing full-fledged MTEFs in developing countries.

MTEFs have also been a subject of recent Bank evaluations. A report prepared by the Quality Assurance Group (QAG) notes that MTEFs have performed differently across regions and have been least successful in Africa (QAG 2008). Working for the Bank's Independent Evaluation Group, Wescott (2008) points to the decisive role of entry points—that is, whether MTEFs are first tried in sectors where they are likely to deliver the most success—in shaping the outcome of MTEF reforms. The QAG concludes, "There is a strong case for a Bank-wide review of the experience with MTEFs and lessons drawn."

This study responds to the QAG's conclusion by reporting on a comprehensive review of the experience with MTEFs that addresses some of the limitations of previous studies. It looks at the experiences of countries with and without MTEFs over the period 1990 to 2008, when most reforms were adopted.[1] It does so by employing a systematic methodological approach that relies on multiple analytical techniques, including event studies and econometric analysis, to obtain results about the impact of MTEFs on fiscal performance. It then draws on case study and other material to (a) determine whether MTEFs should be a common element of public financial management (PFM) systems given differences in country circumstances and (b) provide guidance on the design and implementation of MTEFs in the context of broader advice about PFM reform.[2]

In the process, the study attempts to answer the following policy questions:

- What initial economic, political, institutional, and other conditions determine the success of MTEFs? Are there key country, PFM, and MTEF characteristics that are critical for success?

- How should the implementation of MTEFs be sequenced and coordinated with other budget reforms?
- What role should the Bank, bilateral development partners, and other international agencies play in supporting the adoption of MTEFs?

Based on the answers to these questions, the study then provides guidance on the following:

- Is an MTEF always appropriate, or do differences in country circumstances call for different approaches?
- What characteristics give an MTEF a good chance of succeeding in different country circumstances?
- Are some ways of implementing a new MTEF or strengthening an existing one better than others?

This study is intended first and foremost to inform the World Bank's advice on MTEFs and PFM reform in general. It should also be of interest to other multilateral and bilateral providers of technical assistance in the area of PFM and to country authorities seeking to introduce or strengthen an MTEF.

The report is structured as follows. Chapter 2 provides background on what constitutes an MTEF and what it aims to achieve. It also describes the Bank's engagement with MTEFs, presents main points of debate over the experience with MTEFs, and provides a rationale for this study. Chapter 3 describes the key characteristics of MTEFs, explains the approach used to identify and classify them according to their stage of development, and reviews trends in their adoption. Chapter 4 outlines the methodological approaches used to examine the impact of MTEFs on fiscal performance, formulates the research hypotheses that are tested in the study, and presents empirical findings from the event studies and econometric analysis. It also presents qualitative insights, informed by case studies, on how MTEFs have affected the quality of budgeting. Chapter 5 draws some lessons about the key institutional determinants of MTEF performance. Chapter 6 discusses lessons learned from Bank support for MTEF implementation. Chapter 7 presents the conclusions of the study and discusses their implications for the Bank. Several appendixes provide supporting material, including a country-by-country tabulation of MTEF status, a full discussion of econometric results, and country case studies.

Notes

1. It would be instructive to look at how the onset of and recovery from the recent global economic and financial crisis affected the performance of MTEFs. However, data for some key variables used in the analysis are available for 2009, but not for 2010. The results will be revisited once data for 2010 and 2011 become available.

2. Detailed operational advice on the implementation of MTEFs will be provided in follow-up work.

References

QAG (Quality Assurance Group). 2008. "Improving Public Sector Governance Portfolio: Quality Enhancement Review." QAG, World Bank, Washington, DC.

Wescott, C. 2008. "World Bank Support for Public Financial Management: Conceptual Roots and Evidence of Impact." IEG Working Paper, Independent Evaluation Group, World Bank, Washington, DC.

CHAPTER 2

What Are MTEFs and What Can They Do?

Medium-term expenditure frameworks (MTEFs) constitute an approach to budgeting and public financial management (PFM) that addresses well-known shortcomings of annual budgeting, including short-sightedness, conservatism, and parochialism (Wildavsky 1986). Most public programs require funding and yield benefits over a period of years, but annual budgeting largely ignores future costs and benefits. Multiyear budget planning is the defining characteristic of MTEFs. Annual budgets typically start with the previous year's budget and modify it in an incremental manner, making it difficult to reprioritize policies and spending.[1] As a result, spending patterns become entrenched, even in the face of changing needs. MTEFs take a strategic forward-looking approach to establishing priorities and allocating resources, which allows the level and composition of public expenditure to be determined in light of emerging needs. MTEFs also require policy makers to look across sectors, programs, and projects to see how spending can be restructured to best serve established policy objectives. As a consequence, the opportunistic interests of spending agencies and beneficiaries that are a feature of annual budgeting should no longer dominate to the same degree. However, for these benefits to materialize, an MTEF cannot be regarded as separate from and only loosely related to the annual budget. MTEFs must eventually replace the annual budget as the centerpiece of the budget process. Indeed, an MTEF requires budget preparation to go beyond the annual budget to take account of the medium term.

MTEFs translate macrofiscal objectives and constraints into broad budget aggregates and detailed expenditure plans, guided by strategic expenditure priorities. When an MTEF is implemented well, public expenditure is limited by the availability of resources, budget allocations reflect spending priorities, and public goods and services are delivered cost-effectively. MTEFs therefore offer the prospect of achieving the three high-level objectives of public expenditure management: aggregate fiscal discipline, allocative efficiency, and technical efficiency (level-one, -two, and -three budgetary objectives).[2] Traditional annual budgeting often falls short of meeting these objectives. Moreover, with macrofiscal policy increasingly being framed in a medium-term context, guided by debt sustainability analysis, multiyear fiscal targeting, and in some cases permanent fiscal rules, MTEFs establish a formal link between broad fiscal policy objectives and budgeting, which can strengthen the credibility of both. This can be particularly important when countries are implementing a medium-term fiscal adjustment program, since an MTEF can signal a government's commitment to high-quality adjustment based on prioritization of spending and reduction of waste, which are often key to successful adjustment.

MTEFs can also leverage the fact that aggregate fiscal discipline, allocative efficiency, and technical efficiency are closely linked objectives. Governments can focus more on the microeconomic challenges of improving expenditure efficiency when they do not have to address the adverse macroeconomic consequences of persistent fiscal imbalances.[3] Conversely, efficient public spending makes it easier to maintain fiscal discipline, since both allocative and technical efficiency reduce waste and thus alleviate the overall resource constraints. While the search for allocative efficiency does this by squeezing unproductive expenditure programs, technical efficiency requires pursuing objectives with fewer resources. Moreover, when the government is committed to fiscal discipline, new expenditure needs are more likely to be accommodated by reallocating spending than by providing additional funding. Finally, both fiscal discipline and expenditure efficiency create fiscal space that can support productive spending on economic and social infrastructure as well as on other high-priority areas. Fiscal space can also be used to respond to upcoming fiscal challenges (for example, population aging, climate change) as well as ever-present fiscal risks (for example, calls on government guarantees, natural disasters). MTEFs provide a basis for considering these fiscal management challenges and the links between them within a consistent framework.

The power of MTEFs to generate good fiscal performance derives from their impact on the quality of budgeting and budget credibility. MTEFs help to reduce shortcomings of annual budgeting by achieving the following:

- *Budget realism.* The revenue that the government can reasonably expect to collect and the new borrowing that it can safely undertake should place an upper limit on spending. This contrasts with the fairly common situation where governments formulate ambitious annual spending plans based on unreasonable expectations about potential revenue and borrowing capacity.

- *Spending driven by medium-term sector strategies.* Rather than preparing an annual budget by making incremental changes to current programs, determining priorities based on the latest political imperative, budgeting separately for capital and current expenditures, ring-fencing chosen programs and projects, and building other rigidities into the budget, resource allocation should reflect an assessment of priorities within and between sectors based on agreed objectives and policies.

- *Spending agencies with a voice.* Instead of focusing primarily on compliance with expenditure controls, ministries, departments, and other spending agencies should have significant input into the design of sector strategies and some flexibility in managing their resources to pursue sector objectives and implement sector policies efficiently.

- *Budgets containing multiyear spending allocations.* To the extent possible, spending agencies should have a predictable resource envelope to ensure effective decision making, which is lacking when budgeting involves annual negotiations over incremental resources. With an MTEF, spending agencies have reasonable assurance about the resources they are likely to receive over the medium term. This not only makes it easier to plan multiyear expenditures, but also gives spending agencies the confidence to change policy direction.

- *Budget funding linked more closely to results.* A shift in focus from control of inputs to flexibility in the mix of inputs to produce specific outputs and outcomes allows greater emphasis on allocating resources according to the results achieved by spending programs and provides more discretion over the choice of inputs used to achieve particular results.

- *Greater fiscal transparency and accountability.* MTEFs provide a clear-cut mechanism for monitoring government performance against approved plans, which makes it easier to hold governments accountable for their choice of fiscal policies.

The Debate over MTEFs and the Role of the Bank

MTEFs are not a recent innovation, but their spread around the world is a recent phenomenon. In one form or another, MTEFs have been around since at least the early 1980s, when Australia launched its forward estimates system.[4] A few industrial countries followed suit in the 1980s and early 1990s (Denmark, New Zealand, the Netherlands, and Norway), but some African countries implemented MTEFs only in the late 1990s. The specific context in these countries (with the exception of South Africa) was the need to ensure a multiyear commitment of resources to policies included in poverty reduction strategy papers (PRSPs). Donors played an important role in encouraging the implementation of MTEFs. Part of their motivation was to improve public financial management as a means to ensure that external assistance and domestic resources would support development programs directed toward poverty alleviation.

Consequently, the World Bank built MTEFs into the standard budgeting toolkit that it was recommending to client countries at the time. This toolkit became an integral part of the *Public Expenditure Management Handbook*, which says that an MTEF "facilitates the management of policies and budget realities to reduce pressure throughout the whole budget cycle, … results in better control of expenditure and better value for money within a hard budget constraint, and resolves the tensions between what is affordable and what is demanded" (World Bank 1998, 9).[5]

Over the period from 1991 to 2010, the Bank was directly involved with MTEF reform in 109 low- and middle-income countries in all six regions.[6] Products focusing on MTEFs were mainly lending operations, analytical and advisory activities, and, to some extent, technical assistance. As figure 2.1 shows, the number of products has increased significantly over time, especially in the late 1990s and early 2000s, with the total number of products reaching 691 by 2010.[7] The Bank provided advice on

Figure 2.1   MTEF Bank Products in 109 Countries, by Region and Year, 1991–2010

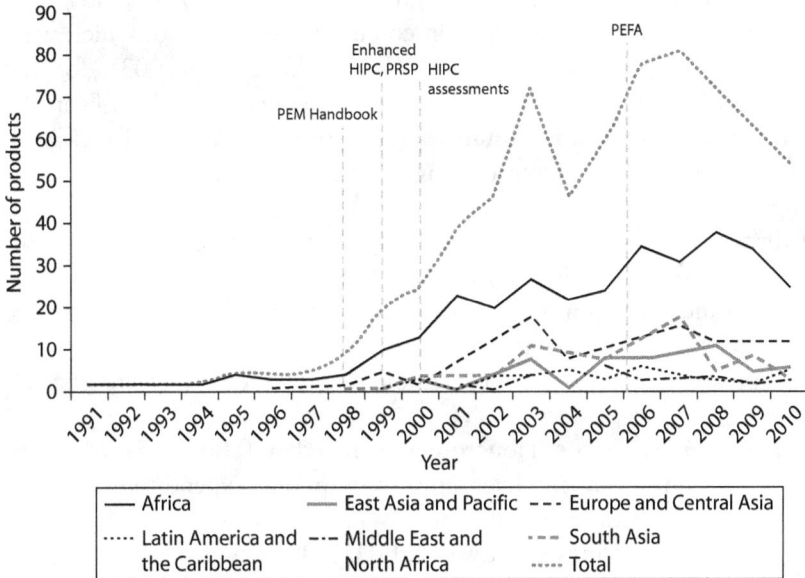

Source: World Bank.
Note: HIPC = Heavily Indebted Poor Countries Initiative; MTEF= medium-term expenditure framework; PEFA = public expenditure and financial accountability assessment; PEM = Public Expenditure Management; PRSP = poverty reduction strategy paper.

MTEFs most actively in Africa (354 products) and in Europe and Central Asia (152 products), mainly in low-income countries. The spikes in the Bank's engagement with MTEF reforms shown in figure 2.1 tend to be associated with broader Bank initiatives in the area of public financial management, such as publication of the *Public Expenditure Management Handbook* (World Bank 1998), the launch of the enhanced Heavily Indebted Poor Countries (HIPC) and PRSP Initiatives, and the introduction of the public expenditure and financial accountability (PEFA) framework or work at the country level, such as the preparation of a PRSP or a PEFA assessment. The objectives most commonly pursued in the context of MTEF reforms supported by the Bank are allocative efficiency, followed by aggregate fiscal discipline. Appendix A provides more detail on Bank operations focusing on MTEFs.

The Bank's involvement with MTEFs picked up significantly despite early concerns that MTEFs might not be living up to expectations. Following some initial reviews that raised issues about MTEF implementation (see, for example, McNab, Martinez-Vazquez, and

Boex 2000; Oxford Policy Management 2000), two studies examined MTEFs in Africa. Le Houerou and Taliercio (2002), in a Bank study, draw lessons from MTEFs in 13 African countries, all but one of which were introduced with Bank support. Holmes and Evans (2003), for the Overseas Development Institute, review experience with MTEFs in the context of PRSPs in nine countries (eight of which are in Africa). Both studies identify similar shortcomings of the MTEF reforms:

• Initial country conditions, especially with regard to basic aspects of budget management, are not taken sufficiently into account.
• With the exception of a few cases, inadequate attention is paid to the political and institutional aspects of the reform process.
• Operational MTEFs do not resemble their textbook counterparts.

However, while Le Houerou and Taliercio (2002, 25) conclude, "MTEFs alone cannot deliver improved [public expenditure management] in countries in which other key aspects of budget management remain weak," Holmes and Evans (2003, 31) conclude more optimistically, "MTEFs are progressing, albeit unevenly, and . . . in many cases they have both facilitated and are being strengthened by the current emphasis on implementing PRSPs." These studies are summarized in more detail in appendix B.

The experience with MTEFs has also increasingly become a subject of other reviews. Oxford Policy Management (2008, 2009) has followed up on its 2000 assessment with suggestions on how to make MTEFs more effective. Filc and Scartascini (2010), Kasek and Webber (2009), and Oyugi (2008) examine the experience with MTEFs in Latin America, emerging Europe, and Southern Africa, respectively. These studies, which are summarized in appendix B, largely confirm the above observations about MTEF performance.

Rationale for This Study

On the basis of these studies, it may seem that there is little need for another assessment of the experience with MTEFs. Rather, the focus should now be on strengthening existing MTEFs as well as providing a blueprint for the successful implementation of new MTEFs. However, the available studies have significant limitations. First, their conclusions are derived mainly from country case studies, which lack empirical evidence supported by quantitative analysis. Second, they focus on a relatively small sample of countries. The emphasis to date has been on countries with MTEFs, especially in Africa and where the World Bank has supported their implementation. Third, MTEFs have become much more popular since the late 1990s, so studies undertaken in the early 2000s had relatively little experience to work with or time series to analyze.

This study aims to undertake a more comprehensive review of the experience with MTEFs and to address the limitations of the previous assessments. This is accomplished in the following way:

- *Methodological approach.* While it is not unusual to employ country case studies when reviewing the experience with policy reforms, there is scope to apply a wider range of analytical techniques to the available qualitative and quantitative information, with a view to identifying economic, political, institutional, and other (for example, regional) patterns that may be helpful in understanding differences in country experiences with MTEFs as well as in examining the effect of MTEFs on fiscal performance. Therefore, this study relies on multiple techniques, including event studies, econometric analysis, and case studies.
- *Country coverage.* This study looks at the experience of countries with and without MTEFs. Even if the goal is to improve World Bank advice on MTEFs to its clients, much can be learned from the experience of all countries that have introduced MTEFs and, for benchmarking purposes, of those that have not.
- *Timing.* MTEFs can take many years to implement in full, which means that having an additional five or more years of experience to examine is significant and can potentially yield meaningful insights.[8]

Notes

1. While incremental budgeting can work well in times of revenue growth, it comes under particular pressure when revenue falls, becomes more volatile, or reaches its natural limit, because this is when expenditure prioritization takes on increased importance.

2. These objectives cannot be viewed in isolation. Success in meeting them requires that budgetary and PFM systems function well, a subject discussed later in the book. There is also a link to broader economic developments (Campos and Pradhan 1996). Improved fiscal outcomes contribute to higher growth, lower inflation, and macroeconomic volatility. In addition, as the quality of spending improves, higher incomes should be accompanied by lower poverty rates, while better infrastructure should contribute to even higher growth and further poverty reduction.

3. Some argue that, in fact, large deficits prompt better expenditure prioritization; however, the lessons from fiscal adjustments around the world suggest
that spending cuts are borne disproportionately by high-priority spending,
especially public investment in infrastructure, with adverse consequences for
future growth (see, for example, Easterly, Irwin, and Servén 2008). Lewis and
Verhoeven (2010) report that the growth of public social spending has dipped
as the global financial crisis has put fiscal positions under pressure and suggest
that this "risks setting back achievement of human development goals."

4. Australia replaced annually negotiated expenditure appropriations with
policy-based medium-term allocations that were updated periodically to
reflect new economic and programmatic developments. New policies were
included as decisions were made (see Keating 2001). The United Kingdom
had an embryonic MTEF system going back to the 1960s, when public expenditure survey committees were introduced, although the process was not
called an MTEF in those days.

5. While recognizing the importance of multiyear planning, the International
Monetary Fund (IMF) did not explicitly recommend MTEFs in its PFM
guidelines (Potter and Diamond 1999). However, the IMF views MTEFs as
good for fiscal transparency, for the same reasons that the Bank advocates
them (see IMF 2007).

6. If products focusing on high-income countries are included, the total number
of countries is 110. There are six such products and they comprise countries
that reached high income level recently.

7. Out of this total, project documents are available for only 363 products.

8. On average, countries that take a gradual approach to implementation
(as recommended later in this study) need about six years on average to
put in place a full-fledged MTEF. Some countries have taken or will need
much longer.

References

Campos, E., and S. Pradhan. 1996. "Budgetary Institutions and Expenditure
Outcomes." Working Paper 1646, World Bank, Washington, DC.

Easterly, W., T. Irwin, and L. Servén. 2008. "Walking up the Down Escalator: Public
Investment and Fiscal Stability." *World Bank Research Observer* 23 (1): 37–56.

Filc, G., and C. Scartascini. 2010. "Is Latin America on the Right Track? An
Analysis of Medium-Term Frameworks and the Budget Process." RES
Working Paper 4659, Inter-American Development Bank, Research
Department, Washington, DC.

Holmes, M., and A. Evans. 2003. "A Review of Experience in Implementing
Medium-Term Expenditure Frameworks in a PRSP Context: A Synthesis
of Eight Country Studies." Overseas Development Institute, London.

IMF (International Monetary Fund). 2007. *Manual on Fiscal Transparency*. Washington, DC: IMF.

Kasek, L., and D. Webber, eds. 2009. *Performance-Based Budgeting and Medium-Term Expenditure Frameworks in Emerging Europe*. Washington, DC: World Bank.

Keating, M. 2001. "Public Management Reform and Social Development." *OECD Journal on Budgeting* 12 (1–2): 141–212.

Le Houerou, P., and R. Taliercio. 2002. "Medium-Term Expenditure Frameworks: From Concept to Practice (Preliminary Lessons from Africa)." Africa Region Working Paper 28, World Bank, Washington, DC.

Lewis, M., and M. Verhoeven. 2010. "Financial Crisis and Social Spending: The Impact of the 2008–2009 Crisis." *World Economics* 11 (4): 79–110.

McNab, R., J. Martinez-Vazquez, and L. Boex. 2000. "Multi-Year Budgeting: A Review of International Practices and Lessons for Developing and Transitional Economies." *Public Budgeting and Finance* 20 (2): 91–112.

Oxford Policy Management. 2000. "Medium-Term Expenditure Frameworks: Panacea or Dangerous Distraction?" Oxford Policy Management Review Paper 2, Oxford Policy Management, Oxford, U.K.

———. 2008. "Making Medium-Term Budgets Effective." Oxford Policy Management Briefing Note, Oxford Policy Management, Oxford, U.K.

———. 2009. "A Suggestion for Making MTBF Reforms Simpler and More Achievable." Oxford Policy Management Briefing Note, Oxford Policy Management, Oxford, U.K.

Oyugi, L. 2008. "Experiences with Medium-Term Expenditure Framework in Selected Southern and Eastern African Countries." SEAPREN Working Paper 7, Southern and Eastern Africa Policy Research Network.

Potter, B., and J. Diamond. 1999. *Guidelines for Public Expenditure Management*. Washington, DC: International Monetary Fund.

Wildavsky, A. 1986. *Budgeting: A Comparative Theory of Budgetary Processes*. New Brunswick, NJ: Transaction Books.

World Bank. 1998. *Public Expenditure Management Handbook*. Washington, DC: World Bank.

CHAPTER 3

MTEF Foundations

This chapter describes the general characteristics of medium-term expenditure frameworks (MTEFs), explains the approach used to identify and classify them according to their stage of development, and reviews trends in their adoption in countries and regions worldwide.

General Characteristics

As noted, multiyear budget planning is the defining feature of MTEFs. The approach to planning can be thought of as a three-stage process.

- *Specifying a medium-term envelope of aggregate resources (the top-down approach).* The Ministry of Finance (MoF) or other ministry responsible for preparing the budget, in conjunction with other economic ministries and usually the central bank, uses a macro-fiscal framework and forecasting models to assess the availability of total resources. This reflects the potential collection of tax and non-tax revenue, borrowing capacity and availability of loans, and aid committed to support budget programs and projects. Resource availability is translated into initial allocations for spending agencies, based on past spending, new priorities and policies, and relevant guidance provided by the cabinet, council of ministers, or a similar body.[1]

- *Determining medium-term resource needs of spending agencies (the bottom-up approach).* Spending agencies prepare spending plans based on sector strategies and the estimated costs of continuing and new activities. These are translated into multiyear budget requests. In formulating their requests, spending agencies typically have to use centrally provided cost assumptions (for example, assumptions about salaries and prices) presented in the budget circular. In addition, the Ministry of Finance usually specifies initial allocations, in which case budget requests are a vehicle for spending agencies to justify requests for allocations that are different from those of the MoF.

- *Agreeing on expenditure allocations and finalizing the annual budget (the reconciliation process).* The ministry reviews the budget requests of spending agencies, taking into account sector strategies and the resource envelope. Based on discussions with spending agencies, additional guidance provided by the cabinet, and consideration of the required trade-offs, decisions are made, and agreement is reached on multiyear allocations for spending agencies and possibly programs. The annual government budget is prepared, endorsed by the cabinet, and submitted to parliament for approval. Spending agencies subsequently finalize their sector strategies and spending plans.[2]

MTEFs can also be viewed as a sequence of three increasingly demanding stages. This view is based on an approach to breaking down MTEFs suggested by Castro and Dorotinsky (2008), but it is applied differently. According to them, and most others who adopt a similar approach, a country's MTEF status is determined by the combination of stages adopted. For the purposes of this study, a country's MTEF status is defined by the highest MTEF stage achieved, assuming that the previous stages are in place. This approach has been chosen to facilitate the study's empirical work, which requires that MTEF stages be mutually exclusive. The three stages for an MTEF are as follows:

- *A medium-term fiscal framework (MTFF).* This encompasses the top-down specification of the aggregate resource envelope and the allocation of resources across spending agencies. Putting in place an MTFF is desirable regardless of a country's level of budgeting capacity, because providing a medium-term macro-fiscal framework for budget preparation can improve the quality of even quite basic input-oriented annual budgeting.

- *A medium-term budgetary framework (MTBF).*[3] In addition to the features of an MTFF, an MTBF includes both the bottom-up determination of spending agency resource needs and reconciliation of these with the resource envelope. Taking a medium-term approach to budget planning can improve expenditure prioritization even when emphasis is placed on the inputs needed to meet broad sector objectives and allocations are specified solely at the spending agency level. However, a more advanced MTBF can be combined with program budgeting to produce a programmatic MTEF, where allocations are linked to the objectives of and specified for individual programs. In the process, an MTBF can be a step in the direction of output-oriented budgeting.

- *A medium-term performance framework (MTPF).* Starting from an MTBF, an MTPF completes the shift in focus from inputs to outputs, with an emphasis on the measurement and evaluation of performance. Thus it serves not only as a means of promoting results but also as a way of using budget allocations to encourage better performance (that is, by linking funding to results). An MTPF, and therefore a full-fledged MTEF, is a pinnacle reachable only by those countries that have implemented a well-functioning MTBF.

Spending strategies play a key role in determining the effectiveness of an MTEF. More specifically, under an MTBF spending agencies have to justify their budget requests by referring to *sector or agency strategies* that support them. This is the case whether the approach to budgeting is input or output oriented. If the former, input needs are explained by referring to strategic objectives (that is, placing more emphasis on preventive health necessitates hiring X doctors and Y nurses); if the latter, emphasis is placed on the cost of meeting output targets (that is, increasing primary school enrollment by X percent requires increasing the allocation for primary education by Y percent). A *national strategy*, which is a top-down statement of high-level expenditure priorities, is also needed. There is a presumption that sector strategies are consistent with a broader national strategy and that decisions about resource allocation across sectors are guided by such a strategy. However, national strategies often do not exist, at least not explicitly, in which case there is little to guide decisions about the budget allocations of different sectors. Moreover, when they do exist—for example, in countries that have introduced an MTEF but retained multiyear national planning—the two are often quite separate. It is also the case that the links are quite weak between poverty reduction strategy papers (PRSPs), which are a limited form of national strategy, and budget allocations (World Bank 2007). The lack of a national strategy is a significant gap in the design of MTEFs and a potential obstacle to their effectiveness.

Specific Design Issues

Several design issues have to be addressed in implementing MTEFs. Countries have options when it comes to determining the key features of their MTEFs.

Coverage

Which levels of government should be included and what categories of spending should be constrained? Broad coverage is the most effective because it ensures that all spending is subject to scrutiny and prioritization under an MTEF.

A central government MTEF only covers central transfers to subnational governments. Ideally, a government-wide MTEF should cover subnational governments that have substantial budgetary responsibilities, but this may not be feasible when subnational governments have a significant degree of spending autonomy, at least with regard to using an MTEF for making decisions about general government spending as a whole. However, larger subnational governments should be encouraged to adopt their own MTEFs. Moreover, for analytical purposes at the national level, attention should always be paid to the size, structure, and efficiency of general government spending.

There is a tendency to frame the debate about the appropriate coverage of an MTEF in terms of what is and is not nondiscretionary spending. Thus some governments exclude interest and entitlements from MTEF coverage because of their nondiscretionary nature. Others exclude a wider range of spending (for example, aid-financed spending, capital spending). However, in principle, all spending programs (at the relevant level of government) should be covered, and attempting to distinguish discretionary from nondiscretionary spending misses the point: the larger the share of total spending that is excluded from scrutiny under the MTEF, the larger the potential fiscal discipline and efficiency gains that are forgone. Moreover, the distinction between discretionary and nondiscretionary spending can be manipulated to lessen scrutiny. It is also the case that some spending, while fixed in the short term, can be changed over the longer term as priorities shift and new policy options emerge.[4] Australia, for instance, applies its MTEF to all spending, even though close to three-quarters of spending is appropriated via permanent or standing appropriations as opposed to annual appropriations.

Off-budget spending also creates a challenge for MTEFs, since it routinely falls outside normal budget scrutiny, especially in countries with substantial natural resource revenues. However, spending agencies often pursue important policy objectives through extrabudgetary funds, in many cases using earmarked revenue, and this fact should be taken into account in determining medium-term budget allocations. Similarly, insofar as governments provide guarantees that could have implications for future spending, expected calls on guarantees should be taken into account in making spending decisions. While there may be a case for placing limits on the stock of guarantees or new guarantees (as part of debt management) to limit future spending arising from guarantees, an MTEF contingency reserve is needed to accommodate the potential impact of guarantees on costs and other fiscal risks.

Detail

How disaggregated should an MTEF be by spending agency and program? It is usual to specify expenditure allocations under an MTEF at the spending agency level since this is the level at which spending is controlled. Where allocations are specified at the program level, they are often indicative, and spending agencies have some freedom to switch spending between programs. In any event, allocations for capital and current spending should be clearly distinguished. Under program budgeting, specifying program allocations (that is, moving to a programmatic MTEF) is justified, although too detailed a program breakdown can leave spending agencies with insufficient discretion. Moreover, large programs cut across spending agencies; insofar as possible, these should be broken into subprograms specific to one spending agency, so that joint responsibility for program implementation does not result in coordination failures and undermine accountability.

Time Frame

How long a time period should an MTEF cover, and how frequently should it be revised? Nearly all MTEFs cover three or four years. First-year allocations overlap with those of that year's annual budget, in some cases (for example, France and the United Kingdom) second-year allocations are fixed, and out-year allocations are indicative, in the sense that they convey to spending agencies what they can reasonably expect to spend in those years based on unchanged (that is, existing and planned) policies, current macro-fiscal projections, and other relevant factors (such as the separately projected costs of entitlement programs). It is therefore understood that out-year allocations can be changed to reflect policy, economic, and other developments. An MTEF that is partly or wholly fixed for the time period it covers is, in effect, a multiyear budget, although multiyear appropriations are unusual. Out-years are rolled forward each year, with the first out-year providing the basis for the next year's budget (or the following year's where the second MTEF year is fixed). In rolling forward, policy adjustments may have to be assumed and allocations altered if, for example, adverse economic developments imply budget outcomes that are inconsistent with broader macro-fiscal targets. In other words, the out-years of the MTEF have to be plausible. An initial MTEF should be revised to reflect final budget allocations.

Expenditure Ceilings and Forward Estimates

How should an MTEF seek to constrain spending? MTEF spending allocations are often specified as expenditure ceilings, which are regarded as the ultimate disciplining mechanism under an MTEF. However, while first-year annual budget ceilings are usually hard in the sense that they can be relaxed only in exceptional circumstances, out-year ceilings tend to be no more than indicative. However, with multi-year budgeting, ceilings can be binding over the life of an MTEF, either in nominal or in real terms. Denmark and the Netherlands set real ceilings for each year of a four-year MTEF, while Sweden sets nominal ceilings for its entire four-year MTEF. The case for the former as opposed to the latter approach rests largely on the unpredictability of inflation and a desire to limit countercyclical fiscal impulses to the revenue side of the budget (for more detail about the use of expenditure ceilings in Denmark, the Netherlands, and Sweden, see Ljungman 2008). Forward estimates can refer to different things. Sometimes they amount to no more than projections of spending based on unchanged policies that are used as a guide for determining final spending allocations reflecting new priorities and for setting ceilings. As such, they are a routine input into MTEF preparation.[5] However, they can (as in Australia) represent a commitment of the resources that a spending agency will receive if policies, projections, and so forth do not change; as such, they can be regarded as conditional out-year ceilings. While an MTEF can signal that governments are committed to sound fiscal policies, ceilings could be cast as expenditure rules to make them more effective in disciplining spending agencies, with explicit sanctions if spending exceeds ceilings (budgets could be cut or spending agency heads could be penalized). While expenditure rules are a useful disciplinary device, coverage can become an especially contentious issue if there are sanctions, since a spending agency does not want to be held accountable for something it cannot control.[6]

Margins

How should scope be provided to respond to unanticipated developments? Margins can be implicit or explicit. The use of conservative macroeconomic and revenue forecasts often provides an implicit margin, although if forecasts are systematically biased in this way, spending agencies are likely to anticipate this and reflect it in their budget requests. Conservative forecasts are in part a reaction to past optimism bias (which contributed to deficits and debt by treating bloated expenditure allocations as entitlements). Aiming to overperform relative to fiscal targets also provides an implicit margin. The intent and transparency of such approaches are difficult to defend. It is far better to use realistic forecasts (possibly reflecting independent input) and targets, which make the budget expenditure envelope more credible. Reliance should then be placed on contingency reserves to respond to revenue shortfalls and legitimate expenditure overruns. However, contingency reserves are meant to allow normal and modest budget deviations, both negative and positive, to be managed in a routine manner. The causes and consequences of larger deviations should be assessed and responded to appropriately through budget adjustments. Contingency reserves can be held by the central government for distribution across spending agencies, by spending agencies for distribution across programs, or by both. The last makes the most sense. The MoF can also ask spending agencies to identify programs and projects they would expand or new initiatives they would implement if resources are higher than projected and those they would cut if they are lower.

Institutional Responsibilities

Which agency should oversee application of the MTEF? It is often argued that a strong MoF is needed to steer the MTEF process to conclusion, although some say that an overly intrusive MoF can undermine the legitimacy and effectiveness of the process. Whether the MoF is in a position of institutional strength may depend more on the budget legacy than on any decision made in connection with an MTEF. In any event, solid support from parliament and the cabinet is needed if an MTEF is to succeed. Spending agencies also have to be fully engaged. Institutional responsibilities are discussed in more detail below.

MTEF Good Practices

Countries have MTEFs with different characteristics and features. While it is possible to distill these as a set of *best* practices, these would be drawn largely from advanced economies with the best-functioning budget systems. More helpful for developing countries is a set of *good* practices to which most could aspire as they develop an MTEF, especially as they move through the three stages of an MTFF, MTBF, and MTPF. Box 3.1 contains such a set of MTEF good practices.

Data and Classification

This study uses a wide range of source material to determine the status of a country's MTEF. However, establishing which countries have an MTEF and what type of MTEF they have (fiscal, budgetary, or performance)—defined by the highest stage achieved—is sometimes unclear from what is known about a particular country's approach to budgeting. This study uses an indicators-based approach to identify and classify MTEFs, relying on a wide range of information, and then checks its classification with public financial management and country experts inside and outside the Bank, revising the classification as necessary. Box 3.2 summarizes how MTEFs are classified, and appendix C discusses in more detail the data and approach to classification and presents the full coding by country.[7] In the final analysis, a country's status is a judgment call. Moreover, as the description of MTEF characteristics suggests, not all MTFFs, MTBFs, and MTPFs are the same, and it is necessary to be alert to the possible implications of heterogeneity within MTEF stages.

MTEFs around the World

As of end-2008, 132 countries—more than two-thirds of all countries—are considered to have implemented a formal MTEF or an equivalent

Box 3.1

Guide to MTEF Good Practices

Medium-term fiscal framework

- Debt and deficit targets are established using model-based debt sustainability analysis, taking into account constraints imposed by policy rules.
- Revenue forecasts are based on revenue department or other tax and non-tax receipt models.
- Independent macroeconomic forecasts are used, and fiscal forecasts are subject to scrutiny by an audit office, fiscal council, or similar consultative body.
- Aid commitments are covered by debt sustainability analysis and revenue forecasts.
- The Ministry of Finance (MoF) issues a background paper on macro-fiscal objectives to inform budget decision making and form part of the budget documentation.

Medium-term budgetary framework

- The MoF issues a budget strategy paper describing the macro-fiscal framework and providing a broad indication of national development and budgetary priorities for the medium term.
- A budget circular is sent to spending agencies outlining the basis on which they should prepare their medium-term budget requests. This circular indicates the availability of budget resources, usually in the form of provisional agency or program expenditure ceilings, and the aggregate cost assumptions to be used, including changes in inflation and public sector pay.
- The budget requests of spending agencies reflect strategic objectives, the cost of current and new activities, expected cost recovery, and other relevant factors.
- Final expenditure ceilings are reflected in the annual budget submitted to the legislature for consideration.
- Spending agency budgets are finalized, and sector strategies are revised to reflect budget realities.
- Spending agency budgets and sector strategies are published.

Medium-term performance framework

- Sector strategies discuss program outputs, outcomes, and performance.
- Agency output, outcome, and performance indicators are used to establish budget targets.
- Spending agencies report on results relative to targets. Comprehensive spending reviews are conducted periodically.

Box 3.2

MTEF Classification and Indicators Used in This Study

A *medium-term fiscal framework (MTFF)* determines the availability of aggregate resources as an input into budget formulation and sets expenditure ceilings for spending agencies as a basis for budget implementation. The MTFF is top-down in nature, focuses on allocating resources to purchase inputs, and holds spending agencies accountable for the use of inputs. MTFF indicators include budget or other reports that contain the government's medium-term macrofiscal strategy, macroeconomic and fiscal forecasts, and the results of debt sustainability analysis, as well as agency expenditure ceilings formulated in the absence of an MTBF. Externally imposed MTFFs, such as those embodied in International Monetary Fund programs, poverty reduction strategy papers, or European union stability or convergence program targets, are not counted as MTFFs unless the preceding indicators also suggest that they underpin a country-driven MTFF.

A *medium-term budgetary framework (MTBF)* specifies spending agency and program expenditure ceilings based on a compromise between the availability of top-down resources determined using an MTFF and the need for bottom-up resources to finance sector spending plans. MTBFs are primarily input based, in that expenditure allocations may be determined by reference to outputs or outcomes, but spending agencies are still held accountable for the use of inputs. MTBF indicators include a budget strategy paper detailing budgetary objectives and constraints, spending agency or other reports explaining the objectives and strategies of aggregate and sector expenditures, budget circulars detailing medium-term expenditure allocations, and budget reports containing medium-term expenditure ceilings or forward estimates. In addition to having an MTFF, countries with an MTBF produce such documents or otherwise demonstrate that the allocation of budget resources has a medium-term, strategic focus. Some countries begin by piloting an MTBF for selected spending agencies; this study records a piloted MTBF as an MTFF.

A *medium-term performance framework (MTPF)* shifts the focus of attention from spending agency or program inputs to agency or program outputs and out-comes, holding spending agencies responsible for their performance and linking funding to results. MTPF indicators include budget, spending agency, or other reports explaining program objectives and strategies, listing specific agency or program output targets, and explaining results. In addition to having an MTBF, countries with an MTPF produce this information or otherwise demonstrate that budgeting focuses on performance.

Figure 3.1   Global MTEF Adoption, 1990–2008

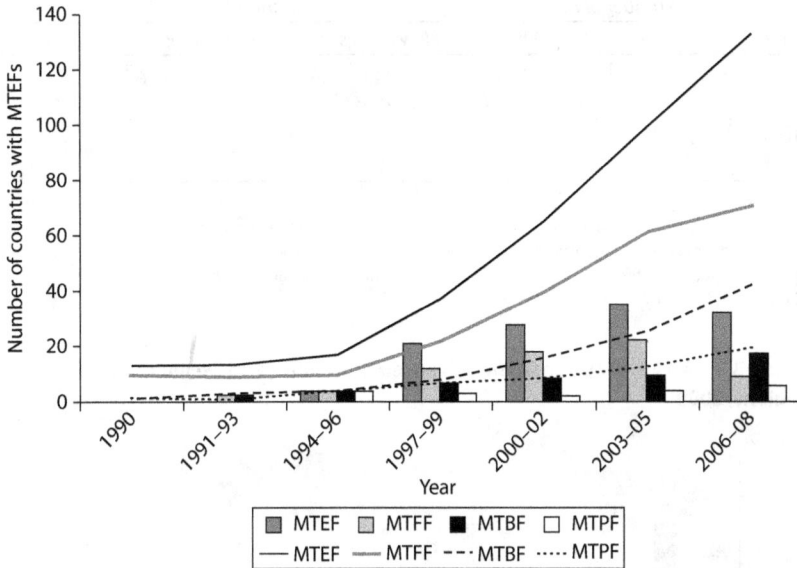

Source: World Bank.
Note: MTBF = medium-term budgetary framework; MTEF = medium-term expenditure framework; MTFF = medium-term fiscal framework; MTPF = medium-term performance framework. The data lines show the cumulative number of countries with MTEFs. The bars show the number of new countries with MTEFs.

arrangement. As figure 3.1 shows, most of these have been implemented since the late-1990s. The widespread adoption of MTEFs coincided with the introduction of PRSPs, the inclusion by the Bank and other donors of an MTEF in their standard advice on budget reforms, and the post–Asian crisis pickup of interest in promoting and safeguarding fiscal discipline. More generally, many low-income and emerging-market countries implemented MTEFs in an effort to improve the link between the mobilization and use of public resources and the achievement of development goals, while several advanced economies embraced MTEFs as interest in modern budget reforms took off. As expected, MTFFs are the most commonly implemented form of MTEF, but recently there has been a shift to MTBFs and MTPFs. In 2008, the composition of MTEFs across countries included 71 MTFFs, 42 MTBFs, and 19 MTPFs, with countries transitioning to MTBFs and MTPFs as opposed to introducing new MTEFs, especially in the case of MTPFs (see table 3.1).

Table 3.1   Sources of MTEF Growth, 1990–2008

	Number of MTEFs		Change, 1990–2008		
Stage	1990	2008	New MTEFs	Transitions	Reversals
MTFF	9	71	104	−41	−1
MTBF	1	42	21	23	−3
MTPF	1	19	0	18	0
MTEF	11	132	125	0	−4

Source: World Bank.
Note: MTBF = medium-term budgetary framework; MTEF = medium-term expenditure framework; MTFF = medium-term fiscal framework; MTPF = medium-term performance framework. The MTFF reversal occurred in Argentina; the MTBF reversals occurred in Argentina, Estonia, and the United States. Out of the 18 transitions to MTPFs, 9 are from MTFFs and 9 are from MTBFs.

Figure 3.2   MTEF Adoption in the Advanced Economies and Developing-Country Regions, 2008

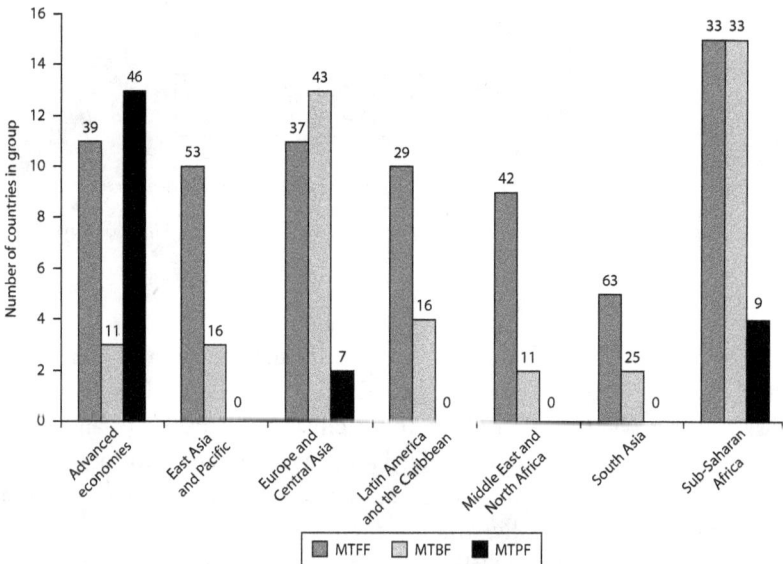

Source: World Bank.
Note: MTBF = medium-term budgetary framework; MTEF = medium-term expenditure framework; MTPF = medium-term performance framework. Percentage of countries in the region are displayed at the top of the bars.

MTEF coverage varies significantly across country groups. Figure 3.2 shows that MTEFs have achieved almost complete coverage of advanced economies where, as can be seen in figure 3.3, MTEFs were adopted in two waves.[8] As noted, in the late 1980s and early 1990s, some countries followed Australia's lead, and then in the late 1990s

Figure 3.3 MTEF Adoption in the Advanced Economies and Developing-Country Regions, 1990–2008

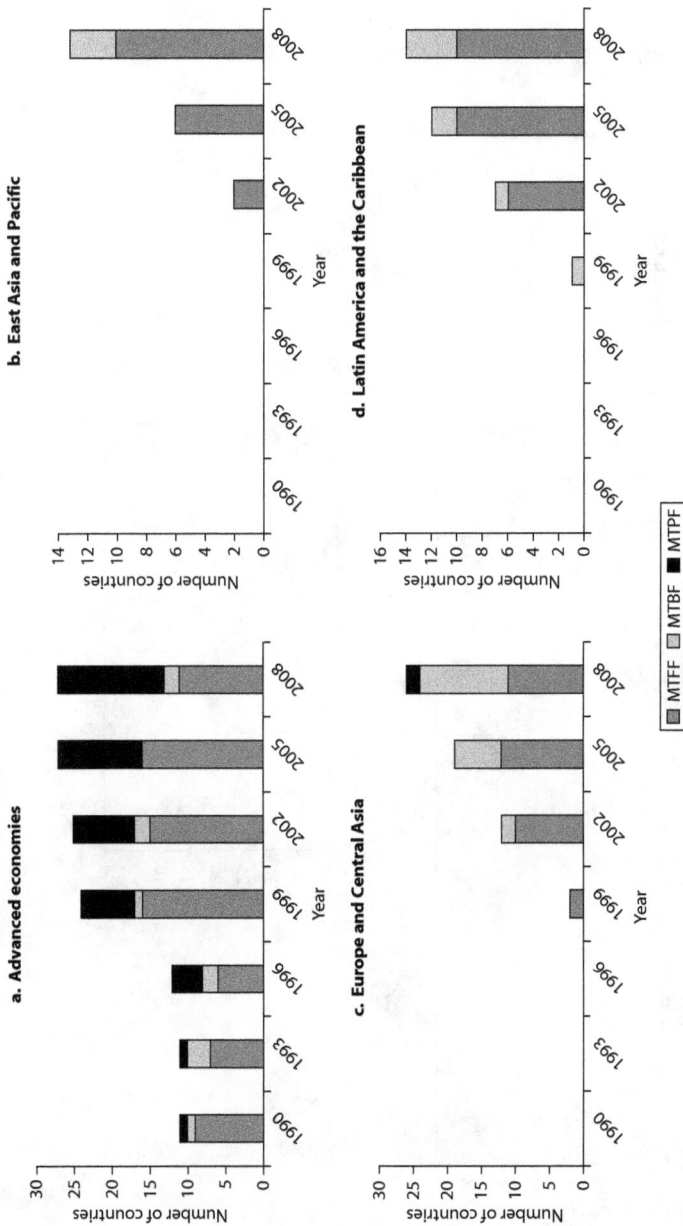

a. Advanced economies

b. East Asia and Pacific

c. Europe and Central Asia

d. Latin America and the Caribbean

MTFF   MTBF   MTPF

(continued next page)

29

Figure 3.3 *(continued)*

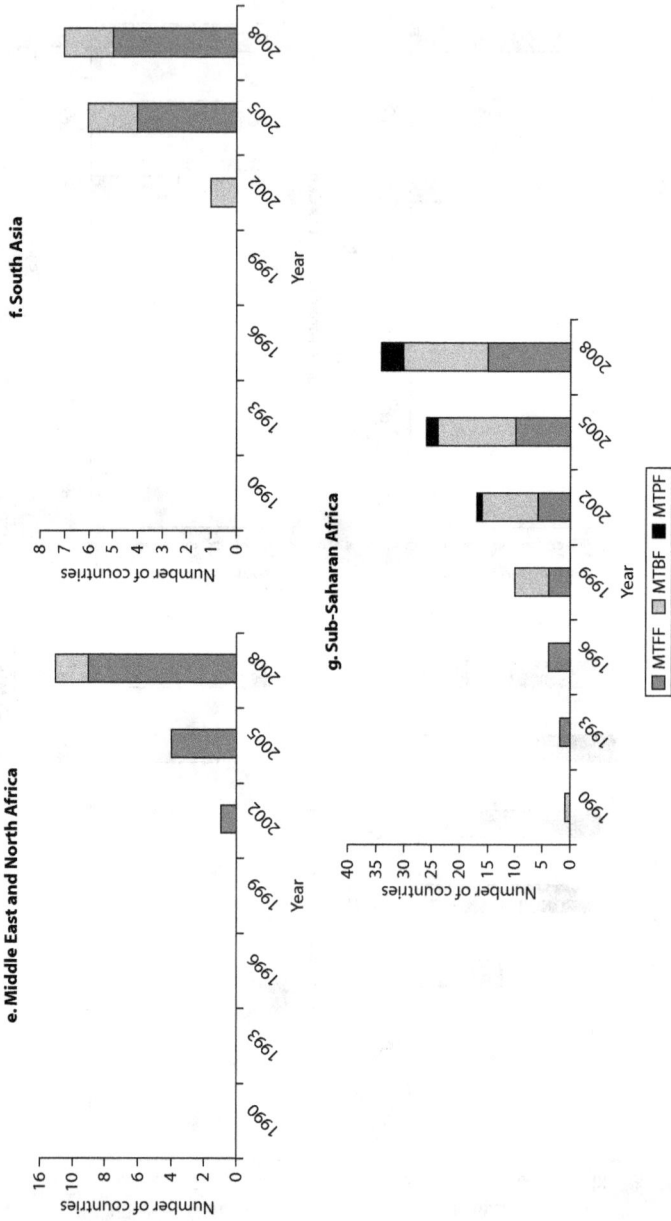

e. Middle East and North Africa

f. South Asia

g. Sub-Saharan Africa

Legend: MTFF ▨ MTBF ▨ MTPF ■

Source: World Bank.
Note: MTBF = medium-term budgetary framework; MTEF = medium-term expenditure framework; MTPF = medium-term performance framework.

MTEFs were introduced mainly in the European Union to support budgetary targets set as a precondition for the monetary union. Just under half of MTEFs are now MTPFs, while there are relatively few MTBFs, suggesting that when advanced economies decide to move beyond an MTFF, focusing on performance is a natural development given the sophistication of their budgeting systems. MTEFs have also achieved broad coverage of the countries in Europe and Central Asia, in part reflecting their universal adoption in Western Europe. As shown in figure 3.4, coverage spread faster and farther in Central and Southern Europe than in the former Soviet Union, but this is not surprising given that the former Soviet Union opened up later and that countries of Central and Southern Europe sought to integrate quickly with Western Europe.[9]

Building on an early start in Uganda, MTEFs spread across Sub-Saharan Africa.[10] Three-quarters of countries in the region had one by the end of 2008. There were an equal number of MTFFs and MTBFs,

Figure 3.4   MTEF Adoption in Europe, by Region, 1990–2008

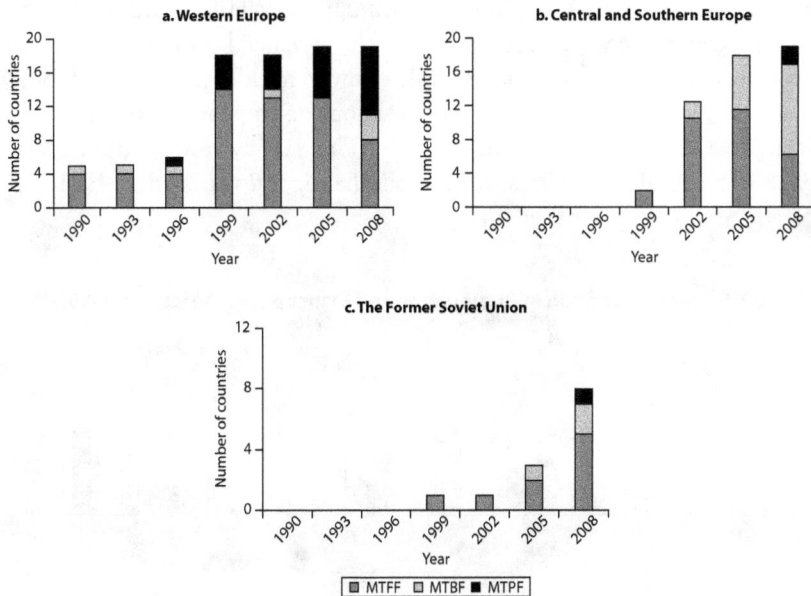

Source: World Bank.
Note: MTBF = medium-term budgetary framework; MTEF = medium-term expenditure framework; MTPF = medium-term performance framework.

and three countries (Burkina Faso, Mauritius, and Namibia) followed South Africa's lead and implemented an MTPF. While MTEFs can be thought of as Anglophone in origin, figure 3.5 reveals that they are now more numerous in Francophone than in Anglophone Africa, taking off, in particular, after France introduced an MTEF in the late 1990s. MTEFs have also been adopted by most countries in South Asia, with Nepal and Sri Lanka having MTBFs.

MTEFs are less widespread in other regions. However, there has been a recent spurt of adoptions in East Asia and the Pacific, including MTBFs in Cambodia, Thailand, and Vanuatu. The situation is similar in Latin America and the Caribbean, where several countries have introduced MTFFs following years of efforts to use similar frameworks to manage fiscal policy under IMF programs. Only four countries have moved beyond this and introduced an MTBF—Argentina, Colombia, Nicaragua, and St. Lucia—although Brazil's budgeting system has the characteristics of an MTBF.[11] In the Middle East and North Africa, MTEFs are a very recent innovation; only Algeria and Jordan have an MTBF, while the major oil-exporting countries (Saudi Arabia and the United Arab Emirates) do not even have an MTFF.

These patterns of adoption translate into fairly uniform coverage across income levels. Apart from the widespread MTEF adoption in high-income countries, which are essentially the advanced economies, there is little difference across upper middle-, lower middle-, and low-income countries; indeed, if anything, MTEF adoption appears to be inversely related to income level (see figure 3.6). This largely reflects the experience in Sub-Saharan Africa, on the one hand, and the Middle East and North Africa, on the other.

Figure 3.5   MTEF Adoption in Anglophone and Francophone Africa, 1990–2008

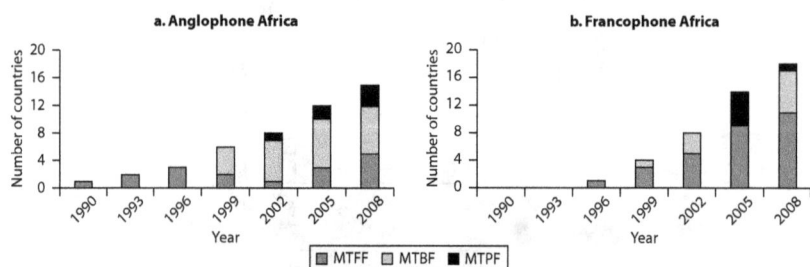

Source: World Bank.
Note: MTBF = medium-term budgetary framework; MTEF = medium-term expenditure framework; MTPF = medium-term performance framework.

Figure 3.6 MTEF Adoption by Income Level, 1990–2008

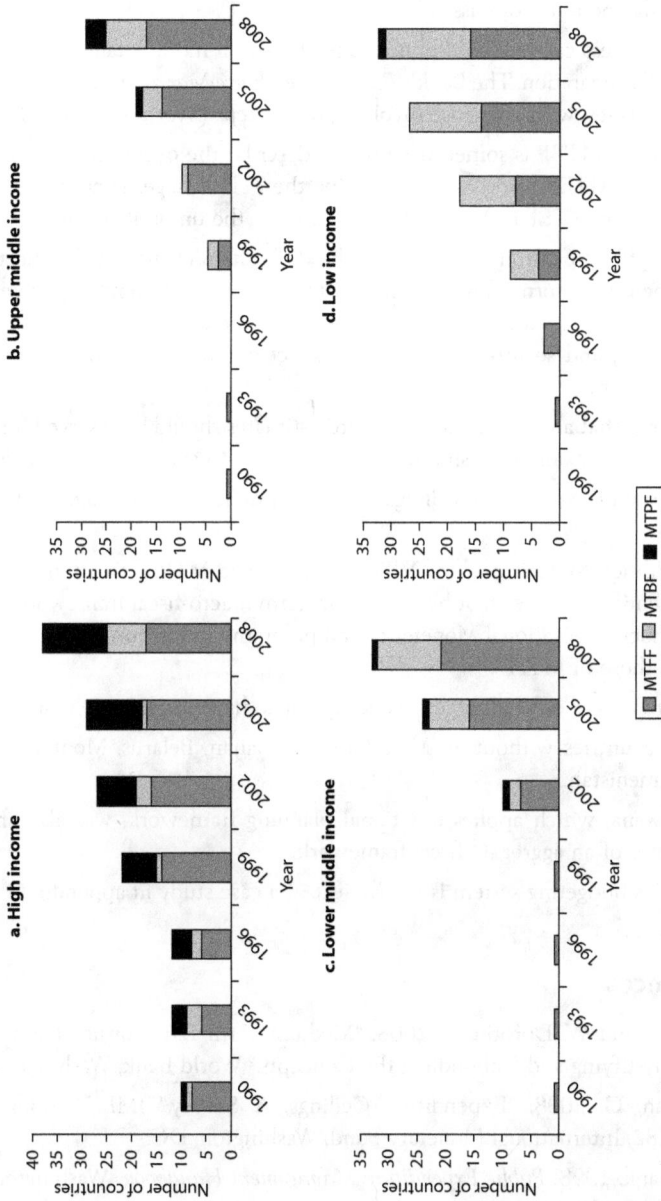

a. High income

b. Upper middle income

c. Lower middle income

d. Low income

Legend: MTFF | MTBF | MTPF

Source: World Bank.

Note: MTBF = medium-term budgetary framework; MTEF = medium-term expenditure framework; MTPF = medium-term performance framework.

33

Notes

1. Allocations across spending agencies can be forward estimates or ceilings. This distinction is discussed below.

2. This process can have additional stages, based on more detailed timelines for MTEF preparation. The Bank's *Public Expenditure Management Handbook* lists seven stages, with one stage involving three steps (World Bank 1998).

3. The term MTBF is sometimes used to describe the overall framework, with the term MTEF being used to describe the MTBF stage. There is some logic to this, but MTEF is more commonly used as the umbrella term.

4. Thus public pension spending may be difficult to change in the short term, but pension reforms (cutting benefits, raising contribution rates, pushing back retirement age, shifting to defined-contribution plans, relying more on private annuities, and so forth) offer the prospect of lower expenditures over the longer term.

5. Ceilings that are not based on forward estimates should be reserved for emergencies; for example, cash limits might be used to avoid a budget crisis.

6. The use of expenditure ceilings to support deficit or debt rules is discussed below.

7. In addition to distinguishing MTFFs, MTBFs, and MTPFs, an attempt is made to identify countries that have medium-term macro-fiscal frameworks agreed to under International Monetary Fund programs and to compare their effects with those of MTFFs.

8. Cyprus is the only advanced economy not to have implemented an MTEF.

9. The countries without an MTEF are Azerbaijan, Belarus, Montenegro, and Turkmenistan.

10. Botswana, which applies a national planning framework, was also an early adopter of an aggregate fiscal framework.

11. Brazil's budgeting system is the subject of a case study in appendix G.

References

Castro, I., and W. Dorotinsky. 2008. "Medium-Term Expenditure Frameworks: Demystifying and Unbundling the Concepts." World Bank, Washington, DC.

Ljungman, G. 2008. "Expenditure Ceilings: A Survey." IMF Working Paper 08/282, International Monetary Fund, Washington, DC.

World Bank. 1998. *Public Expenditure Management Handbook*. Washington, DC: World Bank.

———. 2007. "Minding the Gaps: Integrating Poverty Reduction Strategies and Budgets for Domestic Accountability." World Bank, Washington, DC.

CHAPTER 4

What Works and Why

Medium-term expenditure frameworks (MTEFs) can promote fiscal discipline by addressing several causes of deficit bias. By specifying an overall resource constraint, MTEFs rein in the political tendency to overcommit public resources (the common pool problem) by requiring policy makers to acknowledge that the total amount of resources is limited, to negotiate collectively, and to commit themselves to detailed multiyear fiscal constraints. Further, by imparting a medium-term perspective to budgeting and taking into account the future fiscal costs of government policies and programs, an MTEF can fill information gaps that allow politicians to renege on their commitments to implement affordable policies (the time consistency problem). A medium-term perspective also encourages governments to conduct discretionary stabilization in a symmetric, countercyclical manner, rather than with the sort of asymmetry (countercyclical in bad times and procyclical in good times) that leads to rising deficits and debt (Kumar and Ter-Minassian 2007).

In that they set a top-down resource constraint, medium-term fiscal frameworks (MTFFs) should have a significant impact on fiscal discipline. Of course, gains in fiscal discipline are predicated on having an MTFF that works as intended. If spending agencies view allocations or ceilings as minimum entitlements rather than as constraints, MTFFs could be a source of fiscal indiscipline and deficit bias (Schick 2010).

Since medium-term budgetary and performance frameworks (MTBFs and MTPFs, respectively) incorporate an MTFF, they should have an increasingly stronger effect on fiscal discipline than an MTFF alone. This is, in part, because countries that have the capacity to implement an MTBF or an MTPF will have greater success in working with an MTFF. It is also a consequence of better prioritization and more emphasis on performance, which can bring into sharper focus the payoff to fiscal discipline and the costs of arbitrary fiscal adjustment.

Prioritization guided by longer-term sector strategies should improve the allocation of resources. Insofar as spending agencies prepare sector strategies, identify their resource needs, and allocate their budgets according to strategic priorities, this bottom-up prioritization should produce a shift to spending with higher economic and social returns. However, the full payoff to prioritization requires deciding how to allocate resources across sectors, which is done as part of the reconciliation between the top-down and bottom-up approaches involving a lead agency, normally the Ministry of Finance (MoF), and spending agencies; in connection with this, less strategic guidance may be available (for example, in the form of a national economic or development program or plan). Moreover, as discussed later, these may be new roles for all the agencies involved, and considerable learning by doing may be necessary before the potential gains are fully realized. In addition, difficult decisions have to be taken to cut low-priority but often politically sensitive spending.

The outcome of effective prioritization should be a shift away from unproductive spending. Poor-quality investment, distorting and untargeted subsidies, bloated civil services, and the like should not survive scrutiny under an MTEF, while productive spending on economic and social infrastructure, health and education services, and other growth- or development-friendly activities should be favored. So the introduction of an MTBF should certainly be associated with an increase in the total share of productive spending, and for an MTPF the impact should be somewhat stronger. An MTFF alone may also have a beneficial effect on resource allocation in that a medium-term resource constraint should lead to some reexamination of spending even with annual, input-focused budgeting.

Spending should also become less volatile. Since the path of spending should reflect the medium-term rather than the short-term availability of resources, total expenditures should be less volatile, with an MTFF having the main influence in this connection. There should also be a contribution from an MTBF—and to a lesser extent an MTPF—since better prioritization should lead to a more stable level of spending.

The volatility of the composition of spending should also be affected. In the short term, compositional volatility should increase following implementation of an MTBF, as spending is reallocated to more productive sectors and programs. Thereafter, insofar as spending decisions are guided by strategic priorities with a longer-term focus, the composition of spending should become less volatile. However, this depends on how previous spending has responded to short-term variations in the availability of resources.

If, on the one hand, agency and program allocations are subjected to ad hoc changes as aggregate spending responds to short-term variations in resources, then longer-term compositional volatility would probably decline. If, on the other hand, spending is cut and restored across the board or a few spending items are adjusted up and down, volatility would probably increase. On balance, based mainly on cross-country evidence that fiscal adjustment is often of low quality, it seems more likely that longer-term compositional volatility would decline (for a description of the characteristics of large fiscal adjustments, see Tsibouris et al. 2006). An MTPF could lead to some additional reduction in compositional volatility, while an MTFF could have a modest beneficial effect.

Technical efficiency is concerned with the link between inputs and outputs. Ideally, the link would be with outcomes, not outputs. Spending programs are typically directed toward achieving economic and social outcomes, such as stable growth, poverty reduction, social protection, law and order, and national security, but final outcomes such as these are often influenced by a wide range of factors other than government spending and are difficult to measure.

Outputs are measurable indicators linked with final outcomes, although some can be thought of as intermediate outcomes. Thus education spending to build more schools is an input, enrolling more children in school is an output, increasing literacy is an intermediate outcome, and poverty reduction and economic growth are final outcomes from education spending. The tendency is to measure a mix of outputs and intermediate outcomes in assessing agency performance and to be imprecise in describing them as either outputs or outcomes. With this distinction in mind, the idea in thinking about technical efficiency is that a spending agency is undertaking a constrained optimization exercise and is trying either to maximize outputs or outcomes with a given amount of budget resources or to minimize the budget resources used to achieve a given set of outputs or outcomes.

Budget allocations deriving from such an exercise are technically efficient (although they may not be allocatively efficient because the government could function cost-effectively but do the wrong things). Improved technical efficiency may follow from an MTFF but is more likely a consequence of an MTBF and MTPF, with the latter likely to have the largest effect, as budget funding is influenced by results in the form of outputs or outcomes.

Measurement and Hypotheses

This study uses the following measures of fiscal performance:

- *Fiscal discipline*—the overall balance of the central government as a share of gross domestic product (GDP) (fiscal balance). Central government data provide limited coverage of government revenue and spending, especially in countries where subnational governments have significant fiscal responsibilities, but a time series of general government data is not available for all countries. Other fiscal indicators can also be used to measure fiscal discipline. Government debt is an obvious candidate, but it is influenced by factors that lead to stock adjustments (for example, debt relief, recapitalizations) that are decided outside the MTEF. There are also alternative measures of the fiscal balance (for example, the primary, current, and operational balance), but the overall balance, which measures the government's borrowing requirement, is appropriate for measuring the impact of an MTEF intended to ensure that total spending is constrained by the government's envelope of total resources.

- *Allocative efficiency*—volatility of total central government expenditure as a share of GDP (total expenditure volatility), general government health expenditure as a share of total expenditure (health expenditure share), and volatility of general government health expenditure as a share of total expenditure (health expenditure volatility).[1] Volatility is measured by changes in the deviation from trend.[2] Health spending is only one component of productive spending, but the main sources of internationally comparable expenditure data for the other sectors, especially the Government Finance Statistics of the International Monetary Fund (IMF), have too many gaps across countries and over time to be usable. Health spending data are only available for general government. It is important to acknowledge that the general applicability of the results of this study is limited by the exclusive focus on health spending.

- *Technical efficiency*—the difference between actual life expectancy and maximum life expectancy for a given level of health spending per capita (cost-effectiveness of health expenditure).[3] This measure of technical efficiency has clear limitations, both because it is just one indicator of health outcomes and because life expectancy is determined by a wide range of factors not taken into account by the analysis in this study.

Based on these measures, the following hypotheses are tested:

- *Fiscal discipline*—an MTEF improves the fiscal balance. An MTFF has the largest effect, with an MTBF and MTPF having an additional impact.

- *Allocative efficiency*—an MTEF reduces total expenditure volatility, increases health expenditure share, and reduces health expenditure volatility. With regard to total expenditure volatility, an MTFF has a large effect that is bolstered by an MTBF, while an MTPF may or may not have much of an additional effect. An MTBF has the largest effect on the share and volatility of health expenditures, an MTPF has an additional impact, and an MTFF may or may not have a significant effect.

- *Technical efficiency*—an MTEF increases the cost-effectiveness of health expenditure. An MTPF has the largest positive effect, and an MTBF has a smaller impact. Again, an MTFF may or may not have a significant effect.

Investigative Approaches

Three approaches are employed to examine the links between MTEFs and fiscal performance: event studies, econometric analysis, and case studies.

Event studies are a simple graphic description of the behavior of a variable of interest on either side of a particular event. The event in this case is the adoption of an MTEF, while the fiscal performance measures referred to above are the variables of interest. Event studies are based on the identification of a window of time around MTEF adoption. If the MTEF has its anticipated effect, during this window of time variables of interest should move in a direction consistent with improvements in fiscal discipline, allocative efficiency, and technical efficiency. Moreover, the period after adoption should be characterized by better fiscal outcomes than the period before adoption.

Event studies simply compare the values of key variables before and after MTEF adoption; they say nothing about correlation and causation. Therefore, the econometric analysis exploits variations in the data on MTEF status, fiscal performance, and other relevant variables in an attempt to discover whether MTEF adoption has a statistically significant impact on fiscal discipline, allocative efficiency, and technical efficiency.

Case studies can also throw light on whether country experience affects the impact of MTEFs, especially insofar as MTEFs might influence fiscal performance via their impact on the quality of budgeting.

The Hypothesis

It is important to state at the outset of the discussion of the report's empirical work that the econometric analysis has to address a potentially serious reverse causality (or endogeneity) problem. The hypothesis being tested is that MTEFs have a positive influence on fiscal performance. Lying behind this is the idea that countries are persuaded to adopt MTEFs because they want to improve fiscal discipline and spending efficiency. However, there is another possibility, which is that countries do something else to improve fiscal performance and then adopt an MTEF only after they have achieved a fiscal improvement on which to consolidate and build. This may be an easier option insofar as governments are not preoccupied with addressing fiscal imbalances and reducing wasteful spending. The reverse causality problem means that the latter effect may be mistaken for the former.[4] This is obviously more than an econometric issue, in that it addresses a key policy question.

To address the reverse causality problem, the econometric analysis uses instrumental variables techniques designed specifically for this purpose, with the result that this study can make some of the strongest statements to date about correlation and causation, especially with regard to the positive impact of MTEFs on fiscal discipline. Moreover, although the econometric analysis validates these statements, the event studies, which are described first, provide a clear indication of fiscal performance before and after MTEF adoption.

Event Study Comparisons

This section presents the methodology and results of the event study comparisons.

The event studies were conducted in the following way. The implementation date of each country's MTEF is normalized to year t, distinguishing between MTFFs, MTBFs, and MTPFs. The measures of fiscal discipline, allocative efficiency, and technical efficiency, together with some supplementary variables, are averaged across countries and plotted for years $t-3$, $t-2$, $t-1$, t, $t+1$, $t+2$ and $t+3$, along with 95 percent confidence intervals. Given an interest in whether MTEFs spur better fiscal outcomes, it is instructive to compare years $t-3$, $t-2$, $t-1$ with years $t+1$, $t+2$ and $t+3$, and so averages for these periods are indicated in the boxes on each figure.[5] For example, as shown in figure 4.1, the average fiscal balance in the three years following MTEF implementation was -0.4 percent of GDP, compared with an average fiscal balance of -3 percent of GDP

Figure 4.1   MTEFs, the Fiscal Balance, Expenditure, and Revenue

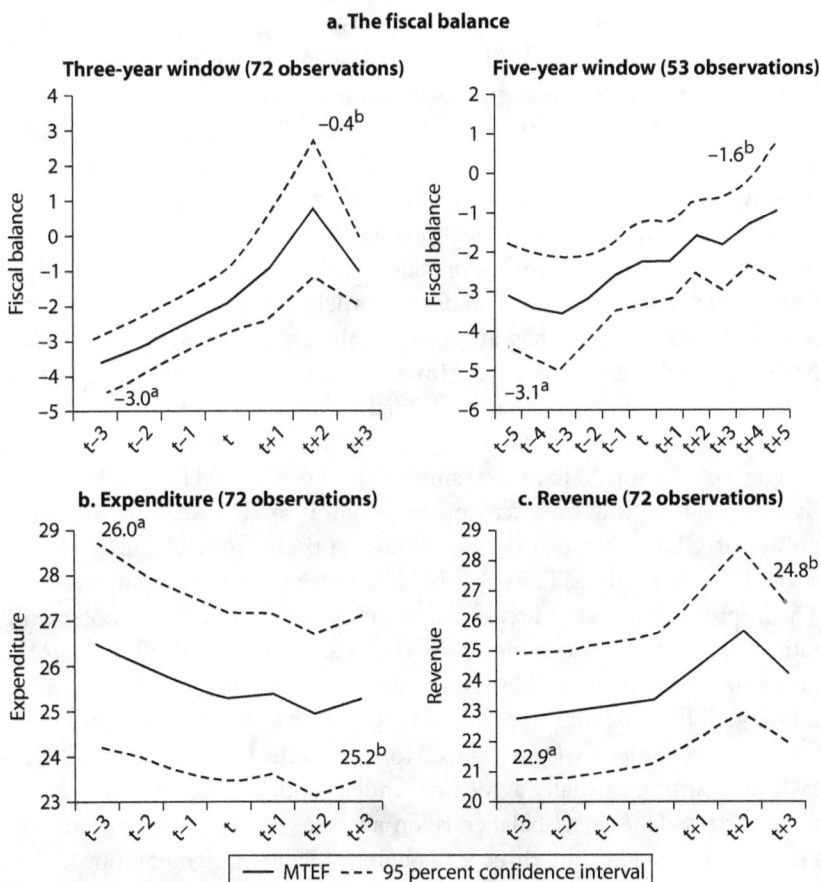

a. The fiscal balance

b. Expenditure (72 observations)

c. Revenue (72 observations)

— MTEF --- 95 percent confidence interval

Source: World Bank.
Note: MTEF = medium-term expenditure framework.
a. Pre-MTEF mean.
b. Post-MTEF mean.

prior to implementation. Not all countries that have implemented MTEFs can be included in the event studies. This is because some MTEFs were in place or introduced very early or late in the 1990–2008 period. Also, since MTPFs are a relatively recent innovation, few countries have them. The event studies are based on a maximum of 72 MTEFs (40 MTFFs, 20 MTBFs, and 12 MTPFs).

The event studies suggest that fiscal discipline is stronger after MTEF implementation. Figure 4.1 shows that the fiscal deficit is, on average, around 2.6 percentage points of GDP lower in the three years following MTEF implementation than in the three years preceding it.[6] The fiscal improvement appears to be short-lived, with the fiscal balance weakening three years after MTEF implementation. However, an event study with a five-year window (panel a of figure 4.1) points to an improvement in the fiscal balance beyond the third year of MTEF implementation.[7] Figure 4.1 also indicates that the source of fiscal improvement is both lower spending and higher revenue, but more than two-thirds of the improvement comes from higher revenue. This could be interpreted as saying that improved fiscal positions reflect other policy changes that have led to improved revenue. In this connection, one possibility is that the adoption of MTEFs around the world coincided with the introduction of value added taxes that have considerable potential to generate revenue. Since MTEF implementation has attracted significant donor support, it may have triggered grant assistance. However, in both cases, the role of the MTEF may be to ensure that additional revenue is used at least in part to reduce deficits rather than being automatically spent.

The results for MTFFs are similar to those for MTEFs. However, figure 4.2 shows that the fiscal improvement is smaller, at 2.2 percentage points of GDP. This also derives almost entirely from higher revenue, suggesting that only MTBFs and MTPFs foster expenditure adjustment. The improvement in the fiscal balance before and after MTFF implementation looks much the same as in the years before and after an IMF program is put in place. This is not surprising because the macro-fiscal framework that anchors an MTFF is very similar to the one that underlies fiscal targets under IMF programs. However, as is clear from figure 4.2, IMF programs are usually agreed on under conditions of relatively great fiscal distress (the fiscal balance is, on average, 2.9 percentage points of GDP weaker than in the three years before MTFF implementation). The fiscal improvement is also slightly larger and sustained for longer.

The implementation of both MTBFs and MTPFs is associated with larger improvements in the fiscal balance than the implementation of MTFFs. As figure 4.3 reveals, these improvements are 3.3 and 3.4

Figure 4.2   MTFFs, IMF Programs, and the Fiscal Balance

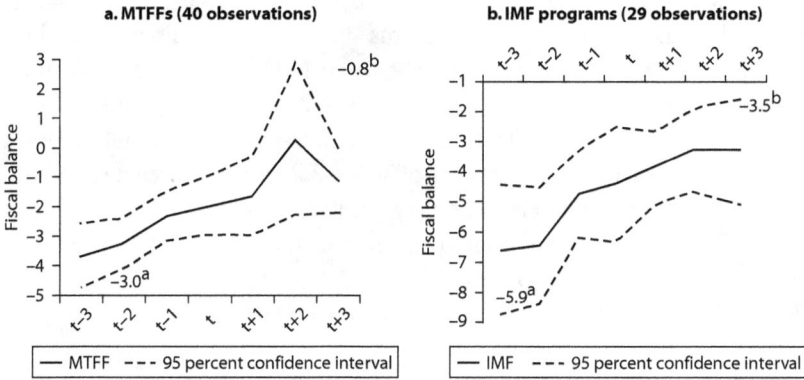

a. MTFFs (40 observations)   b. IMF programs (29 observations)

Source: World Bank.
Note: IMF = International Monetary Fund; MTFF = medium-term fiscal framework.
a. Pre-MTEF mean.
b. Post-MTEF mean.

Figure 4.3   MTBFs, MTPFs, and the Fiscal Balance

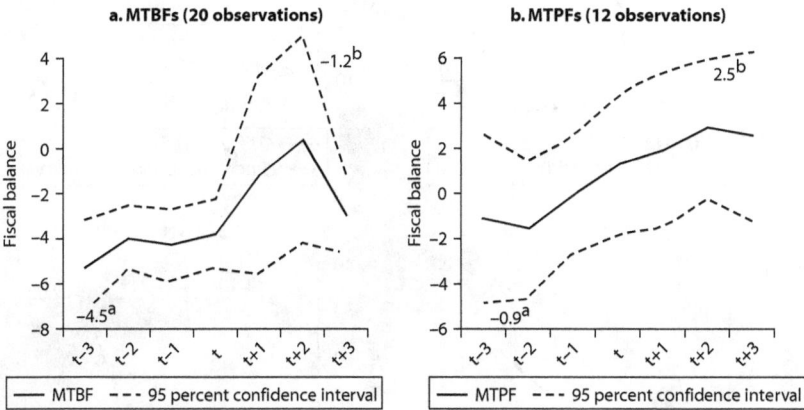

a. MTBFs (20 observations)   b. MTPFs (12 observations)

Source: World Bank.
Note: MTBF = medium-term budgetary framework; MTPF = medium-term performance framework.
a. Pre-MTEF mean.
b. Post-MTEF mean.

percentage points of GDP, respectively. MTPFs are also implemented in the context of much stronger fiscal positions, which could point to how a record of fiscal discipline provides countries with the opportunity to focus on improving efficiency as a means of further strengthening their fiscal position. That said, the small number of MTPFs means that this interpretation must be treated with caution.

It is useful to distinguish between the implementation of new MTEFs and the transition between MTEF stages and between full and piloted

MTEFs. In the case of MTBFs, where a distinction can be made between countries that introduce an MTBF with and without previously having an MTFF, the approach taken seems immaterial to fiscal discipline. Figure 4.4 shows that moving straight to an MTBF is associated with an improvement in the fiscal balance of about 4.2 percentage points of GDP, while implementing an MTFF (figure 4.2) and transitioning to an MTBF are each associated with improvements of about 2.2 and 2.4 percentage points, respectively. These outcomes are very similar. As indicated in box 3.2 in chapter 3, MTBFs that are piloted in select sectors are recorded as MTFFs,

Figure 4.4   MTEF Transitions, Pilots, and the Fiscal Balance

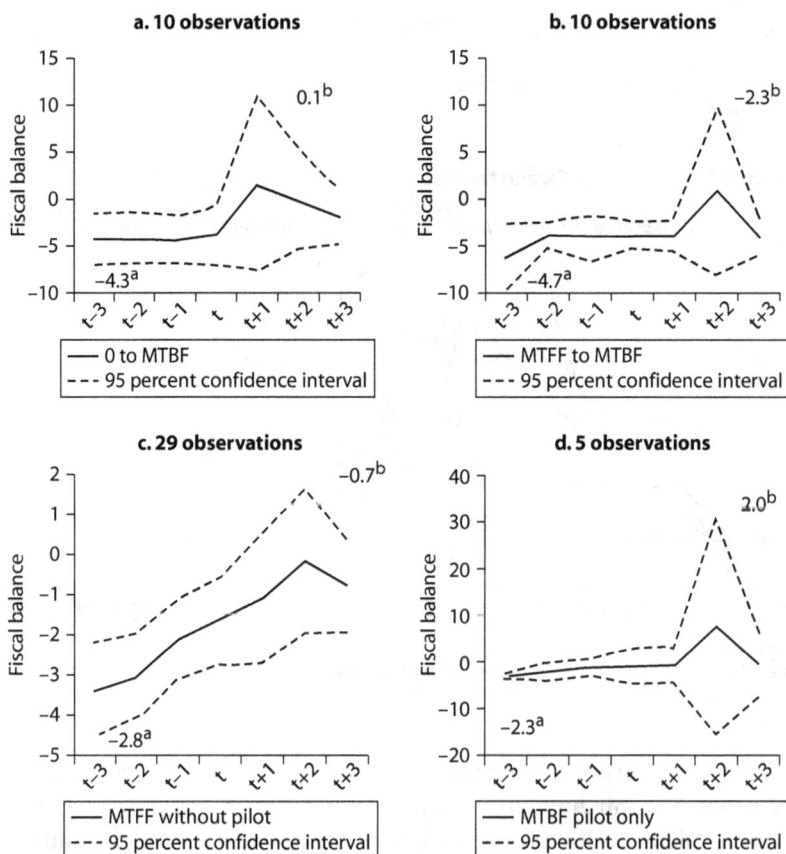

Source: World Bank.
Note: MTBF = medium-term budgetary framework; MTEF = medium-term expenditure framework; MTFF = medium-term fiscal framework.
a. Pre-MTEF mean.
b. Post-MTEF mean.

because it is assumed that the pilot is intended to test the MTBF approach and the systems designed to support it rather than to achieve significant improvements in resource allocation. However, figure 4.4 suggests that piloted MTBFs are associated with a fiscal improvement that is twice the size of the improvement associated with MTFFs alone. This suggests that an MTBF may have a large additional impact on fiscal discipline, but the sample of MTBF pilots is very small.

MTEFs are also associated with some improvement in efficiency. With regard to allocative efficiency, figure 4.5 points to less volatility in total expenditures, driven mainly by the impact of MTBFs (figure E.1 in appendix E). The health expenditure share increases only modestly, with little difference for the three MTEF stages (figure E.2 in appendix E), which may suggest that health spending was a sufficiently high priority before

Figure 4.5   MTEFs and Efficiency

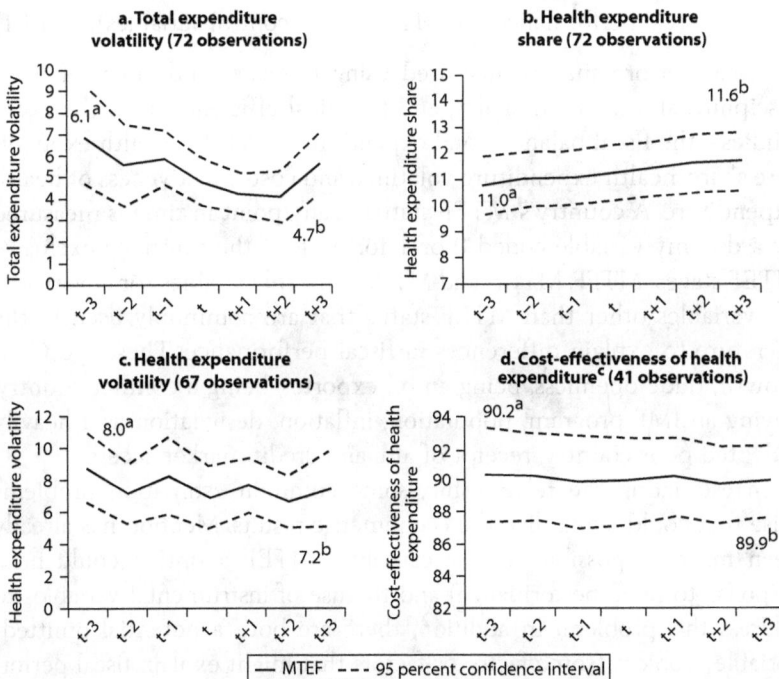

a. Total expenditure volatility (72 observations)

b. Health expenditure share (72 observations)

c. Health expenditure volatility (67 observations)

d. Cost-effectiveness of health expenditure[c] (41 observations)

— MTEF   --- 95 percent confidence interval

Source: World Bank.
Note: MTEF = medium-term expenditure framework.
a. Pre-MTEF mean.
b. Post-MTEF mean.
c. A lower value of the index means an improvement in cost-effectiveness.

MTEF implementation and that any reallocation of expenditures occurred elsewhere.[8] However, health expenditures are less volatile after MTEF implementation. As for technical efficiency, the cost-effectiveness of health expenditures is much the same before and after MTEF implementation. Only an MTBF appears to be associated with any improvement (figure E.4 in appendix E). While MTPFs should be associated most closely with improved cost-effectiveness, the small sample of MTPFs prevents anything meaningful from being said about them, while the minimal variation in life expectancy and the short sample period are limiting factors affecting the analysis of technical efficiency more generally.

Econometric Analysis

The econometric analysis attempts to identify causal relationships between MTEFs and fiscal performance. The basic empirical relationship is as follows:

$$\text{fiscal performance} = f\,(\text{MTEF status, control variables}). \qquad (4.1)$$

Fiscal performance is measured using the same indicators of fiscal discipline, allocative efficiency, and technical efficiency as in the event studies—the fiscal balance, total expenditure volatility, health expenditure share, health expenditure volatility, and cost-effectiveness of health expenditure. A country's MTEF status at any point in time is measured by a dummy variable coded 0 or 1 for each of the mutually exclusive MTEF stages: MTFF, MTBF, and MTPF. Control variables (or covariates) are variables other than MTEF status that are commonly used in the literature to explain differences in fiscal performance. These are GDP growth, trade openness, being an oil exporter, being a conflict country, having an IMF program, population, inflation, designation as a heavily indebted poor country, receipt of aid, and credit market access.

In estimating the relationship, some common estimation problems arise that could jeopardize the econometric results. Mention has already been made of possible reverse causality (MTEF adoption could be a response to fiscal performance) and the use of instrumental variables to address this problem. In addition, there are both a potential omitted-variable problem (some factor or factors that might explain fiscal performance may not be taken into account) and a possible errors-in-variables problem (fiscal performance, MTEF status, and other variables may not be measured correctly). The response to the omitted-variable problem is to include fixed country and time effects that control for country characteristics, such as culture and norms, and for global factors, such as oil price shocks, while the errors-in-variables problem is partially solved by the care taken to code countries' MTEF status, which is the only variable constructed specifically for this study.

Overall, nine econometric specifications are applied to pooled cross-section and time-series data. These are based on ordinary least squares with and without fixed effects, differences-in-differences with fixed effects and with and without regional trends, and generalized method of moments (GMM) techniques with and without static instrumental variables and year effects.[9] The static instrumental variable used to correct for the endogeneity of MTEF status is MTEF diffusion, which measures the geographic spread of each MTEF stage among a country's neighbors. The idea is that a country's MTEF status may be correlated with that of its neighbors, but its fiscal performance will be independent of the MTEF status of its neighbors. The GMM specifications include lagged dependent variables, which also control for the persistence of fiscal performance over time.

Table 4.1 provides a qualitative summary of the quantitative results reported in appendix E.

MTEF adoption has a significant positive effect on fiscal discipline. For the preferred specification (GMM with instrumental variables and year effects; column 8 in table F.2 in appendix F), an MTFF, MTBF, or MTPF increases the fiscal balance by 0.9, 1.0, and 2.8 percentage points of GDP, respectively. This means that, comparing years in which a country has an MTEF with years in which it does not, the fiscal balance improves more in countries that implement an MTEF than in those that do not. Moreover, the improvement is larger for more advanced MTEF stages. This result is qualitatively the same as that from the event studies, although the marginal impact of an MTPF (compared to an MTBF) is considerably larger. However, quantitative comparisons between the econometric and event study results are not valid given the differences in the two approaches.[10] That said, the marginal impact of MTPF adoption is implausibly large, and this may reflect the stronger fiscal position of advanced countries in the period considered. In the preferred specification, being an oil exporter has a positive influence on the fiscal balance, presumably because it implies higher revenue, while being a conflict country and receiving aid have a negative influence, in the first case because conflict goes hand-in-hand with economic collapse and in the second because the provision of aid is often associated with fiscal need.

The results for an alternative empirical relationship are reported for fiscal discipline. Appendix F describes and discusses the inclusion in the

Table 4.1 Summary of the Econometric Results

Variable	Fiscal discipline — Fiscal balance (1)	Allocative efficiency — Total expenditure volatility (2)	Allocative efficiency — Health expenditure share (3)	Health expenditure volatility (4)	Technical efficiency — Cost-effectiveness of health expenditure (5)
MTEF variables					
MTFF	0.85**	−1.74***	0.40***	−2.66***	0.11
MTBF	0.99*	−2.38***	0.48***	−2.95***	0.07
MTPF	2.82***	−3.42***	1.04***	−2.19	0.51***
Conditioning variable					
OECD	+✓✓				
Control variables					
Lag GDP growth	+✓	−✓			
Trade openness					
Oil exporter	+✓✓	+✓✓	−✓✓		
Conflict	−✓✓		−✓		
Lag IMF program					
Population			−✓		
Population square		+✓✓	+✓		
Inflation	−✓	+✓✓			
Heavily indebted poor country					+✓✓
Aid	−✓✓	+✓✓	−✓	+✓✓	
Lag credit market access					
Other variable					
Lag dependent variable	+✓✓	+✓✓	+✓✓	+✓✓	+✓✓

Source: World Bank.

Note: GDP = gross domestic product; IMF = International Monetary Fund; MTBF = medium-term budgetary framework; MTEF = medium-term expenditure framework; MTFF = medium-term fiscal framework; MTPF = medium-term performance framework; OECD = Organisation for Economic Co-operation and Developement. Coefficients from the preferred specifications are from column 8 of table E.2 in appendix F. * = significant at 1C percent; ** = significant at 5 percent; *** = significant at 1 percent; + = positive coefficient; − = negative coefficient; ✓ = significance with the preferred specification; ✓✓ = significance with other specifications yielding similar MTEF results as the preferred specification.

regressions of conditioning variables that the literature suggests could enhance the impact of an MTEF on the fiscal balance. Five such variables are included: the presence of a fiscal rule, which is justified by the fact that many countries have put in place fiscal balance, debt, expenditure, or revenue rules to bolster the credibility of fiscal policy; political cohesion, which makes it easier to implement reforms; democracy, because fiscal imbalances are likely to be larger when there is disagreement about spending priorities; membership in the Organisation for Economic Co-operation and Development (OECD), which creates peer pressure to adopt reforms that enhance fiscal discipline; and technical assistance from the IMF, which indicates support for the implementation of such reforms. Conditioning variables are included both as independent variables and interacted with MTEF status. Of these variables, only OECD membership is significant and only for MTPF adoption. This is not entirely surprising given that MTPFs are found mainly in these countries. Moreover, the large marginal impact of MTPFs on fiscal balances disappears when OECD membership is taken into account, confirming the advanced-country effect.

MTEF adoption also has a payoff in terms of allocative efficiency. Based on the same preferred specification, total expenditure volatility declines, starting with an MTFF and becoming stronger moving to an MTBF and then to an MTPF. Higher GDP growth in the previous year reduces the volatility of total expenditures, because more resources are available. Being an oil exporter, experiencing higher inflation, and being an aid recipient all increase the volatility of total expenditures, reflecting the fact that oil revenue and aid are themselves volatile, while inflation can create volatility in the availability of resources. The health expenditure share increases, with the more demanding MTEF stages having an increasingly strong effect. Being an oil exporter reduces the health expenditure share, presumably reflecting other expenditure priorities in these countries. Finally, health expenditure volatility also declines. A surprising finding is that an MTFF has a larger impact on the volatility of health expenditures than on total expenditures, which could be a consequence of coding piloted MTBFs, which often cover the health sector, as MTFFs. MTBFs still have a stronger effect than MTFFs, while MTPFs have a weaker effect. This could again be an advanced-country effect, since these countries are usually less volatile and typically have well-established, stable health sectors. Aid is the only significant control variable; it increases health expenditure volatility, again because aid is volatile and because donors favor health spending. Overall, these results are very much as predicted, and they provide stronger evidence of improvements in allocative efficiency under MTEFs than the event studies.

The impact of MTEF adoption on technical efficiency is less pronounced. Only MTPFs have a noticeable impact on the cost-effectiveness of health expenditures, which is as expected, but the effect is not that significant. Inflation increases cost-effectiveness, perhaps because higher costs prompt the search for cost savings. As noted for the event studies, the ability to say much about technical efficiency is hampered by the small number of MTPFs, limited variation in life expectancy, and the short sample period.[11]

Case Study Insights about the Quality of Budgeting

The impact of MTEFs on fiscal performance works mainly through changes in the quality of budgeting. Because of data limitations, it is not possible to investigate this channel in the event studies or econometric analysis. Rather, reliance is placed mainly on case studies and other sources to reveal how MTEF implementation affects the quality of budgeting. To this end, it is important to ask whether an MTEF provides a basis for preparing the annual budget and influences key budget decisions, the MTEF and annual budget are based on reasonable forecasts of key variables, existing and new programs are properly costed, spending decisions are guided by strategic considerations, and agency performance is used to guide the allocation of budget resources. In addition, cross-country assessments provide some insight.

Cross-Country Assessments

Several instruments were used to assess various aspects of a country's budgeting and broader public financial management (PFM) systems and to compare them across countries. Most notable in this regard is the public expenditure and financial accountability (PEFA) framework, which specifically addresses budget credibility as reflected in deviations of revenue and expenditure (and expenditure composition) from the budget. Final or draft PEFA reports are available for 100 developing countries. The International Budget Partnership's Open Budget Index (OBI) focuses on transparency—access to information, public participation, and accountability—but provides a proxy for the quality of budgeting in 85 advanced and developing countries. The Budget Institutions Index (BII) is quite broad in scope, in that it covers transparency, fiscal rules, budget scrutiny, accountability, and other PFM characteristics.[12] Although it does not deal specifically with MTEFs, the BII does provide a broad picture of the quality of PFM systems in 72 low-income countries. Finally, the Public Investment Management Index (PIMI) captures the institutional environment underpinning public investment management across four stages—project appraisal, selection, implementation, and evaluation—in 71 countries (Dabla-Norris et al. 2011).

PEFA, OBI, BII, and PIMI scores are higher in countries with MTEFs. Figure 4.6 indicates that the results from each assessment instrument and their components show consistently better scores for MTEF countries than for non-MTEF countries. While none of the instruments especially favors MTEF characteristics, PEFA deals separately with budget credibility—by comparing budgets and out-turns—where an MTEF is expected to have a direct beneficial effect. That said, MTEF countries

Figure 4.6   PEFA, OBI, BII, and PIMI Scores in MTEF and Non-MTEF Countries, as of 2008

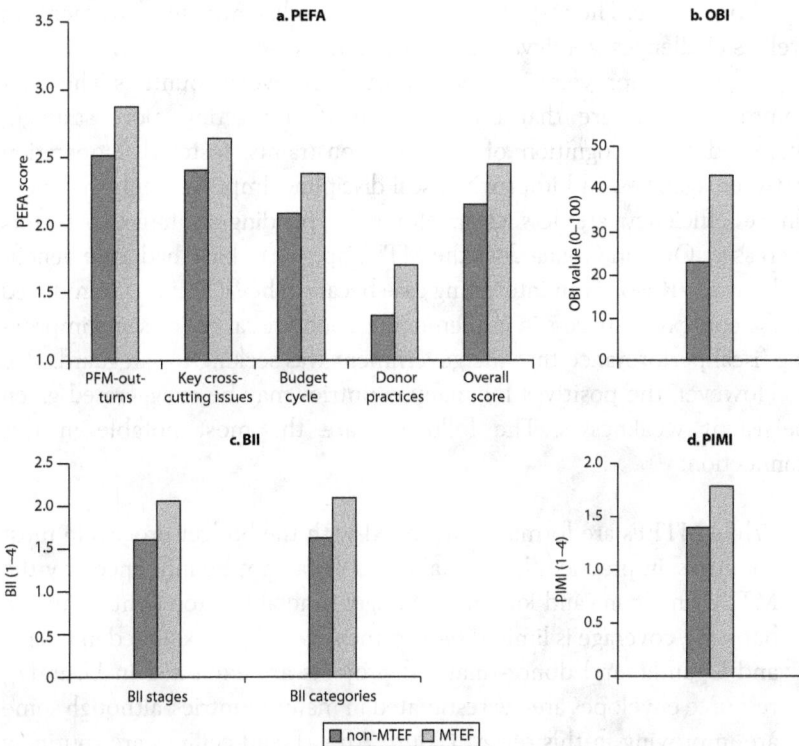

Sources: Public Expenditure and Financial Accountability for PEFA scores, International Budget Partnership for OBI, Dabla-Norris et al. (2010) for BII, and Dabla-Norris et al. (2011) for PIMI.
Note: BII = Budget Institutions Index; MTEF = medium-term expenditure framework; OBI = Open Budget Index; PEFA = public expenditure and financial accountability; PIMI = Public Invesment Management Index.

outperform non-MTEF countries across all PEFA components. However, PEFA scores tend to deteriorate as the budget cycle proceeds (de Renzio 2009), which may mean that MTEFs add more to budget preparation than to budget execution. Moreover, the fact that PEFA scores are higher to the extent that budget decision making is more concentrated (Andrews 2010) could be linked to the benefits of an MTEF led by the Ministry of Finance.

Case Studies

Several case studies were undertaken in an attempt to derive some lessons about the experience with MTEFs. Appendix G reports in detail on the 10 countries covered by the case studies—Albania, Armenia, Brazil, Ghana, Jordan, Republic of Korea, Nicaragua, the Russian Federation, South Africa, and Uganda. The case study questionnaire asked for comments on various aspects of MTEF experience related to the quality of budgeting. The responses suggest both substantial improvements as well as challenges in relevant budget practices.

Budgeting improvements were reported for several countries. The most common claims are that the MTEF made budgeting more strategic, increased the recognition of resource constraints, fostered cooperation between agencies, and improved fiscal discipline. Improvements in expenditure efficiency are less clear, although spending in targeted sectors increased. Only in Ghana does the MTEF appear to have had little beneficial impact. Russia is an interesting case because the MTEF was introduced in the context of success in implementing sound fiscal policies and improving fiscal performance that the government was seeking to safeguard.

However, the positives for many countries may be exaggerated given persistent weaknesses. The following are the most notable in this connection:

- While MTEFs are formally integrated with the budget process in most countries, in practice the annual budget may not be influenced by the MTEF (in Ghana and Jordan the budget timetable is too tight for this to happen), coverage is limited (government wages are excluded in Ghana and Uganda, and donor-financed projects are excluded in Uganda), resource envelopes are overestimated in many countries, although some are improving in this regard (South Africa), and ceilings are routinely ignored (Korea, Uganda). In some cases, budgeting seems to have remained incremental in nature (Ghana), although even well-functioning MTEFs retain some incremental elements (Uganda).

- While sector strategies are usually prepared, this is sometimes a pro forma exercise (South Africa), coverage of government expenditure is limited (Russia), or programs are not costed properly (Korea, Nicaragua). When public investment plans or programs are supposed to guide national priorities, links to the MTEF and budget are weak (Albania, Armenia), often because the country is not resource constrained (Albania).

- When a performance element is introduced, this is often based on an excessive number of indicators (Ghana) or on indicators of dubious quality (South Africa), is ignored in the decision-making process (Armenia, Jordan, Nicaragua), and is weak at the budget execution stage (Russia).

The case studies also suggest that implementation of an MTEF can run ahead of itself. MTEFs undoubtedly introduce additional complexity into budgeting, especially MTBFs and MTPFs. When countries move too fast, an advanced MTEF is likely to be badly designed and poorly implemented, which makes it less effective than a more basic MTEF. Ghana is a case in point. A consultant-led push to jump immediately to an MTPF before the required systems and skills had been developed meant that public financial management is less advanced now than if a more measured approach to MTEF implementation had been adopted. Moreover, in some areas it may be weaker than before MTEF adoption.

The recent global economic and financial crisis has tested MTEFs. Countries suspended their MTEFs for a year or more in response to the crisis (Armenia, Russia) or did not fully internalize its impact (Albania, Jordan). To some extent, this is understandable given that the sharp slowdown in growth worldwide and recession in many countries, together with the uncertain prospects for recovery, made macroeconomic and fiscal forecasting and thus preparing an MTEF unusually difficult. At the same time, the fiscal consequences of declining revenue, fiscal stimulus programs, and bank bailouts made expenditure prioritization even more important, and a realistic MTEF could have been helpful in determining how to accommodate these fiscal pressures. Russia is again a relevant case in point. Restarting the MTEF effort relatively soon after the crisis, in the 2010–12 budget cycle, allowed the country to sustain improvements in its fiscal position.

Notes

1. The general government data on health expenditure are sourced from the World Health Organization, while the central government data are sourced from the International Monetary Fund's *World Economic Outlook*.

2. The precise measure is the absolute value of the year-on-year change in the percentage deviation of the expenditure share from trend calculated using a Hodrick-Prescott (HP) filter.

3. This is measured as the distance from a frontier defined by the countries that are the most efficient in increasing life expectancy given their level of health spending per capita. In effect, it measures inefficiency or waste.

4. The reverse causality problem is described in more detail in appendix F.

5. A case can be made for including year t as the first year of the post-MTEF period since the MTEF was in effect that year. However, in some cases it is unclear whether an MTEF became operational in the year of implementation, especially in cases where the calendar and fiscal years do not coincide; hence the implementation year is treated as transitional.

6. The fiscal balance begins to improve in the year of MTEF implementation. If the MTEF became fully operational in that year, this could reflect the immediate impact of the MTEF. However, there are reasons to treat this as a transitional year and not part of the post-MTEF period.

7. The three- and five-year event studies are not directly comparable because of differences in sample size.

8. Limitations on data availability mean that, while 72 MTEFs are used for the event studies on fiscal discipline and total expenditure volatility, 67 are used for the event studies on health expenditure share and volatility and only 43 are used for the event study on cost-effectiveness of health expenditures.

9. A region-specific time trend controls for regional shocks. Year effects control for global factors.

10. The event study for the fiscal balance describes whether, on average across countries that adopted an MTFF, the fiscal balance improves in the years after MTFF adoption compared to the years before adoption.

11. Grigoli, Mills, Verhoeven, and Vlaicu (2012) use the same dataset but another approach involving Difference (or D-) GMM rather than system GMM. They arrive at very similar findings for the impact of MTEFs on fiscal performance (see Appendix F). This adds further evidence on the robustness of this study's results.

12. The BII by Dabla-Norris et al. (2011) includes three budgetary stages: planning and negotiation, approval, and implementation. Each of these budgetary stages is made up of five cross-cutting categories: (a) top-down procedures, (b) rules and controls, (c) sustainability and credibility, (d) comprehensiveness, and (e) transparency.

References

Andrews, M. 2010. "How Far Have Public Financial Management Reforms Come in Africa?" Faculty Research Working Paper RWP10-018, Harvard Kennedy School, Cambridge, MA.

Dabla-Norris, E., J. Brumby, A. Kyobe, Z. Mills, and C. Papageorgiou. 2011. "Investing in Public Investment: An Index of Public Investment Efficiency." IMF Working Paper 37, International Monetary Fund, Washington, DC.

De Renzio, P. 2009. "Taking Stock: What Do PEFA Assessments Tell Us about PFM Systems across Countries?" ODI Working Paper 302, Overseas Development Institute, London.

Grigoli, F., Z. Mills, M. Verhoeven, and R. Vlaicu. 2012. "MTEFs and Fiscal Performance: Panel Data Evidence." Policy Research Working Paper, World Bank, Washington, DC.

Schick, A. 2010. "Fiscal and Budget Institutions: Consolidators or Accommodators?" IMF Fiscal Forum, Washington, DC.

Tsibouris, G., M. Horton, M. Flanagan, and W. Maliszewski. 2006. "Experience with Large Fiscal Adjustments." Occasional Paper 246, International Monetary Fund, Washington, DC.

CHAPTER 5

Requirements for Effective MTEFs

This chapter discusses key institutional determinants of the performance of medium-term expenditure frameworks (MTEFs). Earlier assessments suggested that MTEFs have not lived up to expectations and attributed the failure to a variety of institutional factors. While the results of this study point to a positive impact of MTEFs on certain aspects of fiscal performance, the case studies suggest that MTEFs could achieve more if their potential to improve the quality of budgeting was exploited more fully. This chapter highlights what countries should be focusing on if they are to implement an MTEF that stands a good chance of succeeding. The discussion in this chapter is organized under four headings:

- Commitment to a new approach to budgeting
- Organizational adaptability and technical capacity
- Appropriate macro-fiscal policies and institutions
- Sound budget systems and properly sequenced public financial management (PFM) reforms.

Commitment to a New Approach to Budgeting

Political support for an MTEF is essential for its success. This support has to extend far beyond endorsing MTEF adoption. It has to include sustained backing for and involvement in a new way of doing government business. Without this support, the MTEF may be seen as a technical exercise parallel to the budget that preempts a lot of administrative resources with little apparent payoff. An MTEF is more than the elements, such as strategic planning, multiyear estimates, and expenditure ceilings, that characterize its more advanced stages. It is even more than a key component of the budget process. Rather, it constitutes a different approach to budgeting. In the best of circumstances, this new approach may offer such compelling benefits that politicians will willingly commit to an MTEF. In the Russian Federation, for example, the MTEF was seen as a way to institutionalize sound fiscal policies and achieve better fiscal performance. More realistically, politicians may have to be persuaded that an MTEF should be adopted, in which case strong political leadership is needed not only to mobilize support for the MTEF, but also to prevent the MTEF from being implemented in a manner that limits its effectiveness.

One challenge in this connection is to bring about necessary changes in political behavior. An MTEF prevents opportunistic interests that facilitate spending on whatever is politically expedient or benefits narrow constituencies from dominating the allocation of resources. Moreover, while MTEFs introduce additional complexity into budgeting, this should not translate into less transparency that could make it easier for politicians to push through unrealistic budgets, lower the productivity of spending, and delay expenditure reform. There has to be willingness to set priorities subject to resource constraints and to end the culture of entitlements in which expenditure allocations are regarded as floors that will always be raised rather than as ceilings that could be lowered. Only if this happens will MTEFs be able to deliver fiscal discipline and efficiency.

The MTEF and the annual budget also have to be well integrated. Box 5.1 presents a stylized version of an integrated MTEF and budget process. A key feature of this process is the continuous involvement of parliament, the cabinet, the Ministry of Finance (MoF), and spending agencies, which is a clear indication of broad-based commitment to a new approach to budgeting. The parliament and cabinet, in particular, play a key strategic role, which requires not only that they accept the centrality of the MTEF, but also that they fully understand how it functions and their role in making it work well and they are willing to fulfill this role.

Unfortunately, high-level support for MTEFs is sometimes missing or only transitory. The problem is that political leaders find it very difficult

Box 5.1

An Integrated MTEF and Budget Preparation Process

9–12 months before the new fiscal year
- Cabinet and spending agencies set out national and sector strategic priorities.
- The Ministry of Finance (MoF), in consultation with other economic agencies, develops the macro-fiscal framework and determines the medium-term expenditure framework (MTEF) resource envelope, based on the previous year's medium-term expenditure framework (MTEF)and high-level fiscal targets and rules.
- Spending agencies cost existing and new programs.
- The MoF prepares a medium-term budget strategy paper and budget or MTEF guidelines that include provisional expenditure ceilings.

6–9 months before the new fiscal year
- The cabinet reviews and endorses the medium-term budget strategy paper and provisional ceilings.
- The budget strategy paper is submitted to parliament for information.
- Budget and MTEF guidelines are circulated to spending agencies. (The nature of the guidelines will depend on whether the MTEF is a medium-term budget with hard multiyear ceilings or an annual budget combined with forward estimates, hard budget-year ceilings, and indicative out-year ceilings.)
- Spending agencies prepare their budget and MTEF submissions, taking into account sector strategies, program costs, and proposed ceilings.

3–6 months before the new fiscal year
- The MoF reviews the submissions of spending agencies, and hearings are held between the MoF and spending agencies to resolve technical differences.
- The cabinet is consulted about policy differences and other issues that could require significant reallocation of budget resources across spending agencies or programs.
- The MoF updates the macro-fiscal framework.
- The MoF prepares the final budget and MTEF, incorporating revised expenditure ceilings.

0–3 months before the new fiscal year
- The cabinet reviews the final budget or MTEF, endorses ceilings, and submits the budget to parliament for approval.
- Spending agencies revise sector strategies and prepare business plans consistent with their ceilings.

to reconcile their ambitions with the constraints implied by resource scarcity. An MTEF may be seen as a useful budgeting tool, but it requires sustained commitment in practice. The case studies reveal that political support has been strong and sustained in some countries (the Republic of Korea, Russia, South Africa) and has built up over time elsewhere (Uganda), but it has also been fragmented and inconsistent (Albania) and focused on form rather than substance (Ghana). Buy-in has to extend to the executives and high-level technocrats of all the agencies involved. A significant risk is that the MTEF will be seen largely as an initiative of the MoF, perhaps because it places much more emphasis on fiscal discipline than other PFM objectives and is therefore used simply to constrain spending or perhaps to wrest power from other agencies. In most countries, the MoF takes the lead in MTEF implementation, but in Ghana, Nicaragua, and, to a lesser extent, Jordan, MoF leadership has been a source of tension with other agencies.

A comprehensive approach to expenditure planning is also vital. An important element missing in many MTEFs, even well-functioning ones, is top-down guidance on strategic priorities. Thus while spending agencies often prepare sector strategies that can inform prioritization across programs and projects within a sector, there is no national strategy to inform judgments about resource allocation across sectors. This is not to say that governments do not have a view on national spending priorities; they often clearly do and articulate them in different ways. In many countries, this articulation occurs in connection with elections, as part of election platforms or efforts to forge workable coalitions. In some industrial countries, priorities emerge from periodic comprehensive spending reviews. However, the problem in many countries is that what national priorities are and how they affect budget allocations are often unclear. The fear is that allocations within sectors may be the result of a well-functioning MTEF, while allocations between sectors may reflect the shortcomings of annual budgeting. It is therefore important for governments to be explicit about national priorities.

For many developing countries, national economic or development planning has long provided a basis for setting national and sector priorities. There is no reason why this cannot continue with an MTEF, at least for a while. Eventually an MTEF can provide a comprehensive framework for integrating planning and budgeting. But in the interim, as the MTEF is developed, having a well-functioning planning agency, either as a stand-alone entity (a planning ministry) or as part of another entity (such as the prime minister's office), can be workable. In many developing countries, it has proved quite difficult to integrate the MTEF with national development planning because the Ministry of Planning is often more powerful than the Ministry of Finance, institutional rigidities are hard to change, the tradition of collective decision making through the cabinet is weak, and the planning process is regarded as more important than the budget process. At the same time, a developing-country MoF often does not have the resources to take on the responsibility for planning, and its resources are best devoted to building up its MTEF capabilities in its existing areas of competence. That said, the MoF and spending agencies should be engaged in the work of the planning agency, so that national plans, sector strategies, resource projections, and expenditure allocations are determined in a complementary rather than a conflicting manner. In particular, the MoF can curb the tendency for economic and development plans to set unrealistic targets. Ideally, the planning and MTEF processes should become better integrated over time, and ultimately the former could be fully incorporated into the latter. Box 5.2 highlights the difference between national development plans (NDPs), public investment plans (PIPs), and MTEFs and discusses how NDPs and MTEFs can coexist (how PIPs and MTEFs can coexist is discussed below). How this coexistence is achieved and how long it takes will be country specific, depending on factors such as a country's development challenges, overall progress with PFM reform, and success in achieving buy-in from a planning agency that might resist having its responsibilities shifted to the MoF or another central economic agency. The merging of the finance and planning ministries contributed to the integration of planning and the MTEF in Uganda and Korea.

Countries that engage in PIP outside the budget process will have to consider its role in an MTEF. The case studies reveal that the usual approach is to let the MTEF and PIP coexist, as in Albania, Nicaragua, and Uganda. However, if the PIP is not resource constrained, which is the case in Albania, meaningful coordination with the MTEF is not possible. The outcome can also be dual budgets, where public investment is budgeted separately from current expenditures. Oftentimes, overall budgets end up being driven by investment and donors, and capital and current budgets are coordinated poorly. This is most evident in the underprovision for operations and maintenance. In sharp contrast to the dual budget regime of a PIP, an MTEF provides a framework for determining how much and what type of public investment is consistent with medium-term economic and social objectives and links medium-term

Box 5.2

MTEFs, Development Planning, and Public Investment Planning

Medium-term expenditure frameworks (MTEFs), national development planning, and public investment planning play different roles. For a country to consider adopting an MTEF in an environment with a (successful) national development plan (NDP) or public investment program (PIP), it is necessary to judge the advantages and disadvantages of each instrument and the implications for one if the other is introduced. Table B5.2 focuses on the relative strengths and weaknesses of MTEFs, NDPs, and PIPs.

Although there may be some similarities between NDPs, PIPs, and MTEFs, there are also important differences. Ideally, if these planning instruments are to remain in place, they should coexist in a synergistic way. While some countries, such as Korea, have eliminated development plans in the context of introducing MTEFs, this is not always the preferred option, at least initially. While it would be possible to introduce an MTEF without linking it to an NDP or a PIP, doing so might be an inefficient and ineffective way to address the goal of development within fiscal constraints.

Table B5.2   Major Strengths and Weaknesses of NDPs, PIPs, and MTEFs

Indicator	NDPs	PIPs	MTEFs
Strength	Presents a vision for development that can motivate the public and private sectors Identifies major development issues	Identifies priorities for public investment Facilitates project selection using widely accepted criteria	Supports broader fiscal policy objectives Is a concrete medium-term plan, constrained by resource availability
Weakness	Usually lacks specificity and is more aspirational than practical Does not identify direct consequences for the budget	Can create dual budgeting, with underprovision for operations and maintenance Is often not resource constrained	Does not look beyond the government (for example, ignores private sector contribution to development)

Note: MTEF = Medium-term expenditure framework; NDP = national development plan; PIP = public investment program.

(continued next page)

Box 5.2 *(continued)*

Based on the aim of creating synergy across planning instruments, the major options with regard to NDPs and MTEFs are the following:

- *Lengthen the period of the NDP, making it more clearly a long-term vision.* Introduce MTEFs as a separate tool for medium-term resource allocation, which supports the agenda in the national development plan, albeit within fiscal constraints. The strengths are that the distinctive nature of NDPs and MTEFs can be maintained and two development tools can exist in a synergistic way, each adding separate benefits to the development process. However, new coordination procedures may have to be designed and implemented.

- *Infuse MTEF concepts (annual rolling plan and covering the whole budget) into the NDP.* The strengths are that doing so preserves what may be considered highly effective in an NDP, but also allows the introduction of the MTEF. The weaknesses are that, because these two planning instruments have quite different characteristics, it is highly likely that implementation difficulties will emerge. Moreover, this may encourage confusion between public and private resources and imply that the budget is the mechanism by which the national plan will be implemented, whereas in actuality implementation will rely on multiple players and instruments.

operations and maintenance with the stock of public capital and public investment plans. This being the case, the role of the PIP should be limited to identifying public investments of strategic importance, checking that projects pass standard cost-benefit tests, and ensuring that the right projects are chosen for private sector involvement. The MTEF then determines the allocation of resources to public investment. A separate entity, possibly a planning agency, can be responsible for planning private investment as well as for managing public investment projects.

Finally, if development partners operate within the MTEF framework, this can send a strong signal of the importance attached to it. Both bilateral and multilateral donors have in many cases motivated an MTEF as a means of ensuring that their resources are effectively used and have either provided or mobilized assistance with MTEF development. However, development partners can also be blind to some of the constraints on effective MTEF implementation and can push countries into reforms for which they are not ready, which may not have the desired impact and may possibly be harmful.

Governments should decide that an MTEF is appropriate, and an MTEF should be seen to serve the government's broad economic and development objectives rather than the development partners' narrow interests. Aid creates many problems for budgeting because it is volatile and can involve spending rigidities. The MTEF provides a mechanism for reconciling aid volatility (and resource volatility more generally) with expenditure stability and the preferences of donors with those of government. Bringing aid on-MTEF and on-budget is also consistent with the general trend toward using country systems to manage aid.

Organizational Adaptability and Technical Capacity

MTEFs change how budgeting is conducted. Under an MTEF, the cabinet and parliament play a more strategic role, providing guidance on priorities and policies, although they still perform their respective oversight and legislative functions. The MoF focuses on the macro-fiscal framework, the technical aspects of setting spending priorities, and management of the aggregate budget; in most countries, the MoF also oversees all aspects of MTEF preparation, in effect acting as a gatekeeper. Spending agencies are responsible for formulating sector strategies and spending plans and for managing and evaluating programs.

These are quite different from the traditional roles under annual budgeting, where the MoF prepares the budget in accordance with cabinet instructions and manages public funds, parliament approves the budget, and spending agencies implement programs. All participants in the budget process have to adjust to their new roles and work together to make collective decisions regarding resource allocation, but they also must accept that one agency, usually the MoF, is in the lead. For its part, the MoF has to recognize that its task is to provide guidance on intersector priorities, to resolve interagency conflicts, and ultimately to set expenditure ceilings, but not to get involved in the details of spending decisions.

Problems have arisen in trying to implement a new operational model for budgeting. The MoF, spending agencies, or both have not been motivated or prepared to take on their new roles. The MoF can be too authoritarian and spending agencies can be too submissive; both can have little intention of sticking to their budgets. It is better for budget allocations to be contested as part of the budget process than after the fact, and this is what an MTEF allows—competition for resources and commitment to the outcome once it has been decided. In some cases, the cabinet, parliament, or both have not internalized what an MTEF can and cannot (or should not) do and what their roles are in the MTEF process. There have also been coordination problems with national plans, as well as with PIPs, and dual budgeting has been commonplace, while other elements of the budget process have impeded rather than supported an MTEF. Quite often, the MTEF is a new process grafted onto the existing annual budget, with the latter prepared using traditional and often inappropriate procedures. The outcome can be a budget process that is worse rather than better than before and an MTEF that is a means of justifying unrealistic budgets. Even if everybody is on board and committed to the MTEF, the process of change has to be well managed.

With new responsibilities come new requirements such as collective decision making and skills. The cabinet needs to shift its emphasis from authorizing spending to providing effective strategic guidance on priorities and policies. As the MoF seeks to prioritize public resources rather than assert detailed control over budget execution, it has to make informed judgments about priorities across sectors based on cabinet guidance and the link between sector strategies and expenditure allocations. It must also be able to work with macro-fiscal models, produce high-quality fiscal forecasts, and manage public finances more generally.

As spending agencies seek to influence rather than administer budgets, they must be able to cost programs, plan strategically, determine priorities within sectors, and ultimately measure and evaluate program performance. Of course, there are still constraints—aggregate resources and agency or program ceilings—and the aim is to manage for efficiency within these constraints. Doing so places a much greater emphasis on analytical and managerial skills as opposed to political and administrative skills. *A specific requirement is the ability to impart a quantitative dimension to all policies.*

A particular technical challenge is to combine the best available approaches to determining the resource envelope and preparing forward estimates of program costs. This task has three elements:

- *Macro-fiscal modeling*, which is intended to determine how much new borrowing the government can undertake consistent with maintaining macroeconomic stability and debt sustainability.
- *Revenue forecasting*, which assesses the revenue that can be generated by the current tax system and current sources of non-tax revenue given existing administrative capacity and new sources of revenue, including both policy changes and administrative improvements.
- *Cost analysis*, which identifies cost drivers for existing and announced programs and estimates program costs on the basis of projected developments in these cost drivers.

On the one hand, optimism in determining the resource envelope (to justify bigger budgets) is commonplace and likely when preparing forward estimates of program costs (to justify more or larger programs).[1] Fewer resources or higher costs than planned usually compromise fiscal discipline, while hastily implemented spending cuts can harm efficiency. On the other hand, pessimism can leave spending agencies with unbudgeted resources that will likely be saved or more likely be spent in ways that have not been subjected to full budget scrutiny, which undermines efficiency.

The aim should be to use appropriate macro-fiscal models that are well understood, realistic forecasts that are in line with the consensus of other forecasters, and the best available techniques for costing based on a good knowledge of the drivers of costs in different programs. That things may not turn out as expected is an ever-present fiscal risk that should be provided for through an unallocated budget contingency; however, systematic under- or overestimation of resources can be a sign that opportunistic politicians or bureaucrats are striving to sidestep the budget process and reallocate resources to suit their own ends.

The success of an MTEF hinges on the capacity to perform these tasks. The MTEF is often countercultural, especially where government lacks a tradition of collective decision making, and strains the resources of developing-country governments, especially in spending but also in finance ministries. A combination of new hires and retraining is required to ensure that the MoF and spending agencies are appropriately staffed, although the precise requirements will depend on the quality of personnel a country starts with. Civil service reform may be needed to relieve bottlenecks to obtaining the right skills. In any event, the ability to implement the different MTEF stages must influence the speed of their implementation. Parliamentarians and senior executives also need to be well informed about, or at least sensitized to, the role of an MTEF.

Appropriate Macro-Fiscal Policies and Institutions

Reform can be difficult in the context of macroeconomic instability and large fiscal imbalances. Governments seeking to address these problems can become preoccupied with short-term adjustment and lose sight of longer-term structural issues. Unless they are pushed into reform—for example, under an International Monetary Fund (IMF) program—governments often keep reform on the back burner, waiting until they do not have more immediate issues with which to grapple. However, a case can be made that reforms are easier to introduce when the going is tough, in which case the unavoidable need for short-term adjustment should be seen as an opportunity to implement structural reforms. There is no clear-cut answer as to which of these views is right. And while experience suggests that some reforms, such as civil service restructuring, are easier in bad times, this is not necessarily true of other reforms. Indeed, it may be imprudent to rush into reforms that require careful planning and preparation even if immediate circumstances are favorable.

In the case of MTEFs, there is a specific issue as to whether they should be implemented to attain or consolidate fiscal adjustment. The econometric evidence clearly suggests the former—that is, the causation runs from MTEF adoption to improved fiscal discipline. However, the latter cannot be ruled out entirely given that the approach to addressing the reverse causality problem does not eliminate this possibility. Moreover, as a practical proposition, although an MTEF can facilitate fiscal adjustment in many cases, in others a weak fiscal position may be turned around without one. In these cases, there is no reason to expect that an MTEF cannot assist in safeguarding a stronger fiscal position and in the process provide room for flexibility in conducting fiscal policy (for example, to achieve short-term stabilization or to respond to materializing fiscal risks). This seems to be what happened in Russia. But even where it is believed that an MTEF should be introduced to back up a decision to tackle fiscal imbalances, there may be a trade-off. While an MTEF can support and lend credibility to fiscal adjustment, it requires careful preparation and often needs to be accompanied by other budget reforms if its full potential is to be realized. This being the case, there is a risk that a hastily implemented MTEF could compromise adjustment efforts.

On balance, it would seem that an MTEF could safely be adopted to support fiscal adjustment where supporting budget systems are in place. Where this is not the case, the success of an MTEF cannot be taken for granted, and the sequencing of MTEF implementation with other budgeting and PFM reforms becomes an issue. This is discussed in more detail below.

A related issue is whether MTEFs are more effective when accompanied by fiscal rules. The idea is that ceilings become an implementation rule designed to support high-level policy rules (that is, deficit and debt rules or less common aggregate expenditure rules). Such an approach also reflects the fact that spending is a natural candidate for a fiscal control variable, because spending pressure is the main source of deficit bias and the focus of the budget process. However, the econometric analysis does not suggest that MTEFs and rules are complementary. While this study suggests a clear link between MTEFs and fiscal discipline, the record of policy rules in promoting sound government finances is patchy at best, especially with regard to their ability to rein in national as opposed to subnational governments.

Nevertheless, in the period ahead, as many advanced and emerging-market countries have to address the fiscal imbalances that are a legacy of the recent global economic and financial crisis, a combination of fiscal rules and expenditure ceilings is being recommended as a means of disciplining medium-term government finances and securing the required fiscal adjustment (IMF 2009). However, if rules are to be effective, they clearly have to be strengthened. This is not straightforward. The aim is to achieve an appropriate balance between constraining fiscal policy over the medium term and allowing short-term flexibility, usually by strengthening surveillance mechanisms and imposing effective sanctions in the event that flexibility is abused. Unless this is done, rules are unlikely to work any better in the future than they did in the past, and whether ceilings are effective or not will be largely unaffected by the presence of rules (that is, they will work just as well supporting rules or helping to meet headline, but not rules-based, fiscal targets).

Independent input could play a role in improving the performance of an MTEF and promoting good fiscal outcomes more generally. Since optimistic forecasts frequently undermine the credibility of MTEFs, an independent body could validate, or even prepare, the macroeconomic and fiscal forecasts used to determine the resource envelope. A good example of this is Chile, where panels of experts provide the output and copper price forecasts that are used in preparing the medium-term fiscal framework (MTFF). However, several countries have fiscal councils with functions that extend beyond the validation or preparation of forecasts to include advising on fiscal policies, auditing fiscal performance, and costing new programs (for a discussion of the workings of fiscal councils, see Hemming and Joyce 2012; Kopits 2011). There is some cross-country evidence that fiscal councils have a positive impact on fiscal discipline, especially where the council is perceived to be politically independent and can influence the budget (see Debrun and Kumar 2007).

Sound Budget Systems and Properly Sequenced PFM Reforms

One of the most common claims is that MTEFs cannot work in countries where budget systems are weak and annual budgets lack credibility. Reflecting on the experience with MTEFs, Schiavo-Campo (2008) concludes that, while they have raised awareness of the need for a medium-term perspective, for coordination between government agencies, and for paying attention to results, many MTEFs have been less successful than anticipated because they divert attention away from the basic budget reforms that are critical to their success.

Part of the problem may be that major reforms can develop a momentum that is unjustified by the capacity to implement them. According to Andrews (2009), the appetite for certain budgetary reforms is a consequence of isomorphism, where countries seek legitimacy in whatever is being touted as the best budget practice. MTEFs, as what might be termed a "modern budget reform," could be particularly susceptible to isomorphic influences, while underlying budget practices that influence the success of MTEFs tend to be forgotten.

So, when should an MTEF be implemented? It may seem evident that countries that must resort to some of the worst budget practices, such as cash rationing and payment arrears, cannot properly manage an annual budget and therefore are unlikely to see much benefit from moving to an MTEF. But even in this case, while the priority for reform—establishing expenditure control—may seem obvious, it is unclear whether this is a requirement for MTEF implementation. Indeed, an MTEF could be a catalyst for putting in place complementary budget reforms. One question is, Are there budgeting requirements that have to be met before an MTEF should be considered? A closely related, but different, question is, What budgeting foundations should be laid before an MTEF can be expected to succeed?

These questions get to the heart of the debate about PFM sequencing. Two approaches to sequencing have dominated the discussion to date:

- *The basics-first approach* says that modern budget reforms should be put off until basic budget systems are up and running. A leading proponent of this approach, Schick (1998) emphasizes the importance of establishing basic financial compliance by focusing on input-based cash budgeting, putting in place a reliable accounting system, and conducting effective external financial audits. He also warns that modern budget reforms, especially the shift to a performance-based budget system, require a cultural change in how government conducts business that could take years to take root.

- *The platform approach*, proposed by Brooke (2003), says that sets of complementary budget reforms should be packaged into platforms that are technically dependent on one another and should be implemented sequentially. In contrast to the basics-first approach, which addresses immediate technical requirements and lacks a clear vision of where PFM reform is headed, the platform approach requires government to be explicit about its longer-term PFM goals, which can provide a basis for mobilizing and coordinating outside support for reform.

Clearly, the platform approach can provide a framework for planning comprehensive PFM reform programs. Therefore, despite the appealing simplicity of the basics-first approach, the platform approach—if not in name, then certainly in spirit—has gained greater currency among donors and international finance institutions, including the Bank and the IMF, given their predilection for comprehensive reform programs. However, just as the simplicity of the basics-first approach masks a lack of agreement on what constitutes the basics,[2] so the intuitive appeal of the platform approach has been criticized for its lack of clarity as to the desired makeup of the different platforms, with regard to both the goals of each platform and the precise reforms each platform should include.[3] But this should not detract from the fact that the platform approach, because of its forward-looking, aspirational nature, constitutes the more complete response to the issue of sequencing reform.

However, the differences between the basics-first and platform approaches may be more apparent than real. Indeed, equating the basics with the first platform can reconcile the two approaches by highlighting their complementarity. Thus Diamond (2010) proposes an approach to sequencing with three goal-oriented platforms: basic financial compliance, aggregate fiscal discipline, and spending efficiency. Since aggregate fiscal discipline and spending efficiency are the goals of an MTEF, as Diamond acknowledges, basic financial compliance has to be achieved before an MTEF is introduced. However, achieving basic financial compliance is very demanding. The characteristics of basic financial compliance, presented in box 5.3, are rarely present in their entirety. If these are indeed preconditions for an MTEF, hardly any country should have one.

In fact, it is far from clear that basic financial compliance should be the overarching goal of the first platform. Achieving basic financial compliance is concerned with controlling budget execution, while MTEFs are more about preparing the budget. Sound budget preparation—which should always be resource constrained, even if strategic and performance-oriented budgeting has to wait—is widely considered essential to a good PFM system.

Box 5.3

Characteristics of Basic Financial Compliance

- *Realistic budget.* (a) Revenue forecasts are realistic, based on detailed analysis of tax bases, and (b) expenditures are fully costed, with adequate allowance for inflation, exchange rate movements, and recurrent costs of completed investments.
- *In-year control over spending.* (a) Commitments as well as cash are controlled, and (b) the budget is comprehensive and makes adequate provision for contingencies.
- *In-year control over taxes.* (a) Tax administration has capacity to enforce the tax laws, and (b) tax collections are analyzed and compared with estimates.
- *Timely accounting and reporting.* (a) Accounting is comprehensive and timely, (b) bank reconciliation is reliable and timely, and (c) reports are produced with minimal delay so that budget execution can be tracked.
- *Central control over cash.* (a) A treasury single account (or consolidated fund concept) is used, and (b) the use of cash transactions is minimal.
- *Adequate internal control procedures.* (a) Administrative internal controls are in place in all government departments, (b) procurement is transparent, with well-defined regulations, and (c) internal audit functions are adequate.
- *Adequate external control procedures.* (a) External audits address financial irregularities with timely reports to the legislature, and (b) legislative scrutiny is strong, as is follow-up on audit reports.

Source: Diamond 2010.

That is not to say that budget execution does not matter, and improvements to commitment control, the payment process, accounting, and audit have to be part of the reform process from the outset. Indeed, where budget institutions have been severely compromised, as in fragile states, controlling budget execution with a view to ensuring that the basic functions of government can be performed is often a legitimate priority (Symansky 2010). However, as box 5.4 illustrates, fiscal performance has improved in fragile states that have introduced MTEFs. More generally, in normal circumstances, one of the main reasons that budgets go off track is that they were not realistic to start with. Well-prepared budgets are more likely to be executed as planned; furthermore, expenditure ceilings established under MTEFs help to constrain budget execution.

Box 5.4

MTEFs and Fragile States

Fragile states were identified by looking at the World Bank, Organisation for Economic Co-operation and Development (OECD), and European Commission (EC) definitions:

- World Bank (2011) uses the term "fragile states" for countries facing particularly severe development challenges: weak institutional capacity, poor governance, and political instability. These countries often experience ongoing violence as the residue of past conflict.
- According to OECD (2008), a fragile state is unable to meet its population's expectations or manage changes in expectations and capacity through the political process. Questions of legitimacy, in embedded or historical forms, influence these expectations, while performance against expectations and the quality of participation or the political process also produce (or reduce) legitimacy.
- EC (2007) uses the term "fragility" for weak or failing structures and situations where the social contract is broken as a result of the state's incapacity or unwillingness to deal with its basic functions and meet its obligations and responsibilities regarding service delivery, management of resources, rule of law, equitable access to power, security and safety of the populace, and protection and promotion of citizens' rights and freedoms.

If a country appears on at least one of the three lists, which only began identifying fragile states in 2001, it is included in the data used for the panels in figure B5.4. Thus 44 fragile states were identified and 13 (Afghanistan, Bosnia and Herzegovina, Cameroon, Ethiopia, Guinea, Kenya, Mauritania, Nepal, Niger, Pakistan, Papua New Guinea, Rwanda, and Uganda) were used for the event studies, except when looking at the cost-effectiveness of health expenditure, where only seven (Cameroon, Ethiopia, Kenya, Mauritania, Niger, Pakistan, and Rwanda) were used.

Figure B5.4 suggests that the event study results largely carry over to fragile states. Indeed, all of the indicators of fiscal performance show some improvement. In the case of fiscal discipline, this is not unexpected, given the premium that these countries often place on managing within severe resource constraints. But improvements in allocative and technical efficiency, which are much less apparent in countries that have adopted medium-term expenditure frameworks (MTEFs), is a surprising outcome in fragile states given their weak implementation

(continued next page)

Box 5.4 *(continued)*

Figure B5.4   MTEFs in Fragile States

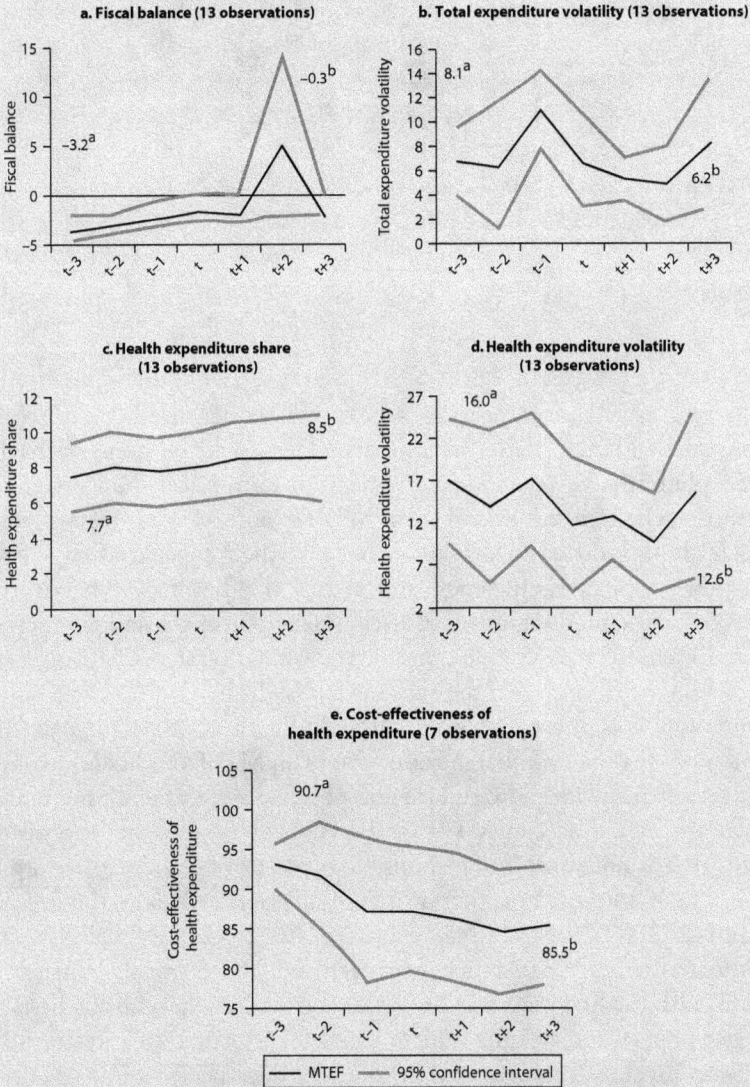

a. Fiscal balance (13 observations)

b. Total expenditure volatility (13 observations)

c. Health expenditure share (13 observations)

d. Health expenditure volatility (13 observations)

e. Cost-effectiveness of health expenditure (7 observations)

MTEF ——— 95% confidence interval

Source: Authors' analysis of World Bank data.
Note: MTEF = medium-term expenditure framework. A lower value of the index means an improvement in cost-effectiveness.
a. Pre-MTEF mean.
b. Post-MTEF mean.

(continued next page)

Box 5.4 *(continued)*

capacity. Of course, the small number of fragile states with MTEFs makes it difficult to reach definitive conclusions. That said, many fragile states have experienced a collapse in administrative capabilities that previously allowed them to manage public finances effectively, and it is only to be expected that some, especially where there has not been a mass exodus of skilled manpower, have been able to rebuild these capabilities quickly. Otherwise, why would seven of the 13 countries have a medium-term budgetary framework (MTBF)? This observation is consistent with other World Bank work that reports rapid PFM improvements in fragile states once political stability and governance structures have been restored (World Bank 2012).

In fact, MTEFs can provide a basis for sequencing budget reform consistent with the platform approach. This could be done by having three platforms corresponding to medium-term fiscal, budgetary, and performance frameworks (MTFFs, MTBFs, and MTPFs, respectively), which are introduced in that order because their concentrations—fiscal discipline, allocative efficiency, and technical efficiency, respectively—reflect the accepted hierarchy of fiscal policy objectives and are increasingly difficult to achieve given that successive MTEF stages become more demanding with regard to the systems and skills needed for their implementation. This approach could certainly be appropriate for countries contemplating the eventual introduction of an MTBF or MTPF. However, while countries with more rudimentary budget systems and poor budget outcomes would see an MTBF and MTPF as reforms for the distant future, the sizable payoff to responsible pursuit of fiscal discipline argues for all such countries making an MTFF a priority. This is the view of Tommasi (2009), for example, who advocates aggregate fiscal discipline as the goal of the basics-first approach, which essentially equates an MTFF with the first platform, on the understanding that it is the basis for budget preparation and the budget has to be executed in a manner that achieves fiscal discipline as envisaged under the MTFF.

Indeed, an MTFF can be the first platform of budget reform even if the budget has, and might retain for some time, a purely annual focus. This is because annual budgets finance multiyear programs, and decisions about allocating resources to such programs should take into account their availability in the budget and subsequent years. This would also be the case if forecasting and modeling skills are rudimentary, and accounting and reporting limitations mean that data are weak. A fiscal constraint with a weak technical and empirical basis is better than none at all, especially if there is a bias toward caution.[4]

The priority then is to develop the foundations needed to ensure that an MTFF can deliver a better-quality assessment of aggregate resource availability and that expenditure ceilings derived from the MTFF and imposed on spending agencies have a good chance of being adhered to. Upgrading the technical skills of forecasters and modelers and improving accounting and reporting principles and practices respond to the first of these needs. Paying attention to the problems with budget execution addresses the second.

A well-functioning MTFF would then provide the basis for shifting to the second platform, an MTBF. A country with a more developed budget system and better fiscal outcomes could begin with this platform, whether or not it has a formal MTFF. As mentioned, an MTBF combines an MTFF with a decentralized, bottom-up assessment of resource needs, guided by both national and sector strategic objectives, in an attempt to ensure that budget resources are allocated to programs, projects, and activities where they have the largest economic and social payoff.

The main foundations of an MTBF are the development and use of national and sector strategies to determine spending allocations as well as effective collaboration between central government and spending agencies to determine spending allocations. An MTBF is also aided by shifting the focus of budgeting to programs, which are the strategic focus, and by adopting at least some accrual principles in accounting, which provide a better indication of medium-term program costs.

In the first instance, an MTBF may not achieve that much. This would certainly be the case if a governmentwide MTBF has only limited strategic input and bottom-up engagement. The most that can be expected is some modest reallocation of resources from obviously wasteful programs, projects, and activities (for example, white elephants) to those with a clearly higher priority (for example, human development). In the first instance, it may be better to phase in the MTBF on a pilot basis. For example, the MTBF could begin with spending agencies responsible for human development programs, which happened in some countries in Africa that introduced MTEFs to secure spending for poverty reduction in the context of a poverty reduction strategy paper.

Alternatively, it could begin with spending agencies that spend heavily on infrastructure (such as the Ministry of Transportation), where the payoff to medium-term planning and funding assurances is likely to be significant. A pilot approach could provide valuable experience, and a more measured approach to implementation may be suitable in the case of an MTBF, as opposed to the case of an MTFF. This is because the argument that it is acceptable to have a fairly weak MTFF, at least initially, would not seem to carry over to an MTBF because a half-hearted attempt to launch a full MTBF could worsen the allocation of resources.

The arguments concerning an MTBF largely carry over to an MTPF, which is the third platform. Certainly, imparting a performance dimension to budgeting has specific requirements. There is also an issue regarding when to transition from an MTBF to an MTPF, especially when assessing and rewarding performance are the latest trend in public management. At some point, the payoff to embarking on an MTPF will exceed that of further refining an MTBF, and this may occur before the MTBF is working perfectly. In part, this decision will depend on the prospects for laying the foundations needed to support an effective MTPF. But it also will require evidence of a more widespread change in how governments conduct their operations and a commitment to foster accountability for results within government agencies.

The basic idea behind an MTEF-based platform approach to sequencing budget reform is fairly simple. The goals of the three MTEF stages— aggregate fiscal discipline, allocative efficiency, and technical efficiency— are compelling and widely supported. It is understood, however, that the mechanisms that MTFFs, MTBFs, and MTPFs put in place will work better when the foundations needed to support them are also in place. Thus while the goals of each platform might be common across countries, different countries will begin with different platforms. Also, the foundations needed to support the platforms will be shared.

Box 5.5 summarizes the requirements of these foundations. However, what needs to be done before any given MTEF stage is functioning properly will differ across countries. In other words, reform strategies still have to be tailored to each country's starting point, capabilities, and institutional setting. An implication of the MTEF-based platform approach is that if MTEFs delivered less than hoped in the past, this was not because an MTEF was the wrong approach to recommend, but rather because it was implemented in the wrong way. More specifically, the stage of MTEF adopted was too advanced because the foundations needed for it to succeed had not been laid. The MTEF-based platform approach not only emphasizes what these foundations are, but also can be a catalyst to building the required foundations.

Box 5.5

Policy, Budgeting, and Technical Enablers for Different MTEF Stages

MTFF

- *Policy requirements.* Set aggregate fiscal targets (fiscal balance, revenue, expenditure) and agency and possibly program expenditure ceilings, consistent with medium-term resource availability
- *Budgeting requirements.* (a) Legal and administrative framework: provide support for an effective cash-based annual budget; (b) accounting, classification, and reporting: employ cash and, possibly, modified cash accounting, an institution- and, possibly, program-based expenditure coding and chart of accounts, and quarterly reporting on budget developments; (c) treasury and information systems: ensure that cash flows are centralized, payments are timely, and the flow of financial information is standardized; and (d) control and audit: establish internal control procedures and external audits to ensure that spending is in line with appropriations
- *Technical requirements.* Employ fiscal forecasting, macro-fiscal modeling, and monitoring of fiscal aggregates and their key components.

MTBF (over and above MTFF requirements)

- *Policy requirements.* Set strategic priorities, both nationally and by sector
- *Budgeting requirements.* (a) Legal and administrative framework: move to program budgeting; (b) accounting, classification, and reporting: employ modified cash or modified accrual accounting and introduce a program classification (if not in place under an MTFF); and (c) treasury and information systems and control and audit: adjust to modified cash or accrual accounting and program classification
- *Technical requirements.* Set up a system of program costing and public investment management.

MTPF (over and above MTBF requirements)

- *Policy requirements.* Measure performance and link the budget to results
- *Budgeting requirements.* (a) Legal and administrative framework: move to performance and possibly accrual budgeting; (b) accounting, classification, and reporting: employ modified accrual or accrual accounting and reporting on program performance; (c) treasury and information systems: adjust to modified accrual or accrual accounting and require annual reporting on performance; and (d) control and audit: introduce performance or value-for-money audit
- *Technical requirements.* Employ performance indicators.

While MTEF implementation can be a guiding framework for budget reform, it need not be. A third of all countries do not have an MTEF, and some may decide it is not for them, at least not for a while and maybe not in name. But the platform approach to sequencing reform still has merit. And while the MTEF-based platform approach dispenses with the notion of basic budget systems and reforms, this idea may still appeal to some countries as a basis for the first platform. What countries do is clearly more important than how they label what they are doing; therefore, the key issue is to get the goals and content of the platforms right. The MTEF-based platform approach emphasizes the importance of establishing a solid foundation for each platform.

Finally, PFM reform does not take place with a clean slate. If the MTEF-based platform approach has merit, it will usually be introduced against a background where elements of the three MTEF stages—MTFF, MTBF, and MTPF—are in place, but none is working well. In this case, the idea is not to abandon more advanced stages; the focus is entirely on developing the MTFF until it is working well. MTBF and MTPF capabilities will eventually be needed, and some of the basics of effective MTBFs and MTPFs may be in place. These basics need to be built upon to enhance MTBF and MTPF capabilities. In general, it is inefficient to abandon existing processes and rebuild them later. In these cases, the emphasis should be on using additional and, possibly, redeploying some resources and efforts to developing an effective MTFF, but at the same time strengthening the foundations for an MTBF and an MTPF. In other words, an MTEF-based platform approach to PFM reform will often involve the sequenced *development*, rather than the sequenced *adoption*, of MTEF stages, and the scope and speed of reform will depend on the starting position of the particular country.

Notes

1. Optimism bias is a long-standing shortcoming of fiscal policy formulation in developing countries, where optimistic revenue forecasts have been used to justify higher spending in the face of fiscal constraints, especially under International Monetary Fund programs (Golosov and King 2002).

2. A recent variant is the accounting-first approach, which pushes for sound accounting—that is, how revenue, spending, and financing items are measured, classified, and reported—as a precondition for effective budget preparation and execution (Vani 2010).

3. For these reasons, Allen (2009) concludes that the platform approach is devoid of operational meaning, arguing that the first platform includes many

measures, such as accounting, budget process, treasury management, government banking, and others, that are difficult to sequence and take a long time to achieve. Thus the first platform is itself ambiguous and could involve reforms that extend beyond the timeline of most governments.

4. This has long been recognized in setting fiscal targets under IMF programs.

References

Allen, R. 2009. "The Challenge of Reforming Budgetary Institutions in Developing Countries." IMF Working Paper 09/96, International Monetary Fund, Washington, DC.

Andrews, M. 2009. "Isomorphism and the Limits to African Public Financial Management Reform." Faculty Research Working Paper RP09-012, Harvard Kennedy School, Cambridge, MA.

Brooke, P. 2003. "Study of Measures Used to Address Weaknesses in Public Financial Management Systems in the Context of Policy-Based Support." Final report produced for PEFA, PEFA Secretariat, World Bank, Washington, DC. http://72.3.224.137/report_studies_file/Study_eng_1193242966.pdf.

Debrun, X., and M. Kumar. 2007. "Fiscal Rules, Fiscal Councils, and All That: Commitment Devices, Signaling Tools, or Smokescreens?" In *Proceedings of the 9th Banca d'Italia Workshop on Public Finance.* Rome: Banca d'Italia.

Diamond, J. 2010. "Towards Good Practice Guidelines in the Sequencing of PFM Reforms." Draft. International Monetary Fund, Washington, DC.

EC (European Commission). 2007. "Toward an EU Response to Situations of Fragility: Engaging in Difficult Environments for Sustainable Development, Stability, and Peace." COM(2007) 643 final, communication from the European Commission to the Council, the European Parliament, the European Economic and Social Committee and the Committee of the Regions, Brussels.

Golosov, M., and J. King. 2002. "Tax Revenue Forecasts in IMF-Supported Programs." IMF Working Paper 02/236, International Monetary Fund, Washington, DC.

Hemming, R., and P. Joyce. 2012. "The Role of Fiscal Councils in Promoting Fiscal Responsibility and Sound Government Finances." International Monetary Fund, Washington, DC.

IMF (International Monetary Fund). 2009. "Fiscal Rules: Anchoring Expectations for Sustainable Public Finances." IMF, Washington, DC.

Kopits, G. 2011. "Independent Fiscal Institutions: Developing Good Practices." *OECD Journal on Budgeting* 11 (3): 1–18.

OECD (Organisation for Economic Co-operation and Development). 2008. *Concepts and Dilemmas of State Building in Fragile Situations: From Fragility to Resilience.* OECD/DAC Discussion Paper. Paris: OECD.

Schiavo-Campo, S. 2008. "Of Mountains and Molehills: 'The' Medium-Term Expenditure Framework." Public Financial Management blog, IMF, Washington, DC, http://blog-pfm.imf.org/pfmblog/2008/09/hype-and-realit .html.

Schick, A. 1998. "Why Most Developing Countries Should Not Try New Zealand Reforms." *World Bank Research Observer* 13 (1): 123–31.

Symansky, S. 2010. "Donor Funding and Public Financial Management Reform in Post-Conflict Countries." Cape-ODI-IMF Discussion Paper, Centre for Aid and Public Expenditure, Overseas Development Institute, London; International Monetary Fund, Washington, DC.

Tommasi, D. 2009. "Strengthening Public Expenditure Management in Developing Countries: Sequencing Issues." European Commission, Brussels. http:// capacity4dev.ec.europa.eu/strengthening-public-expenditure-management-developing-countries-sequencing-issues.

Vani, S. 2010. "Prioritizing PFM Reforms: A Robust and Functioning Accounting and Reporting System Is a Prerequisite." PFM Blog, May 26, http://blog-pfm .imf.org/pfmblog/2010/05/prioritizing-pfm-reforms-a-robust-and-function ing-accounting-and-reporting-system-is-a-prerequisite-.html.

World Bank. 2011. *World Development Report 2011: Conflict, Security, and Development.* New York: Oxford University Press.

———. 2012. *Public Financial Management Reforms in Post-Conflict States: A Synthesis Report.* Washington, DC: World Bank.

CHAPTER 6

Lessons from World Bank Support for MTEF Implementation

Over the last two decades, the World Bank has been a significant player in providing technical advice on and support for implementing medium-term expenditure frameworks (MTEFs) in low- and middle-income countries. The Bank's engagement with MTEFs has grown with the launch of its broader public financial management (PFM) initiatives and related work at the country level. The Bank has supported MTEF reforms primarily through lending operations and analytical and advisory activities (AAAs), which constitute 70 and 30 percent, respectively, of the total number of products. Technical assistance (TA) has been provided mainly as part of economic and sector work, while stand-alone TA has been small.

MTEF reforms are at different stages in different countries. However, in many countries, they are now reaching the point where they are expected to deliver results. This provides a good opportunity to distill lessons about the implementation of MTEFs supported by the Bank and about the impact of Bank projects and other activities that involve support for MTEFs. This chapter summarizes the main findings from a review of Bank lending projects with a substantial MTEF component carried out over the past two decades. It aims to provide more understanding about how to design Bank interventions so that they improve the adoption and implementation of MTEFs. The analysis was undertaken to summarize the lessons learned from different country settings and thus to inform future MTEF-related operations. These lessons may provide useful hints about the approach to take when a country and the Bank together prepare an MTEF-related project.

Methodology

The review focuses on Bank lending operations because ex post evaluation reports are available only for Bank lending. Implementation Completion Reports (ICRs) mark the transition from the implementation of a Bank project to the operation of targeted policies or institutional arrangements at the country level (see box 6.1) and therefore make it possible to analyze the design and impact of Bank interventions at the country level.[1] The sample of relevant Bank operations comprises 104 lending projects out of 691 MTEF-related operations and includes both lending and AAAs.[2] When taking stock of the Bank's MTEF-related products, it is important to bear in mind that client countries often introduce and then

---

Box 6.1

Implementation Completion and Results Reports

Implementation Completion Reports (ICRs) are an integral part of the World Bank lending cycle. They provide a complete and systematic account of the performance and results of each operation. The Bank requires an ICR for each lending project, and all ICRs are delivered within six months of the project's closing date.
ICRs have the following objectives:

- Provide a complete and systematic account of the performance and results of each operation.
- Capture and disseminate the experience learned from one operation to improve future operations and ensure greater impact.
- Provide accountability and transparency with respect to the activities of the Bank, borrower, and involved stakeholders.
- Provide a vehicle for realistic self-evaluations of performance by the Bank and borrower.
- Contribute to databases for aggregation, analysis, and reporting, especially by the Independent Evaluation Group, on the effectiveness of lending operations in contributing to development strategies at the sector, country, and global levels.

suspend or even abandon MTEF reforms for a while. This happens especially when their fiscal position deteriorates due to an external shock or
an economic crisis. When economic circumstances become more
favorable, they usually resume their MTEF efforts.

The 104 loans cover 47 countries, with a comparable number of low-
and middle-income countries and projects in those countries (see
figure 6.1). The share of high-income countries is small, represented by
two lending operations, one in Croatia and one in the Slovak Republic.
Both countries became high income during the implementation of the
reviewed loans. One project is shared by two countries, namely Chad and
Cameroon. Based on the typology of different country settings, countries
included in the review are categorized by income per capita and grouped
as follows: nine are considered fragile, 12 are considered resource rich, and
eight are in transition.[3] Some countries belong to more than one category.

The geographic composition of the sample of lending projects includes
all Bank regions. However, consistent with the distribution of MTEF
adoption worldwide, two regions—Sub-Saharan Africa and Europe and
Central Asia—constitute the largest share, by both number of projects
and number of countries (see figure 6.2).

All three stages of an MTEF are represented in the countries reviewed
(see figure 6.3), with the first and second stages predominating—a
medium-term fiscal framework (MTFF) and a medium-term budget
framework (MTBF). However, more than 60 percent of Bank lending

**Figure 6.1   Reviewed Bank Loans with Substantial Support for MTEFs, by Country
Income Group**

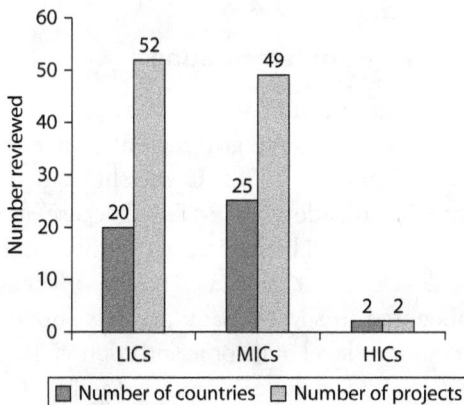

Source: World Bank data.
Note: HIC = high-income country; LIC = low-income country; MIC = middle-income country.

Figure 6.2   Reviewed Bank Loans with Substantial Support for MTEFs, by Region

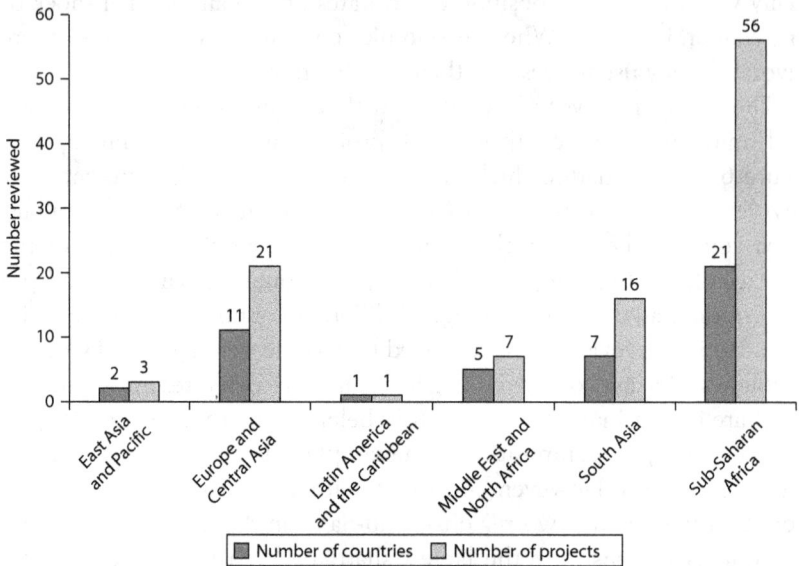

Source: World Bank data.
Note: MTEF = medium-term expenditure framework.

projects have supported a generic MTEF, without specifying what particular stage has been implemented. Bank projects that take a platform approach for MTEFs have focused mainly on MTBFs and, to a lesser extent, on MTFFs. At the same time, only a few Bank projects have addressed the transition from an MTFF to an MTBF.

Bank-Supported MTEF Implementation

In common with most reforms supported by the Bank and the International Monetary Fund (IMF), broad-based government ownership is fundamental to successful adoption of an MTEF. Ownership is defined as the willingness of government to adopt an MTEF because it is expected to improve budget outcomes and benefit the economy, not just because it is recommended by development partners. The importance of government ownership is highlighted in several Bank projects supporting an MTEF, regardless of the country's level of income and context. Relevant examples span different regions and include Morocco, Zambia, Guinea, Pakistan, Uganda, Georgia, Mauritius, Jordan, Tajikistan, and others. Moreover, even Ministry of Finance (MoF) support cannot be taken for granted. In Guinea, for instance, after MTEF processes were decided and required

Figure 6.3   MTEF Adoption by Countries Included in the Sample of Reviewed Bank Loans with Substantial Support for MTEFs, 1990–2008

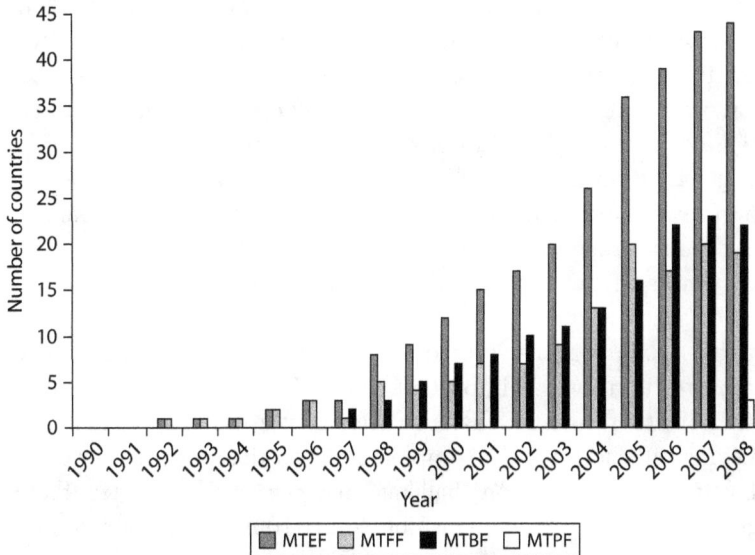

Source: World Bank.
Note: MTBF = medium-term budgetary framework; MTEF = medium-term expenditure framework; MTFF = medium-term fiscal framework; MTPF = medium-term performance framework.

manuals were drafted, implementation stalled when the MoF questioned their purpose and usefulness.[4] On the whole, projects characterized by broad-based government commitment tend to be rated satisfactory.

However, government and bureaucratic support is a necessary, but not a sufficient, condition for effective MTEF implementation. When ownership is weak, Bank teams are encouraged to engage in a period of sensitization to foster a better understanding of potential MTEF benefits, including the positive impact of budget reform on growth and poverty reduction. The Public Sector Capacity Building Project in Mauritius illustrates this point.[5] A Bank country team anchored an MTEF in the government's New Economic Agenda, which sought to align public expenditure with national strategic priorities and to ensure fiscal sustainability. It then used a Country Assistance Strategy policy matrix to monitor MTEF implementation. In addition to government support for implementation, political and bureaucratic will should be underpinned by incentives for change management. The experience of Bangladesh indicates that, even when government ownership is present, targeted, and tailored, engagement and communication with all stakeholders can create appropriate incentives and contribute to deepening ownership and support for an MTEF.[6]

Country context also matters, and successful implementation depends on how well the MTEF is adapted to country circumstances. Bank-supported MTEF interventions have been somewhat more satisfactory in middle- and high-income countries than in low-income countries. Thus the design of MTEF reform should take into account initial preconditions, such as a country's income level, human capital, as well as economic and institutional capacities and constraints. Simplicity and selectivity in defining MTEF objectives can facilitate implementation in low-income countries, which usually have weaker implementation capacity than middle-income countries. In Niger, for example, initial stages of the MTEF and sector spending frameworks in health and education were successfully introduced with Bank support. The fact that a comprehensive medium-term policy agenda included very few prior actions was an important factor.[7] In general, the evidence suggests that other country characteristics play a more important role in achieving satisfactory MTEF implementation than income per capita.

Distinct implementation challenges have emerged in postconflict and fragile states, countries in transition, and resource-rich countries.[8] In a fragile and postconflict environment, MTEF reforms alone are unlikely to trigger systemic budget changes because policy and institutional capacity is insufficient and forceful agents of change are often missing. But even in relatively low-capacity environments, political commitment and popular support for reform can be harnessed by reinforcing existing capacities and strengthening budgetary transparency.

For instance, from the outset in Sierra Leone, the government introduced an MTEF with civil society participation.[9] Budget oversight committees, established in all regions, facilitated the prioritization of expenditures and monitoring of budget execution at the district level. The latter involved using Public Expenditure Tracking Surveys to scrutinize the use of resources by urban and rural communities. These participatory elements fostered acceptance of the MTEF, allowing more effective implementation. At the same time, institutional and management capabilities of the MoF improved substantially over a short period of time, largely as a result of the introduction of a financial management information system.

In countries transitioning from a centrally planned to a market economy, the resistance to change is sometimes strong. This is particularly relevant when a government has isolated itself for a long time from budgetary reforms pursued in other countries. In Algeria, the government considered the timeline set by the Bank for the Budget Systems Modernization Project to be overly optimistic given the country's institutional environment.[10]

In such situations, the groundwork for a Bank project should focus on building political and bureaucratic commitment by outlining a realistic roadmap for reform that clearly explains the benefits and costs of an MTEF. Adapting the pace of reform to existing implementation capacity or strengthening this capacity may be required before introducing an MTEF. The Bank country team used this approach in Albania, which transitioned from an extremely closed autarchic socialist system in the 1990s.[11] Governance and institution building were considered high priorities, and MTEF efforts therefore focused on improving the capacity of the MoF to formulate the budget, based on sound analysis and a medium-term perspective, which was conducive to initial MTEF adoption.

MTEF implementation, similar to PFM reform in general, has achieved mixed success in resource-rich countries. This is despite a clear need to manage revenue flows so that they contribute most effectively to macroeconomic stability and growth. The Petroleum Development and Pipeline Project in Chad and Cameroon used the MTEF to anchor annual expenditures and avoid rapid increases in spending followed by sharp declines due to the volatility of oil revenue.[12] But the MTEF has had insignificant impact due to the lack of medium-term sector strategies. Similarly, in Azerbaijan, an MTEF has not reached its full potential. Although Oil Fund expenditure decisions are made in the context of a consolidated budget that is consistent with the MTEF, line ministries do not participate adequately in its implementation. At the same time, institutional capacity at the central government level remains weak.[13] MTEF implementation has been more successful in the resource-rich countries of Guinea and the Republic of Yemen, highlighting the importance of ensuring political commitment, enhancing institutional capacity, and using participatory approaches to build consensus and overcome initial resistance to the MTEF process.

The sequencing and pace of MTEF reform are particularly important to success. Experience in Ghana suggests that implementation should be gradual and that sequencing should encompass adequate risk management.[14] This approach has involved (a) consolidating an MTFF before transitioning to an MTBF and a medium-term performance framework (MTPF),[15] (b) starting in some pilot sectors before scaling up to the whole budget, and (c) introducing an MTEF first at one level of government before expanding it to the whole country. For example, Kosovo sought to improve macro-fiscal projections and introduce indicative ceilings in order to enhance medium-term fiscal sustainability. The MTFF was an interim step to achieving the medium-term goal of implementing an MTBF.[16]

Mali and Nepal took the second approach, starting with sector pilots before scaling up. Mali, supported by a series of Bank development policy loans (DPLs), gradually introduced medium-term expenditure planning in the education and health sectors and subsequently in transport.[17] Similarly, Nepal launched an MTEF in a few pilot ministries and then applied it to the whole central government. The government focused first on strengthening the predictability of the annual budget, before engaging in other budgetary reforms leading to full MTEF implementation.[18] Vietnam used a combined approach that involved piloting an MTEF in four sectors—education, health, transport, and agriculture—and four provinces with a focus on improving fiscal discipline.[19] The Bank also assisted with MTEF adoption at the subnational level by providing direct lending support to state or provincial governments. In India and Pakistan, the Bank used both sector pilots and stage-oriented MTEF reforms. Thus, for instance, Andhra Pradesh in India introduced an MTBF in health, education, and roads and buildings in a manner that was consistent with corresponding sector strategies and the overall fiscal framework.[20]

In some cases, abrupt or big bang adoption of MTEF, especially if accompanied by complex PFM reforms, can disrupt the budget system and jeopardize the delivery of public services. This approach to sequencing is not the norm, but neither is it the exception. In projects that have tried the big bang approach, reforms have proved to be overly ambitious; as a result, they have had to be scaled down during implementation, and the loan timeline has had to be extended. This happened in Algeria, where the Bank country team, in agreement with the government, revised the reform program to focus on establishing multiyear aggregate fiscal constraints and developing sector strategies. The rollout of an integrated financial management information system was limited to preparation of a master plan, and accrual accounting was excluded from the introduction of program budgeting.

However, sometimes Bank projects have fallen short of taking timely corrective action with respect to the sequencing and pace of an unrealistic MTEF. Ghana, where MTEF adoption was supported by several Bank operations and many bilateral donor projects, is a case in point: the complexity of the underpinning policy reforms and institutional changes envisaged, the large number of subsystems included in the project, and the decision to implement an advanced form of MTEF across-the-board created formidable conceptual, technical, and managerial challenges for the government.[21] As a result, the MTEF had limited impact on macrofiscal planning and resource allocation.

The packaging of MTEFs with other public financial management and broader public sector reforms should be considered with care. Proceeding with too many reforms simultaneously dilutes the focus of the government and strains capacity. This can lead to delays and may jeopardize overall MTEF implementation. Numerous Bank lending projects have combined MTEF adoption with the introduction of new accounting and payroll systems, civil service reform, an integrated financial management information system, and sometimes performance budgeting.

A recent policy lending operation in the Kyrgyz Republic also had an overly ambitious program, including an MTBF and comprehensive civil service reform, with an unrealistic implementation schedule. An ex post review of this project concluded that Bank resources could have been used more effectively if the design of those reforms had taken more heed of the country's capacity constraints.[22] In addition, embracing several budget initiatives can undermine government ownership of some or all components of reform (The Gambia),[23] and exogenous factors such as external shocks can affect the sequencing of MTEF implementation. The recent global economic and financial crisis led to major adjustments in the fiscal agenda of many governments in both low- and middle-income countries and set back MTEF implementation in some countries, as in Armenia.[24]

Strong budget execution clearly contributes to a well-functioning MTEF. This often involves clarifying relationships and accountability between government agencies and providing incentives for budget officials to commit to medium-term expenditure targets. At the same time, more orderly budget execution can contribute to the reliability of the annual budget process and enhance the credibility of the overall macroeconomic framework and budget preparation. For example, in Malawi a series of Bank operations supporting an MTEF since 2000 were rated satisfactory, but the MTEF was still not fully functional in 2010 due to persistent weaknesses in the budget execution process.

An inadequate auditing function and limited parliamentary scrutiny of the budget can also undermine the performance and effectiveness of an MTEF, as occurred in Benin. Conversely, where budget control mechanisms are sufficiently robust, they significantly increase the likelihood of a successful MTEF. Thus in Burkina Faso the requirement to provide the Bank with ex post information on the government annual accounts, audited by the supreme audit institution, and to transmit these budget reports to parliament every year has improved transparency and accountability in the use of public funds. These audited accounts have shed light on the overall financial management of government institutions and facilitated MTEF implementation. Croatia, with Bank support, enacted a law in 2008 making it mandatory for an MTEF, along with the annual budget, to receive parliamentary approval.

Finally, MTEFs implemented with Bank support have resulted in a visible improvement in fiscal discipline and allocative efficiency, but increasing technical efficiency remains a formidable challenge. For example,

- Tunisia prepared an MTEF satisfactory to the Bank, achieving a positive primary fiscal balance in 2008 and contributing to more reliable annual budgeting.[25]

- Niger used the MTEF framework to prepare realistic projections of fiscal revenue and external support from donors, allowing the country to plan high-priority expenditures in core sectors, consistent with poverty reduction strategies.[26] This can be conducive to achieving fiscal stability, reducing spending volatility, and improving allocative efficiency by focusing on the country's development priorities. Niger's experience also shows that technical efficiency cannot be achieved at the sector level unless budget allocations for the sector are stable and predictable.[27]

- As a counterexample, Malawi shows that attempting to introduce a new system of expenditure prioritization by superimposing an MTEF on an inadequate budget allocation system is unlikely to succeed.[28]

- In Pakistan, MTEF implementation in the North West Frontier Province was conducive to better spending prioritization and helped to reduce the volatility of priority spending. When the MTBF was introduced, it contributed to more predictability of the budget and a stronger commitment to maintaining spending in the social sectors benefiting the poor.[29]

- Since the MTEF became an integral part of the budget management process in Nepal, the deviation between budgeted and actual expenditures has fallen sharply and the share of public spending targeting the poor has risen.[30] Similarly, in Tanzania, social spending has received greater funding and support from donors, particularly in the health sector.[31]

- In Burkina Faso the MTEF (a) reinforced fiscal discipline and improved strategic prioritization, (b) highlighted, together with a Public Expenditure Review (PER), the need to improve operational efficiency, including the adoption of efficiency action plans, and (c) led to substantial improvements in budget predictability and fiscal discipline.[32] MTEF implementation was supported by two subsequent programmatic credits, improving the effectiveness of public spending overall.[33]

Lessons about Bank Instruments to Support MTEFs

The Bank has used various lending instruments, including development policy loans and investment loans, to support MTEF adoption and implementation. The majority of the projects reviewed in this analysis have demonstrated good performance and been rated satisfactory or better.[34] To some extent, development policy lending has received a more positive rating than investment lending. However, such ratings encompass all reforms supported by a project, which often cover different segments of economic policy and institution building. The rating for an MTEF component is available for one-third of all projects in the sample and is satisfactory in all but one case.[35] However, positive ratings, both overall and for an MTEF component, need to be treated with caution, because they primarily reflect discrete Bank interventions in support of MTEFs rather than MTEF performance at the country level.

Looking at project ratings by country shows that a series of consecutive Bank operations in support of an MTEF may perform well, but the MTEF may still be not fully operational or its implementation may be stalled. The latter is often a consequence of weak ownership of the MTEF process, a change in government, swings in a government's appetite for reform, an external shock to the economy, or some other factor (Ghana, Guinea, and Tajikistan). Conversely, a Bank intervention to assist MTEF adoption may not be successful due to an overly ambitious reform program, but the country's government may be keen on continuing the reform so that an MTEF gradually takes root (Algeria).

With regard to Bank instruments to assist MTEFs, development policy lending—DPLs, Poverty Reduction Support Credits (PRSCs), or sector-wide approaches (SWAPs)—may be conducive to supporting cross-cutting MTEF implementation. First, these operations provide general budget support, so MTEF ownership is relatively strong. Second, they assist in putting in place a robust MTEF that serves as an anchor for fiscal policy reforms explicitly linked to Bank disbursements. For example, Panama introduced an MTBF with the support of a single-tranche DPL, which provided timely financial and technical support to the government for its implementation.[36]

Third, establishing a fiscal anchor can lead not only to achieving fiscal discipline, but also to receiving more effective external financing from other development partners, which are encouraged to collaborate within an agreed policy framework (Georgia).[37] Incorporating all donor funding into an MTEF remains a large challenge in many countries, especially when a substantial part of aid is still provided through ring-fenced investment lending projects. This undermines the MTEF because project financing is not always well synchronized or consistent with sector budget ceilings. Moreover, inadequate donor cooperation provides the opportunity for line ministries to bypass the MTEF. For instance, in Uganda project aid was poorly integrated into the MTEF, despite an overall improvement in the quality of budgeting and some increase, from 55 to 60 percent, in the share of total overseas development assistance allocated through the MTEF.[38]

More than 70 percent of the DPLs with substantial support for MTEFs specified prior actions for MTEF implementation (see box 6.2).[39] Whereas in most cases their performance was rated satisfactory, there is some evidence that the absence of prior actions pertaining to MTEFs

---

Box 6.2

MTEF Prior Actions in Bank Development Policy Lending

Prior actions involve policy and institutional measures deemed critical to achieving the objectives of a program supported by a development policy operation. Prior actions are met before loan disbursement. In general, good practice principles for prior actions include the following:

1. The policy content and prior actions of an operation should reflect the government's program and priorities developed through a policy-making process that involves broad consultation.
2. Prior actions should be limited to a few key policy and institutional reforms that are critical for achieving expected results.
3. An accountability framework should be agreed on up-front with the government and other development partners.
4. A modality of a development policy operation should be determined based on the soundness of the government's policy framework and monitoring and evaluation system.
5. Progress reviews should be transparent and conducive to predictable and performance-based financial support.

makes such operations less successful. In line with good practice, MTEF-related prior actions tend to be more effective when they involve a limited number of well-defined policy and institutional measures. Conversely, overly general prior actions are more likely to yield less successful results. The same holds for a large number of excessively specific prior actions. Caution is in order, however, because these observations pertain mainly to the DPLs rated moderately satisfactory. Only a fraction of the operations reviewed received a moderately unsatisfactory or unsatisfactory rating overall or for an MTEF component.

In the context of development policy lending, the review suggests that building on Poverty Reduction Strategy Paper (PRSP) interventions makes it more likely that an MTEF will succeed. There is some evidence that a PRSC in support of a PRSP and grounded by a set of government-determined priorities can be conducive to implementing an MTEF. It is more effective when there is strong government ownership and a long-standing relationship of trust between the government and the Bank. This was the case in Armenia, where the government integrated an MTEF with the annual budget and made other improvements in public expenditure management with the support of both DPLs and PRSCs.[40] MTEF implementation was also assisted by a series of PRSCs in Senegal and Mali,[41] where it was gradually introduced correspondingly in 12 and 15 ministries or agencies, reinforcing the link between PRSP development objectives and the budget. However, the overall quality of MTEF implementation in these countries was somewhat lagging behind the pace of the reform. In addition, other budget support loans—for example, the Albania Structural Adjustment Credit[42]—also facilitated MTEF adoption by requiring the preparation of strategies to facilitate prioritization and rationalization of public spending in several sectors. Furthermore, programmatic adjustment loans can be useful in assisting gradual MTEF implementation. Morocco is a case in point: Morocco introduced an MTFF for the first time in the 2007 and 2008 budgets in the context of a broad program of public administration reform, following the recommendations of the 2002 PER and supported by two adjustment lending operations.[43]

Moreover, when combined with basic preexisting institutional capacity for planning and implementation and strong political support, Bank operations grounded in MTEFs can focus on specific sectorwide reforms (SWAPs). A sector program that includes sector-specific interventions and cross-cutting fiscal and fiduciary measures is more likely to yield results that can be sustained. This approach is particularly useful in sectors requiring emergency support, such as health and education, and there are many examples of Bank SWAPs in these sectors. The education sector loan to Sindh Province in Pakistan is a good illustration. The provincial government developed a sector MTBF that gave high priority to pro-poor education spending and helped to reduce its volatility.

In Uganda, Bank support to the education sector explicitly linked conditions for tranche releases to agreements in education policy that were incorporated in an MTBF.[44] In Lesotho, the health SWAP introduced an MTBF in the health sector, with a firm commitment of the government at the highest levels to achieving better health outcomes.[45] At the same time, MTEFs constitute a suitable anchor for sector budget support—SWAPs or program for results (PforRs)—by providing an adequate framework for measuring sector outputs and outcomes against inputs, which facilitates Bank operations and disbursements.

However, moving away from projects and toward a sectorwide approach requires substantial capacity support in order to develop a sector strategy that facilitates MTEF implementation. Additional efforts to capture synergies and cross-sector linkages are often needed, as revealed in the context of the Rwanda PRSC and the India Andhra Pradesh Power Sector Restructuring Project. During the initial stages of implementation in Rwanda, sector allocations in the budget were not strongly linked to an MTEF. However, significant progress has recently been made in most sectors, with movement toward an MTPF.[46] In Andhra Pradesh, integrating the financing requirements of power utilities in an MTEF at the state level helped to improve transparency in public expenditure.[47] This consolidation also facilitated a realistic assessment of public finances and public policy choices.

Synergies between Bank development policy lending (DPLs, PforRs, SWAPs) and investment lending, especially TA loans, can support more successful MTEF implementation. Investment operations have been instrumental in building capacity, transferring resources, and paving the way for implementation. However, adjustment operations have provided the momentum in addressing challenging cross-cutting institutional and policy issues in MTEF reform. In low-capacity environments, TA lending may even be considered a prerequisite for a policy-based budget support loan to ensure the smooth implementation of an MTEF. In Burundi, well-designed technical assistance helped to ensure that MTEF tools were standardized across government agencies and mainstreamed in the budget preparation and execution processes.[48] However, the experience in Nepal shows that even well-designed TA projects may not fully succeed in assisting with MTEF reform due to weak institutional capacity.[49]

The evidence suggests that synchronizing the two instruments—investment and development policy lending—properly is likely to support MTEF implementation better than using either instrument alone (Nicaragua, Georgia, and Albania). For instance, twinning the public sector TA loan and a policy-based loan in Albania assisted in building necessary capability in government. This allowed the government to extend the MTBF from four to 10 line ministries as well as to set expenditure priorities.[50] Furthermore, a pragmatic and incremental approach to technical assistance in support of MTEFs is preferred to large multiyear TA programs, which tend to be more rigid in design and may even strain the limited implementation capacity of the government, as happened in Tajikistan.[51]

Investment lending operations aimed at supporting MTEF adoption in sectors, in contrast to SWAPs, appear to have been quite ineffective. Part of the explanation is that their funding is tied to specific expenditures, which creates rigidity in the implementation of cross-cutting MTEF reform. However, a frail MTEF process can hinder progress with specific sector reforms supported by investment lending. This is illustrated by the ex post evaluation of the Chad Health Sector Support Project, which acknowledged that sector linkages to an MTEF should have been a precondition for project preparation.[52] A sector investment loan appears to be more successful if it supports an MTEF at the subsector level. This happened in the HIV/AIDS (Human Immunodeficiency Virus/Acquired Immune Deficiency Syndrome) Disaster Response Project in Kenya, where additional allocations for prevention and relief, financed from internal and external sources, were fully integrated into an MTEF in order to ensure proper planning and timely execution.[53]

Finally, a steady commitment to advisory and analytical work in public finance management can enable the Bank to respond quickly with lending operations when the political commitment to MTEF adoption and implementation is strong. The most commonly used instruments are PERs at the country level and nonlending technical assistance to the country's central finance agencies. PERs are intended primarily to facilitate allocative efficiency and are undertaken in countries prior to or during MTEF implementation. Therefore, they have usually helped to sharpen the focus on strategic expenditure priorities, to bring to the forefront trade-offs in sector policy choices, and to identify institutional weaknesses in public expenditure management (Tanzania, Niger, Lesotho, Uganda, and Morocco).[54] In Uganda, PER workshops, which are open to all stakeholders, are held every year to review the MTEF. Other Bank AAA products with some relevance to MTEF implementation include country financial accountability assessments, country public procurement assessments, and development policy reviews.

Nonlending technical assistance generally involves technical advice on policy and management from the Bank to central finance agencies in the form of policy notes focusing on targeted issues, workshops, consultations, and hands-on training. Such advice often provides an entry point for Bank TA lending operations encompassing more comprehensive capacity-building interventions. For instance, this was the case in Slovakia, where the Bank provided initial technical advice to the MoF on a set of broader and more specific PFM issues. This helped to build the foundations for the country's long-term aspirations to join the European Union and subsequently contributed to MTBF implementation, supported by a PFM technical assistance loan.

The lending program, which aimed to strengthen the MoF's capacity in medium-term macro-fiscal forecasting and expenditure reviews and organizational capability, assisted in establishing the MTBF as a hard baseline for continuing existing programs, and line ministries came to accept the program limits. Economic growth provided resources to expand or add new programs decided annually on top of the baseline. According to line ministries, the development of the MTBF on a rolling three-year basis has provided greater predictability of resources and enabled better planning decisions.[55]

In sum, this review suggests that choosing Bank instruments more carefully and adopting a selective approach to prior actions may be conducive to MTEF implementation (see table 6.1). A medium-term rather than a longer-term approach to formulating an MTEF reform agenda, in both lending operations and advisory and analytical work, appears more suitable to managing various risks and more likely to yield positive results. Instruments with more flexibility, such as development policy and performance-based loans, are more appropriate for assisting MTEF adoption and operationalization. They allow cross-cutting and complex issues to be addressed and timely adjustments to be made as needs arise. However, fewer prior actions can also facilitate more sustained progress with an MTEF. Governments can adapt the design, sequencing, and pace of MTEF reform according to their institutional capacity and environment. Finally, an MTEF can act as a catalyst for developing a culture of monitoring and evaluation in program performance. This may require the Bank to shift more resources from investment projects to medium-term budget support programs and performance-based loans (such as PforRs).

Table 6.1   World Bank Lending Projects Substantially Supporting MTEFs, by Country Setting

Income level	Country setting			Country	Type of product lending
	Fragile	Resource rich	Transitional		
Low income	✓	✓		Guinea	APL, 2 DPL SAL
				Sierra Leone	DPL SAL
Low income	✓			Afghanistan	DPL DP
				Chad	SIL
				Nepal	TAL, DPL PRSC, SIL
Low income		✓	✓	Kyrgyz Republic	DPL SAL
Low income			✓	Tajikistan	TAL, DPL SAL, DPL DP
Low income				Bangladesh	DPL SAL
				Benin	DPL SAL
				Burkina Faso	4 DPL PRSC, 2 DPL SAL
				Gambia, The	SIL
				Kenya	2 TAL, DPL SAL, APL
				Madagascar	DPL DP
				Malawi	2 DPL SAL, TAL, SIL
				Mali	2 DPL DP, 2 DPL SAL
				Mozambique	DPL SAL
				Niger	2 DPL DP, 3 DPL SAL
				Rwanda	DPL DP, DPL SAL
				Tanzania	DPL SAL, 2 DPL SAD, APL
				Uganda	DPL SAD, 3 DPL PRSC, DPL DP
Middle income	✓	✓		Yemen, Rep.	DPL SAL
Middle income	✓		✓	Georgia	DPL DP, SIL, DPL SAL
Middle income	✓			Bosnia and Herzegovina	TAL, DPL SAD
				Kosovo	SIL, DPL SAL
Middle income		✓	✓	Azerbaijan	DPL PRSC, DPL SAL
				Vietnam	DPL DP, SIL
Middle income		✓		Algeria	SIL
				Ghana	TAL, APL, DPL SAL
				Indonesia	DPL DP
				Jordan	2 DPL PSAL
				Zambia	APL, DPL SAL, DPL DP
Middle income			✓	Albania	DPL SAL, TAL
				Armenia	DPL DP, 3 DPL SAL
				Romania	TAL
Middle income				Bhutan	DPL DP
				India	2 DPL SAL, APL, SIL, DPL PSAL
				Lesotho	2 APL

(continued next page)

Table 6.1   *(continued)*

Income level	Country setting Fragile	Resource rich	Transitional	Country	Type of product lending
				Mauritius	DPL SAL
				Morocco	2 DPL DP, DPL SAL
				Pakistan	2 DPL SAL, DPL SAD, DPL DP
				Panama	DPL DP
				Senegal	DPL DP
				Sri Lanka	DPL PRSC
				Tunisia	DPL SAL
High income			✓	Croatia	DPL PSAL
				Slovak Republic	TAL
Low income	✓			Chad	SIL
and middle income		✓		Cameroon	SIL

Source: World Bank data.

Note: Low-income, middle-income, and high-income countries are based on the World Bank list of economies as of July 18, 2011. Economies are divided among income groups according to 2010 gross national income per capita, calculated using the World Bank Atlas method. The groups are low income, US$1,005 or less; lower middle income, US$1,006–US$3,975; upper middle income, US$3,976–US$12,275; and high income, US$12,276 or more. Resource-rich countries are rich in hydrocarbons or mineral resources on the basis of the following criteria: (a) an average share of hydrocarbon and/or mineral fiscal revenues in total fiscal revenue of at least 25 percent during the period 2000–03 or (b) an average share of hydrocarbon and/or mineral export proceeds of at least 25 percent of total export proceeds during the period 2000–03 (IMF 2005, 63–64). Transitional countries refer not only to the countries of Central and Eastern Europe and the Russian Federation but also to countries emerging from a socialist-type command economy and becoming a more market-based economy (for example, China, Vietnam; see IMF 2000). Fragile countries are either countries that (a) are eligible for international development assistance and have a harmonized average country policy and institutional assessment (CPIA) rating of 3.2 or less (or no CPIA) or (b) have had a United Nations or regional peacekeeping or peace-building mission present during the past three years. This list includes nonmember or inactive territories and countries. It excludes World Bank–only countries for which the CPIA scores are not currently disclosed. This definition is pursuant to an agreement between the World Bank and other multilateral development banks at the start of the IDA 15 round in 2007 (http://intresources.worldbank.org/INTOPCS/Resources/FCS_List_FY12_External_List.pdf). Lending instruments include development policy loans (DPL). Lending types include Adaptable Program Loan (APL), Specific Investment Loan (SIL), Technical Assistance Loan (TAL), Sector Adjustment Loan (SAD), Structural Adjustment Loan (SAL), Program Structural Adjustment Loan (PSAL), Poverty Reduction Support Credit (PRSC), and Development Policy (DP).

Notes

1. A Bank lending project with substantial support for MTEF adoption is defined here as one in which the objectives, components, and conclusions presented in an ICR refer to an MTEF, a medium-term budgetary framework (MTBF), or a medium-term fiscal framework (MTFF), and these expressions are used more than six times in the ICR document. The selection of projects also considered regional and country coverage as well as different types of lending products.

2. The sample of 691 MTEF-related Bank operations was generated from the World Bank internal database.

3. Chad and Niger are not counted as resource-rich countries in this study. They were not listed as such in the International Monetary Fund list for 2000–03, but they were listed as such in 2009. If Algeria is considered a transition economy, the total number of transition economies is nine.

4. Guinea, Capacity Building for Service Delivery Adaptable Loan, 2005 ICR rated unsatisfactory.

5. Mauritius, Public Expenditure Reform Loan, 2003 ICR rated satisfactory.

6. Bangladesh, Development Support Series Credit (I–IV), 2009 ICR rated satisfactory.

7. Niger, Public Finance Recovery Credit, 2002 ICR rated satisfactory.

8. Fragile states are (a) countries eligible for International Development Association (IDA) support with a harmonized average country policy and institutional assessment (CPIA) rating of 3.2 or lower (or no CPIA rating) or (b) the presence of a United Nations or regional peacekeeping or peace-building mission during the past three years. This list includes nonmember or inactive territories and countries. It excludes World Bank–only countries for which the CPIA scores are not disclosed. This definition is pursuant to an agreement between the World Bank and other multilateral development banks at the start of the IDA 15 round in 2007. Transition economies include not only countries of Central and Eastern Europe but also countries emerging from a socialist-type command economy and moving toward a market-based economy, such as China, Vietnam, and Algeria. According to the IMF's *Guide on Resource Revenue Transparency* (IMF 2005), the following criteria define resource-rich countries: (a) an average share of hydrocarbon and/or mineral fiscal revenues of at least 25 percent of fiscal revenues during the period 2000–03 or (b) an average share of hydrocarbon and/or mineral export proceeds of at least 25 percent of total export proceeds during the period 2000–03.

9. Sierra Leone, Second Economic Rehabilitation and Recovery Credit, 2003 ICR rated satisfactory.

10. Algeria, Budget Systems Modernization Project, 2009 ICR rated moderately unsatisfactory.

11. Albania, Public Administration Reform Technical Assistance Loan, 2007 ICR rated moderately unsatisfactory and MTEF implementation rated satisfactory.

12. Chad and Cameroon, Petroleum Development and Pipeline Project Investment Loan, 2006 ICR rated satisfactory.

13. Azerbaijan, Poverty Reduction Support Credit, 2007 ICR rated moderately satisfactory.

14. Ghana, Public Finance Management Technical Assistance Project, 2004 ICR rated unsatisfactory.

15. For example, Armenia, Burkina Faso, and Mauritius have moved to an MTPF.

16. Kosovo, United Nations Administration Mission, Structural Adjustment Loan, 2004 rated satisfactory and MTEF implementation rated satisfactory.

17. Mali, Fourth Structural Adjustment Credit, 2006 ICR rated satisfactory.

18. Nepal, First Poverty Reduction Support Credit, 2006 ICR rated satisfactory.

19. Vietnam, Poverty Reduction Support Operations (I–V), 2007 ICR rated satisfactory.

20. India, Second Andhra Pradesh Economic Reform Loan, 2005 ICR rated satisfactory.

21. Ghana, Public Finance Management Technical Assistance Project, 2004 ICR rated unsatisfactory.

22. Kyrgyz Republic, Governance Structural Adjustment Credit, 2009 ICR rated moderately unsatisfactory.

23. The Gambia, Capacity Building for Economic Management, 2009 ICR rated moderately satisfactory.

24. Armenia, Poverty Reduction Support Credit (I–VI), 2009 ICR rated satisfactory.

25. Tunisia, Fourth Economic Competitiveness Development Policy Loan, 2007 ICR rated satisfactory.

26. Niger, Second Public Expenditure Adjustment Credit, 2005 ICR rated satisfactory and MTEF implementation rated satisfactory.

27. Niger, Public Expenditure Reform Credit, 2007 ICR rated moderately satisfactory; Rural and Social Policy Reform Credits I–II, 2008 ICR rated moderately satisfactory.

28. Malawi, Fiscal Restructuring and Deregulation Program, 2000 ICR rated satisfactory.

29. Pakistan, Structural Adjustment Credit for the Government of North West Frontier Province, 2003 ICR rated satisfactory and MTEF implementation rated satisfactory.

30. Nepal, First Poverty Reduction Support Credit, 2006 ICR rated satisfactory.

31. Tanzania, Structural Adjustment Credit, 2001 ICR rated satisfactory.

32. Burkina Faso, Third Structural Adjustment Credit, 2000 ICR rated satisfactory.

33. Burkina Faso, Third Poverty Reduction Support Operation, 2004 ICR rated satisfactory.

34. If the operations rated moderately satisfactory are included, the portion of positively rated Bank operations rises to 87.5 percent.

35. The ratings of the MTEF component are distributed as follows: satisfactory or higher, 23 projects; moderately satisfactory, eight projects; and moderately unsatisfactory, one project.

36. Panama, Public Finance and Institutional Development Policy Loan, 2007 ICR rated satisfactory.

37. Georgia, Poverty Reduction Support Operations I–IV and Supplemental, 2009 ICR rated satisfactory and MTEF implementation rated satisfactory.

38. Uganda, Poverty Reduction Support Credits, 2005 and 2006 ICRs rated satisfactory.

39. Source for prior actions is the World Bank Development Policy Actions Database.

40. Armenia, Third Structural Adjustment Credit, 2001 ICR rated satisfactory and MTEF implementation rated satisfactory; Fourth Structural Adjustment Credit, 2003 ICR rated satisfactory; Fifth Structural Adjustment Credit, 2004 ICR rated satisfactory and MTEF implementation rated satisfactory; Poverty Reduction Support Credit (I–IV), 2009 ICR rated satisfactory.

41. Senegal, Poverty Reduction Support Credits I–III, 2008 ICR rated moderately satisfactory. Mali, Third Structural Adjustment Credit, 2004 rated satisfactory and MTEF rated highly satisfactory; Poverty Reduction Support Credits I and II, 2009 ICR rated moderately unsatisfactory and MTEF rated moderately satisfactory.

42. Albania, Public Structural Adjustment Credit, 2001 ICR rated satisfactory.

43. Morocco, Public Administration Reform Loans (I and II), 2009 ICR rated satisfactory, and Water Sector Development Policy Loan, 2009 ICR rated moderately satisfactory.

44. Uganda, Education Sector Adjustment Operation, 2001 ICR rated highly satisfactory.

45. Lesotho, Health Sector Reform Program, 2005 ICR rated satisfactory.

46. Rwanda, Poverty Reduction Support Credit/Grants (I–III), 2008 ICR rated satisfactory.

47. India, Andhra Pradesh Power Sector Restructuring Project (APL 1), 2004 ICR rated satisfactory.

48. Burundi, Economic Reform Support Grant III (DPL), 2010 Implementation Status and Results Report rated satisfactory.

49. Nepal, Economic Reform Technical Assistance Project, 2010 ICR rated moderately unsatisfactory and MTEF implementation rated satisfactory.

50. Albania, Public Administration Reform Technical Assistance Loan, 2007 ICR rated moderately unsatisfactory and MTEF implementation rated satisfactory.

51. Tajikistan, Second Institution Building Technical Assistance Credit, 2006 ICR rated unsatisfactory.

52. Chad, Health Sector Support Project, 2007 ICR rated unsatisfactory.

53. Kenya, HIV/AIDS Disaster Response Project, 2007 ICR rated satisfactory.

54. Tanzania, Structural Adjustment Credit, 2001 ICR rated satisfactory. Niger, Public Finance Recovery Credit, 2002 ICR rated satisfactory and MTEF implementation rated satisfactory. Lesotho, Second Education Sector Development Project, 2004 ICR rated satisfactory and MTEF implementation rated moderately satisfactory. Uganda, Poverty Reduction Support Credits, 2005 ICR rated satisfactory. Morocco Public Administration Reform Adjustment Loan, 2009 ICR rated satisfactory.

55. Slovakia, Public Finance Management Project (TAL), 2007 ICR rated satisfactory.

References

IMF (International Monetary Fund). 2000. "Transition Economies: An IMF Perspective on Progress and Prospects." IMF, Washington, DC, November 3. http://www.imf.org/external/np/exr/ib/2000/110300.htm.

———. 2005. *Guide on Resource Revenue Transparency.* Washington, DC: IMF.

CHAPTER 7

Conclusions and Implications for the Future Role of the Bank

This review has examined the unfulfilled potential offered by medium-term expenditure frameworks (MTEFs) in an effort to satisfy the need for more robust empirical evidence about their influence on fiscal outcomes. Because total spending is limited by the availability of resources and spending agencies are usually constrained by expenditure ceilings, MTEFs should promote fiscal discipline. By providing a clear indication of the future resources to be made available to spending agencies and by holding them accountable for results, MTEFs should result in a more strategic approach to expenditure prioritization and improve cost-effectiveness.

However, the few studies of the experience with MTEFs undertaken prior to this review, which focused on the donor-led push to establish MTEFs in Africa during the 1990s with a view to ensuring adequate funding for antipoverty programs, found MTEFs wanting. In particular, they found that introducing a medium-term focus in countries with weak budget processes and procedures—and therefore ineffective annual budgets—tended to be associated with more unrealistic budgets and worse fiscal outcomes. As this study has shown, MTEFs have spread more widely since the 1990s, and countries are adopting more sophisticated MTEFs and should be more familiar with their use. This has provided an opportunity to take a more comprehensive look at the impact of MTEFs.

Based on analysis using various quantitative techniques, this study offers new empirical evidence that MTEFs improve fiscal discipline. More specifically, it provides the strongest support to date that the relationship between MTEFs and fiscal discipline is causal and not attributable to some simultaneous, unobserved changes or reforms that might have improved fiscal discipline. Not only do medium-term fiscal frameworks (MTFFs) have a strong impact, but medium-term budgetary and performance frameworks (MTBFs and MTPFs, respectively) have an additional positive effect. This result is of considerable significance.

For countries grappling with how to address fiscal imbalances in the aftermath of the recent global economic and financial crisis, the fact that MTEFs turn fiscal plans into budget realities offers the genuine prospect that fiscal adjustment can be delivered and fiscal sustainability is within reach. This prospect exists for all countries that are seeking to restore stability to public finances and promote economic growth and, more generally, for countries that are committed to fiscal discipline in bad and good times. Moreover, with traditional deficit and debt rules proving largely ineffective in preventing fiscal profligacy in the past, relying on expenditure ceilings derived from MTEFs to ensure that fiscal targets are met is likely to be effective whether or not traditional rules are in place, provided, of course, that there is genuine commitment to the MTEF.

The review also presents evidence that MTEFs are associated with gains in allocative efficiency. The impact appears to be greater in the more advanced stages of MTEFs, although the results are not as strong as for fiscal discipline. The study is even less categorical about technical efficiency. There are some indications that MTPFs lead to improvements in this area, but the effects are not nearly as strong or as consistent as with other fiscal outcomes. However, the analysis of spending efficiency is constrained by two factors. First, health is the only sector for which comprehensive spending and outcome data are available, and these data have been used for the empirical work in this study. This imposes some limitations on generalizations about the positive effect of MTEFs on both spending reallocation and value for money. Second, only a few countries have an MTPF, and even for those countries little is known about program outcomes, making it difficult to judge technical efficiency. Trying to put together a more comprehensive expenditure database should be a priority for any work attempting to examine the impact of MTEFs on expenditure efficiency. In the meantime, case studies suggest that MTEFs have resulted in more resources being devoted to high-priority spending (and not just health spending), but they have little to say about technical efficiency.

Case studies also indicate that there are strong links between MTEFs and the quality of public financial management (PFM) more generally. While aggregate data suggest that MTEFs lead to better-quality budgeting, the case studies point to instances where MTEFs are poorly integrated with the budget process, where MTEFs are a pro forma exercise run parallel to but separate from the budget, and where MTEFs have, in fact, set back rather than taken forward PFM reform. This raises an interesting question. If MTEFs are, in fact, less well implemented than is needed to be fully effective, why does MTEF adoption have such a strong influence on fiscal discipline? It is widely understood that poorly implemented reform does not work well, so what is happening? The possibility that an MTEF is part of a broad package of reforms with other elements that improve fiscal discipline, regardless of MTEF adoption, has been ruled out.

A more realistic possibility is that, on balance, MTEFs are not that badly implemented; some are, but most are not. Indeed, a well-implemented MTEF can be a vehicle for supporting changes to budget systems that not only make an MTEF more effective in promoting fiscal discipline, but also have an independent disciplining effect of their own. This illustrates the importance of sequencing PFM reform appropriately, taking advantage of the increasingly demanding requirements of successive MTEF stages—MTFF, MTBF, and MTPF—to use MTEF implementation as the basis for sequencing PFM reform. Of course, the strength of political support for the MTEF and the capabilities and capacity of agencies responsible for its implementation are important determinants of success, and none of these factors can be taken for granted.

There is also evidence that MTEFs implemented with Bank support have helped to improve fiscal discipline and allocative efficiency. Given that the Bank has been a significant player in providing MTEF-related lending support and advice to low- and middle-income countries, this study has tried to distill lessons from a review of the Bank's engagement with MTEFs with a view to determining whether Bank support has been conducive to achieving the expected benefits from MTEFs.

In terms of fiscal stability as well as allocative and technical efficiency of public spending, the review shows that the majority of MTEFs completed have received a satisfactory rating. Moreover, since 2002 the number of lending operations rated less than satisfactory has declined. This suggests that the design and implementation of MTEFs have gradually improved, there has been a supporting approach to fiscal policy and an enabling environment for institutional reform, and MTEFs have successfully linked public funds to outputs and outcomes in a manner consistent with the goals of economic growth and poverty reduction. In some cases, MTEFs have also helped governments to align the use of aid with a country's strategic objectives.

This study has several implications for the work of the World Bank, which has been a strong proponent of MTEFs. Insofar as fiscal discipline is the goal, this study suggests that Bank enthusiasm for MTEFs is warranted and appropriate. However, since the Bank has a core interest in spending efficiency, support for MTEFs is also justified in part by the results of the study and by the premise that well-designed and properly implemented MTBFs and MTPFs include mechanisms to ensure that spending is properly prioritized and offers good value for money. This being the case, the Bank has a stake in ensuring that the requirements are met for MTEFs to succeed and should be prepared to provide backing for MTEFs that are built on sound preparatory work and to scale back its ambitions if the proper groundwork has not been laid.

The Bank also needs to focus on devising a broader PFM reform strategy, but could anchor this with implementing an MTEF that reflects country circumstances. To some extent this is already done, but it needs to be a regular practice. In the first instance, an MTEF should not be considered unless an appropriate PFM diagnostic—at a minimum a public expenditure and financial accountability assessment (PEFA)—has been completed. Where a country's ability to implement an MTEF or a particular MTEF stage is a concern, PFM reforms—that is, both budgetary reform to support MTEF implementation and wider PFM reform to leverage the impact of the MTEF—should be identified before choosing the approach to linking PFM reform with MTEF implementation.

As with any other PFM reform, before embarking on full implementation it is important to foster a better understanding among government and civil society of the potential benefits of an MTEF in order to build ownership. MTEF reforms also need to be sequenced according to the country's institutional capacity so as to consolidate initial accomplishments before undertaking more ambitious reforms. Gradual implementation is usually conducive to better results. This is an argument for staged implementation (MTFF, MTBF, and then MTPF) and possibly for pilots in a few sectors or at subnational levels of government before scaling up.

With respect to the choice of Bank lending instruments supporting MTEF implementation, a well-synchronized combination of Bank budget support operations and technical assistance programs allows for gradually institutionalizing MTEF mechanisms into all government agencies, while also providing adequate leverage for policy reforms. MTEFs can also provide the perfect anchor for loans to support sector budgets, such as development policy loans, sectorwide approaches, or potentially program for results, as they provide an adequate framework for measuring sector outputs and outcomes against inputs, which facilitates Bank operations and disbursements. Regarding technical assistance, a pragmatic and incremental approach is preferable to large multiyear programs, which tend to be more rigid in their design and may even strain the limited implementation capacity of the borrower.

Regardless of the Bank lending instrument chosen, progress will be limited without adequate and timely capacity-building support for senior government officials and other stakeholders involved in MTEF implementation. Analytical work in PFM can be used to prepare budget strategies leading to MTEFs, build consensus and capacity, and enable the Bank to respond quickly when the political environment for an MTEF is ready. To tailor Bank advice on MTEF implementation more closely to country circumstances, a policy note should be prepared to provide operational meaning for the use of MTEF stages as a basis for PFM reform and to address some of the more detailed aspects of MTEF design and implementation.

World Bank Engagement with Medium-Term Expenditure Frameworks

This appendix describes the main trends and patterns associated with the World Bank's engagement with client countries in establishing and implementing medium-term expenditure frameworks (MTEFs). It also explains the data and methodology used to identify and analyze MTEF-related Bank products.

Data and Methodology

The analysis combines both structured data and a qualitative assessment of Bank products supporting MTEFs. It covers all Bank-funded products focused on the development and implementation of an MTEF, including lending, analytical and advisory activities (AAA), and technical assistance.

As a guide to understanding the nature and quality of the Bank's work on MTEFs, the team created a series of questions addressing issues related to quality ratings, coverage, type of MTEF reform advocated, and initial objectives of Bank involvement. The analysis draws conclusions based on answers to the questionnaire presented in box A.1. Questions 1–5 highlight the nature and descriptive facts of the Bank's work, while questions 6–7 investigate the links between MTEF stages in which the Bank has been engaged—a generic MTEF, a medium-term fiscal framework (MTFF),

Box A.1

Bank MTEF History Questionnaire

1. Which unit and region in the Bank provided advice on the medium-term expenditure framework (MTEF)?
   - ☐ Poverty Reduction and Economic Management Network (PREM)
   - ☐ Financial and Private Sector Development (FPD)
   - ☐ Sustainable Development Network (SDN)
   - ☐ Human Development Network (HDN)
   - ☐ Operations Policy & Country Services (OPCS)
   - ☐ Africa (AFR)
   - ☐ East Asia and Pacific (EAP)
   - ☐ Middle East and North Africa (MENA)
   - ☐ South Asia (SAR)
   - ☐ Europe and Central Asia (ECA)
   - ☐ Latin America and Caribbean (LAC)
2. Project approval year _____ and, if applicable, end year _____
3. What is the status of the project?
   - ☐ Closed
   - ☐ Active
4. What type of Bank-funded project was used?
   - ☐ Lending
   - ☐ Analytic and advisory activities (AAAs) or economic and sector work (ESW)
   - ☐ Technical assistance
5. What was the rating of the project?
   - ☐ Implementation Completion Report (ICR) rating: _____
   - ☐ Implementation Status Report (ISR) average rating: _____
6. Which MTEF reform has the Bank advocated?
   - ☐ Medium-term fiscal framework (MTFF)
   - ☐ Medium-term budgetary framework (MTBF)/pilot MTBF
   - ☐ Medium-term performance framework (MTPF)
   - ☐ Generic MTEF
7. What was the initial rationale for the Bank's engagement on MTEF?
   - ☐ Improve fiscal discipline
   - ☐ Improve allocative efficiency
   - ☐ Improve technical efficiency

Box A.2

Methodology

An inventory of medium-term expenditure framework (MTEF)-related project identification numbers was consolidated by extensive searches of the internal data using the following keywords as search terms: medium-term expenditure framework, medium term, medium-term budgetary framework (MTBF), medium-term fiscal framework (MTFF), medium-term performance framework (MTPF), MTEF, MTBF, MTFF, and MTPF. The team reviewed about 1,480 projects and reduced the number to 691 by determining the relevance of each identified product to the Bank's MTEF work.

Based on this set of MTEF-related products, the team examined 242 Implementation Completion Reports (ICRs) looking for trends and conducted more in-depth analysis of a subset of 104 ICRs of the role of the Bank's engagement with MTEFs and lessons learned. The ICRs were selected according to the relevance of the content and the number of times a keyword appeared in the document, using additional criteria such as regional and country coverage and type of Bank products.

To answer these questions, information was gathered from two sources, which serve different objectives and require different methodologies: the internal database and MTEF product documents.

The Bank uses the internal database to monitor its lending and analytical and advisory activities (AAA) products. The database mainly provides information on trends in MTEF-related Bank products covering 110 countries from 1991 to 2010 (figures A.1–A.6 and figures A.9–A.10).[a] These data include information on approval and end dates, type of activity, theme, lending and other resources, deliveries, as well as the ICR and Implementation Status Report ratings.

Qualitative analysis was conducted on 691 MTEF-related products,[b] examining whether Bank support to MTEFs was conducive to achieving the stated objectives (figures A.7–A.8 and tables A.1–A.3). The documents examined include ICRs, project documents, project information documents, project appraisal documents, and other significant AAAs. For this qualitative analysis, the team used Sonar Professional, a tool that helps to search, identify, and analyze a large body of documents by directing the user to a specific document and paragraph according to a chosen search word or a string of search words. For example, in order to identify documents advocating the introduction or implementation of an MTBF pilot, the term medium-term budget framework was searched within

(continued next page)

Box A.2 *(continued)*

100 words of "pilot sector." Similarly, the term medium-term fiscal framework was combined with the words objective, introduction, component, and the World Bank to extract MTFF product documents. Documents for 269 products were available for analysis.

a. Two products focused on high-income countries. Two products were approved in 2011.
b. Country assistance strategies and advisory notes on Poverty Reduction Strategy Papers, which often list MTEF reforms among other components, were not included because they are programmatic documents. The Bank provides support for these reforms through lending, AAA, or technical assistance.

and a medium-term budgetary framework (MTBF)—and the activity's main objectives: fiscal discipline, allocative efficiency, and technical efficiency. Box A.2 presents the methodology used to collect information.

Results

This section examines the trends in Bank support for MTEFs and presents the results of qualitative analysis with regard to implementation status and Bank lending to support MTEFs.

Trends in MTEF Bank History

Five Bank networks and six regional vice presidencies were observed in the period covered by the analysis. As shown in figure A.1, the Poverty Reduction and Economic Management (PREM) network had the largest share of MTEF-related products, followed by the Human Development Network (HDN). The majority of products supporting MTEFs provided assistance to Africa (325) and Europe and Central Asia (134). The Middle East and North Africa region had the lowest number of products (30).

A closer look at the breakdown of AAA (182) and lending (507) products suggests a similar pattern, but the main differences are that Operations Policy and Country Services (OPCS) was the second largest network to provide support for AAA products, and all the MTEF-related work by the Finance and Private Sector Development (FPD) network focused on lending.

The number of Bank products supporting MTEFs rose sharply in 1997–2003, from five to 72 products, showing some volatility during 2003–06 and declining after 2007. The peak was in 2007, with 81 products. Within this period, the number of countries covered

Figure A.1   MTEF-Related Bank Products, by Region and Network, 1991–2010

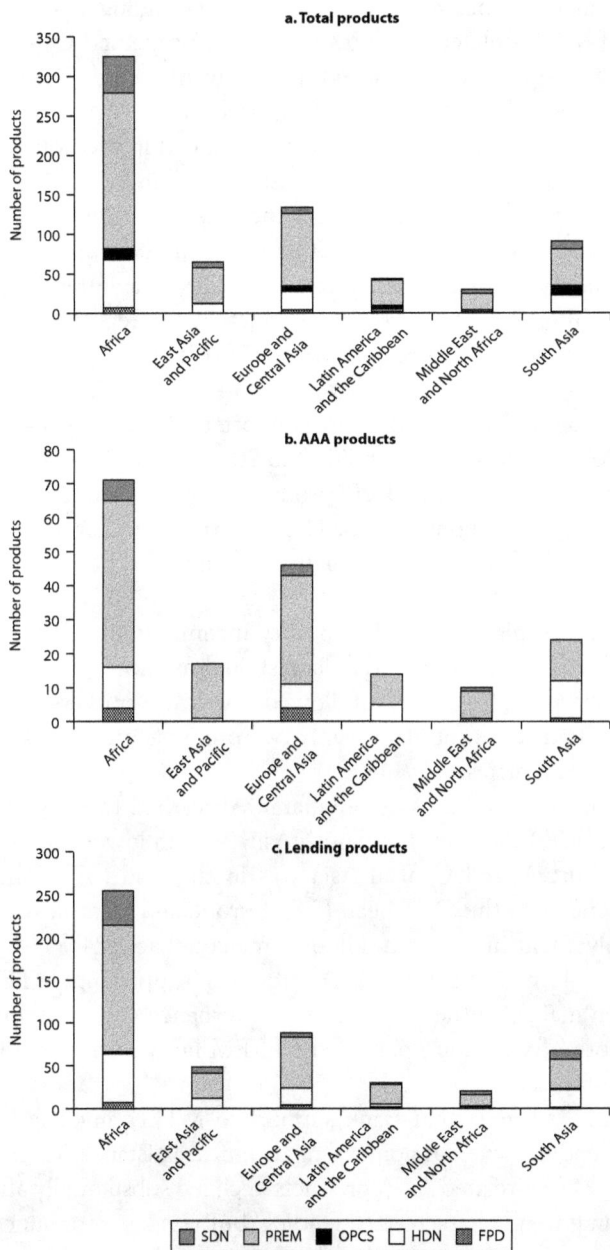

a. Total products

b. AAA products

c. Lending products

SDN   PREM   OPCS   HDN   FPD

Source: World Bank data.

Note: AAA = analytical advisory activities; FPD = Finance and Private Sector Development; HDN = Human Development Network; MTEF = medium-term expenditure framework; OPCS = Operations Policy and Country Services; PREM = Poverty Reduction and Economic Management; SDN = Sustainable Development Network.

expanded from 18 to 99. As shown in figure A.2, Africa had the most consistent increase, beginning in 1998 and continuing until 2008. The number of MTEF-related products spiked in Europe and Central Asia in 2003, declined in 2004, and picked up slowly afterward. The number of products increased in the Middle East and North Africa and in Latin America and the Caribbean in 2010, but declined in the South Asia and Africa regions. It remained at about the same level in East Asia and Pacific and in Europe and Central Asia. This increase generally coincided with broader Bank initiatives, such as publication of the *Public Expenditure Management Handbook*, work related to the Heavily Indebted Poor Country (HIPC) Initiative, Poverty Reduction Strategy Papers (PRSPs) program, and the Public Expenditure and Financial Accountability (PEFA) Program.

The Bank AAA and lending in support of MTEFs reveal different trends. AAA products rose from 2000 to 2003 and declined in 2004. The number remained at around 20 products a year until 2008, when it declined to almost nine products. The pattern of lending was similar in 2000–04, but the number of products nearly doubled between 2004 and 2007, from 27 to 61.

Figure A.3 displays trends by country income group. The number of MTEF-related products was the largest in low-income countries, but declined sharply after 2007, followed by lower-middle-income and upper-middle-income countries. Only two products provided support for high-income countries.

In low-income countries, Sub-Saharan Africa had the largest number of products (269), followed by South Asia (67). In lower-middle-income countries, Europe and Central Asia was in the lead (57), followed by Latin America and the Caribbean (24). Europe and Central Asia topped Bank involvement in upper-middle-income countries (24).

Figure A.4 indicates that Bank products supporting MTEFs were undertaken mainly in the public sector governance and economic policy sectors (both of which are part of the PREM network), each with more than 150 projects.

Figure A.5 suggests that Bank support to MTEFs involved primarily AAA and lending, whereas nonlending technical assistance was minor. The number of MTEF-related AAA products declined substantially after 2007, and the same trend characterized lending, but was less pronounced.

Finally, figure A.6 suggests that both active and closed lending operations have declined since 2009. The number of active lending projects was lower in 2010 than in 2008.

Figure A.2   MTEF-Related Bank Products in 110 Countries, by Region, 1991–2010

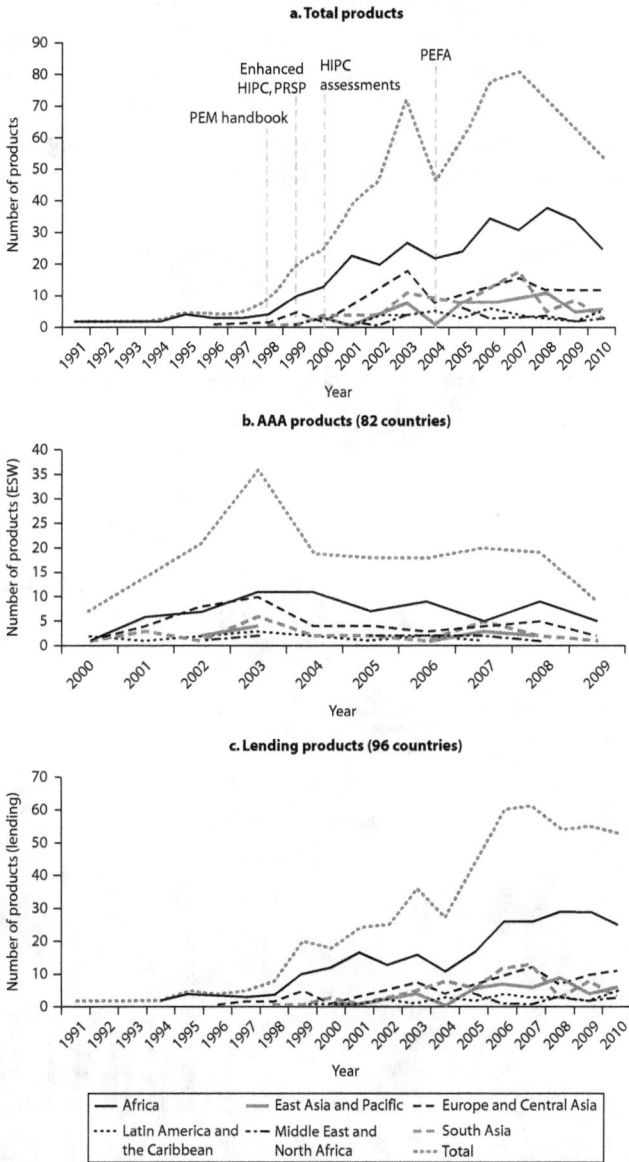

a. Total products

b. AAA products (82 countries)

c. Lending products (96 countries)

Legend:
— Africa   ═══ East Asia and Pacific   – – Europe and Central Asia
···· Latin America and the Caribbean   –·– Middle East and North Africa   ═ ═ South Asia   ····· Total

Source: World Bank data.
Note: AAA = analytical advisory activities; ESW = economic and sector work; HIPC = Heavily Indebted Poor Country; MTEF = medium-term expenditure framework; PEFA = Public Expenditure and Financial Accountability; PEM = Public Expenditure Management; PRSP = Poverty Reduction and Strategy Papers.

Qualitative Analysis

The first part of this section analyzes the status of MTEF implementation, taking into account the stated three-level objectives of fiscal performance (fiscal discipline, allocative efficiency, and technical efficiency) being pursued in MTEF-related lending and AAA products. The second part presents the Bank's assessment of the quality of lending operations supporting MTEFs through ICR and ISR ratings.

Implementation Status. A total of 269 MTEF-related Bank products were available for review (figure A.7, panel a). A large share of them

Figure A.3   MTEF-Related Bank Products, by Country Income Group, 1991–2009

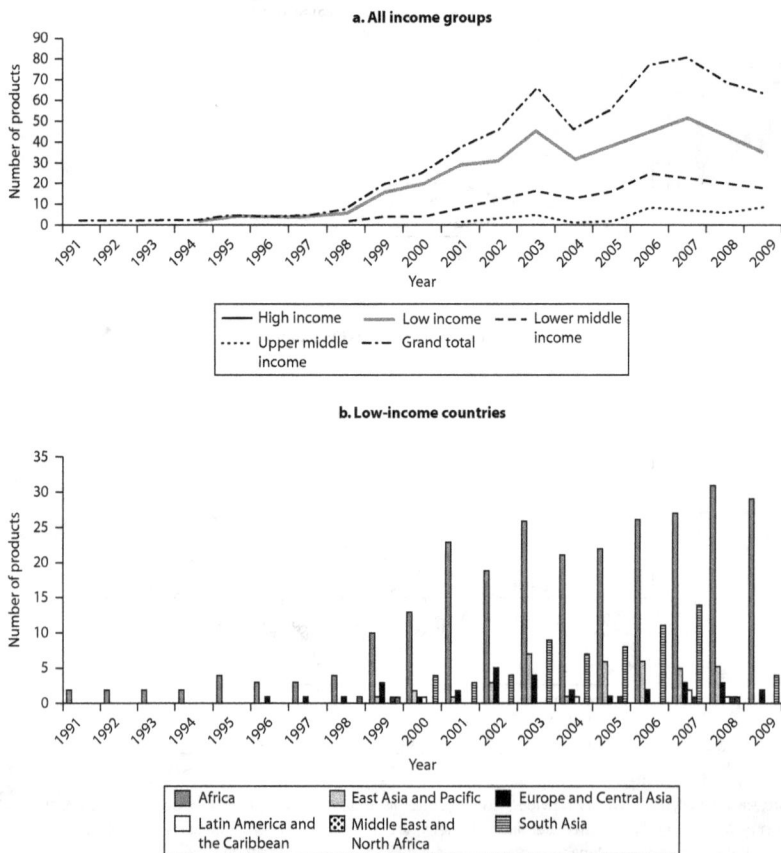

a. All income groups

Legend: High income — Low income — Lower middle income — Upper middle income — Grand total

b. Low-income countries

Legend: Africa — East Asia and Pacific — Europe and Central Asia — Latin America and the Caribbean — Middle East and North Africa — South Asia

(continued next page)

Figure A.3   *(continued)*

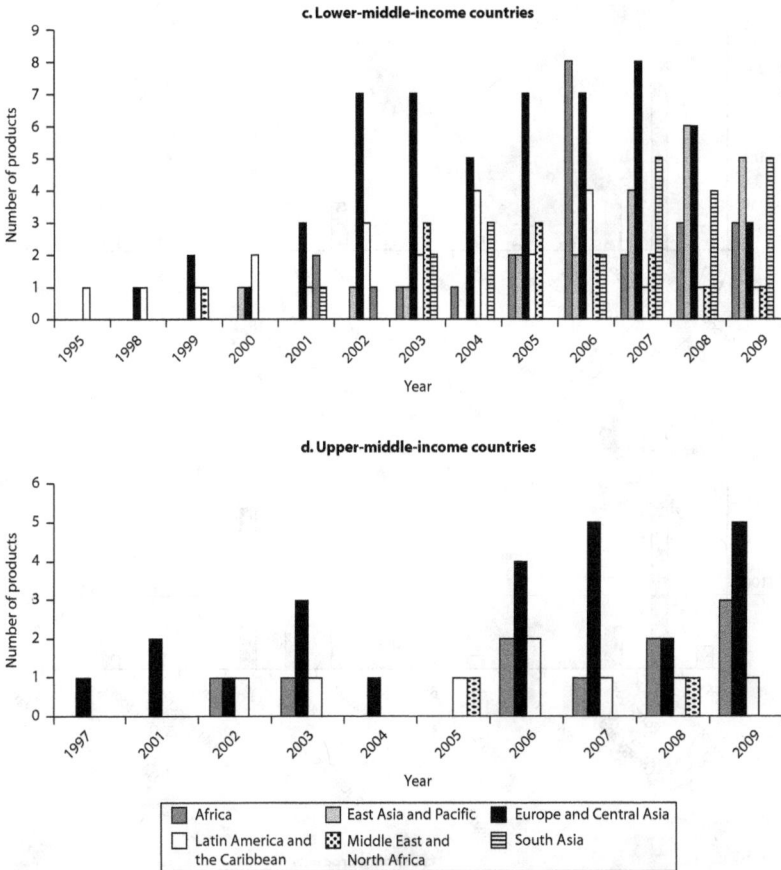

c. Lower-middle-income countries

d. Upper-middle-income countries

Legend:
- Africa
- East Asia and Pacific
- Europe and Central Asia
- Latin America and the Caribbean
- Middle East and North Africa
- South Asia

Source: World Bank data.

(66 percent) supported an MTEF without being specific about the implementation stage pursued; these are identified here as generic MTEFs. However, a closer examination of the documents reveals that both AAA and lending were supportive of MTBFs (the second stage of MTEF implementation, which focuses not only on fiscal discipline but also on allocations among sectors), followed by MTFFs (the first stage of MTEF implementation, which focuses mainly on achieving fiscal discipline and fiscal consolidation). No product focused solely on a medium-term performance framework (MTPF), although some mentioned technical efficiency as a third goal. Figure A.7, panel b, which

Figure A.4   MTEF-Related Bank Products, by Sector, 1991–2010

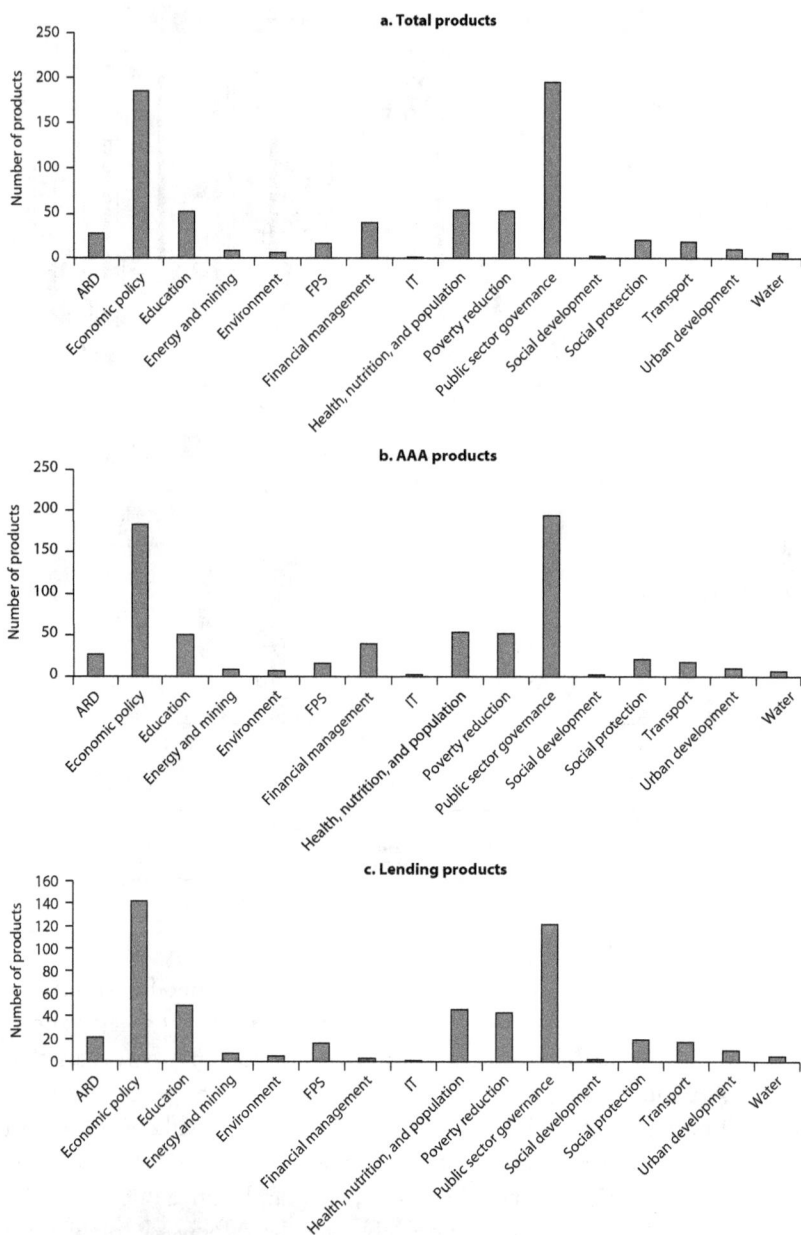

a. Total products

b. AAA products

c. Lending products

Source: World Bank data.
Note: ARD = Agriculture and Rural Development; FPS = Financial Products and Services; IT = information technology; MTEF = medium-term expenditure framework.

Figure A.5   Type of MTEF-Related Bank Products, 1991–2010

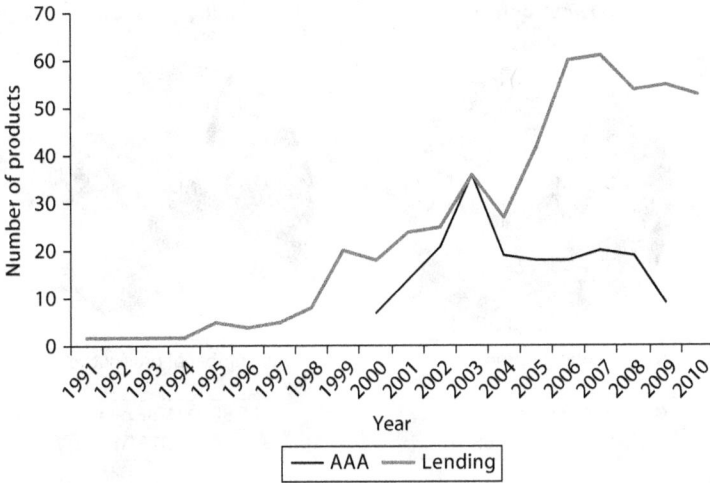

Source: World Bank data.
Note: AAA = analytical advisory activities; MTEF = medium-term expenditure framework.

Figure A.6   Status of MTEF-Related Bank Loans, 1991–2010

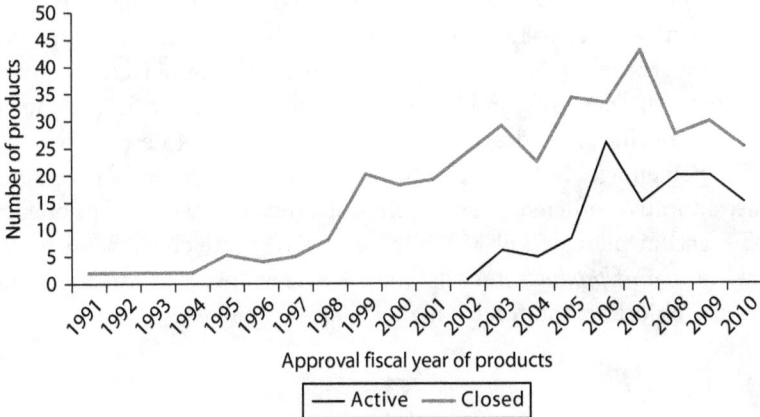

Source: World Bank data.
Note: MTEF = medium-term expenditure framework.

excludes generic MTEFs, confirms that the largest share of Bank MTEF-related products were at an MTBF stage (43 percent), followed by MTFF-focused products (27 percent), and MTBF pilots (24 percent). Only 6 percent of projects described a progression from an MTFF to an MTBF.

Figure A.7   MTEF-Related Bank Products, by Outcome Pursued

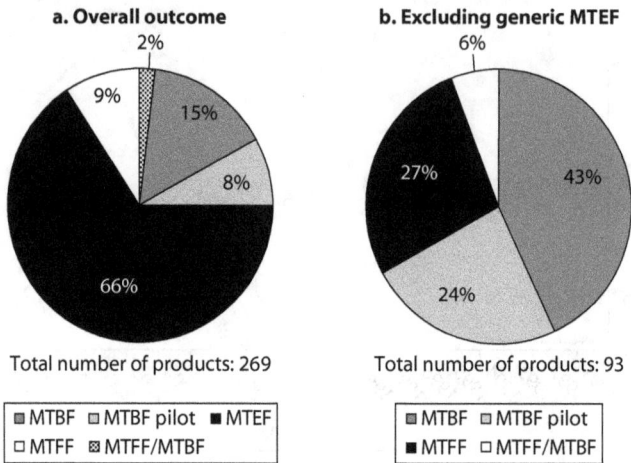

a. Overall outcome

Total number of products: 269

b. Excluding generic MTEF

Total number of products: 93

| ▣ MTBF   ▢ MTBF pilot   ▪ MTEF |
| ▢ MTFF   ▨ MTFF/MTBF |

| ▣ MTBF   ▢ MTBF pilot |
| ▪ MTFF   ▢ MTFF/MTBF |

Source: World Bank data.
Note: MTBF = medium-term budgetary framework; MTEF = medium-term expenditure framework;
MTFF = medium-term fiscal framework.

As shown in figure A.8, out of the 269 products reviewed, 28 pursued clear objectives, such as fiscal discipline, allocative efficiency, and technical efficiency. Most MTEF-related Bank products supported allocative efficiency (39 percent) and fiscal discipline (37 percent), with fewer products specifically addressing technical efficiency (24 percent).

The percentages in table A.1 indicate the number of times fiscal discipline, allocative efficiency, and technical efficiency were mentioned in MTFF and in pilot or full MTBF products, respectively, divided by the total number of *products* in each. Since any given product can have more than one objective, the total is higher than 100 percent:

$$ratio = \frac{\sum O_{i,f}}{\sum P_f} * 100, \tag{A.1}$$

where i denotes the goal (1 = fiscal discipline, 2 = allocative efficiency, 3 = technical efficiency), f denotes framework (MTFF, pilot or full MTBF), O indicates occurrence, and P indicates product.[1]

The percentages in table A.2 indicate the number of times that fiscal discipline, allocative efficiency, and technical efficiency were mentioned

Figure A.8   MTEF Objectives in Bank Products

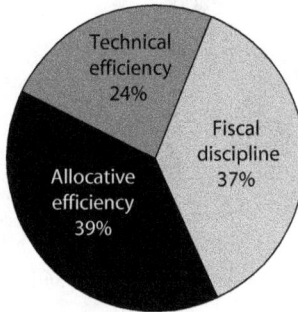

Total number of projects: 28

Source: World Bank data.
Note: MTEF = medium-term expenditure framework.

Table A.1   Goal of Bank Engagement with MTEFs, by Product
% of each goal in total number of products for each MTEF stage

Goal	MTFF	Pilot or full MTBF
Fiscal discipline	100	67
Allocative efficiency	40	83
Technical efficiency	0	50
Total	140	200

Source: World Bank data.
Note: MTBF = medium-term budgetary framework; MTEF = medium-term expenditure framework;
MTFF = medium-term fiscal framework.

Table A.2   Main Goal of Bank Engagement with MTEFs
% of each goal in total goals mentioned

Goal	MTFF	Pilot or full MTBF
Fiscal discipline	71	33
Allocative efficiency	29	42
Technical efficiency	0	25
Total	100	100

Source: World Bank data.
Note: MTBF = medium-term budgetary framework; MTEF = medium-term expenditure framework;
MTFF = medium-term fiscal framework.

in MTFF and pilot or full MTBF products, respectively, divided by the total number of *occurrences* in each:

$$ratio = \frac{\sum O_{i,f}}{\sum O_f} * 100, \qquad (A.2)$$

where i denotes goal (1 = fiscal discipline, 2 = allocative efficiency, 3 = technical efficiency), f denotes framework (MTFF, pilot or full MTBF), and O indicates occurrence.

Tables A.1 and A.2 suggest that, for MTFF-related products, the principal objective was to improve fiscal discipline, while technical efficiency was the least important objective, as expected based on an explicit design. Moreover, an MTFF has fewer objectives per project (140 percent) than an MTBF pilot or a full MTBF (200 percent), most likely because the MTBF is a more advanced stage of MTEF than an MTFF. For the MTBF products, the most common objective was to enhance allocative efficiency, but improving fiscal discipline was also highly relevant.

The percentages in table A.3 indicate the number of times each of the three objectives of fiscal performance was mentioned individually or in combination in MTFF and MTBF pilot or full MTBF products, respectively, divided by the total number of *products* in each.

For example, for fiscal discipline plus allocative efficiency under an MTFF,

$$ratio = \frac{\sum O_{fd,f} + \sum O_{ae,f}}{\sum P_f} * 100, \qquad (A.3)$$

where fd denotes fiscal discipline, ae denotes allocative efficiency, f denotes framework (in this case an MTFF), O indicates occurrence, and P indicates product.

Table A.3 breaks down the fiscal performance objectives addressed by MTEF-related Bank products. These products usually combine lower-level and higher-level goals. For example, for MTFF-related products, 40 percent aimed to improve fiscal discipline and allocative efficiency. For products focusing on MTBF pilots and MTBFs, 17 percent sought to achieve fiscal discipline and allocative efficiency, 17 percent aimed to

Table A.3   Combined Goals of Bank Engagement with MTEFs
% of individual or combined objective in total number of products for each MTEF stage

Goal	MTFF	Pilot or full MTBF
Fiscal discipline	60	17
Fiscal discipline + allocative efficiency	40	17
Fiscal discipline + allocative efficiency + technical efficiency		32
Fiscal discipline + technical efficiency		
Allocative efficiency		17
Allocative efficiency + technical efficiency		17
Total	100	100

Note: MTBF = medium-term budgetary framework; MTEF = medium-term expenditure framework; MTFF = medium-term fiscal framework.

strengthen allocative efficiency and technical efficiency, and 32 percent focused on improving all three objectives.

Lending Operations Supporting MTEFs. To assess the quality of the MTEF-related Bank lending products, two types of ratings are considered: the ICR rating and the ISR rating. The ICR rating, which is used to report on closed Bank-financed operations, uses a five-point Likert scale: unsatisfactory, moderately unsatisfactory, satisfactory, moderately satisfactory, and highly satisfactory scores. The ISR rating, which is a monitoring tool for all current loans and credits financed by the Bank, applies an interval scale of 1–5, with 5 being the highest and 1 being the lowest score.

The analysis in this section is based on a review of 242 ICRs. According to the ICR ratings, approximately 70 percent of the MTEF-related lending products were rated as satisfactory (see figure A.9). During the period 1999–2002, the number of completed lending operations rated as unsatisfactory was quite large, but it has declined since 2002. Since 2004 the share of completed projects rated as moderately satisfactory has increased. This suggests that newer projects have been performing relatively better. Similarly, since 2005 the ISR ratings show a growing number of projects rated 4 and a declining number of projects rated 1.

Conclusion

Bank support for MTEF adoption and implementation has involved lending, AAA, and technical assistance products, implemented mainly by the PREM network, the HDN, and the FPD network. This support has

Figure A.9   Outcome Ratings for MTEF Lending Projects, 1991–2011

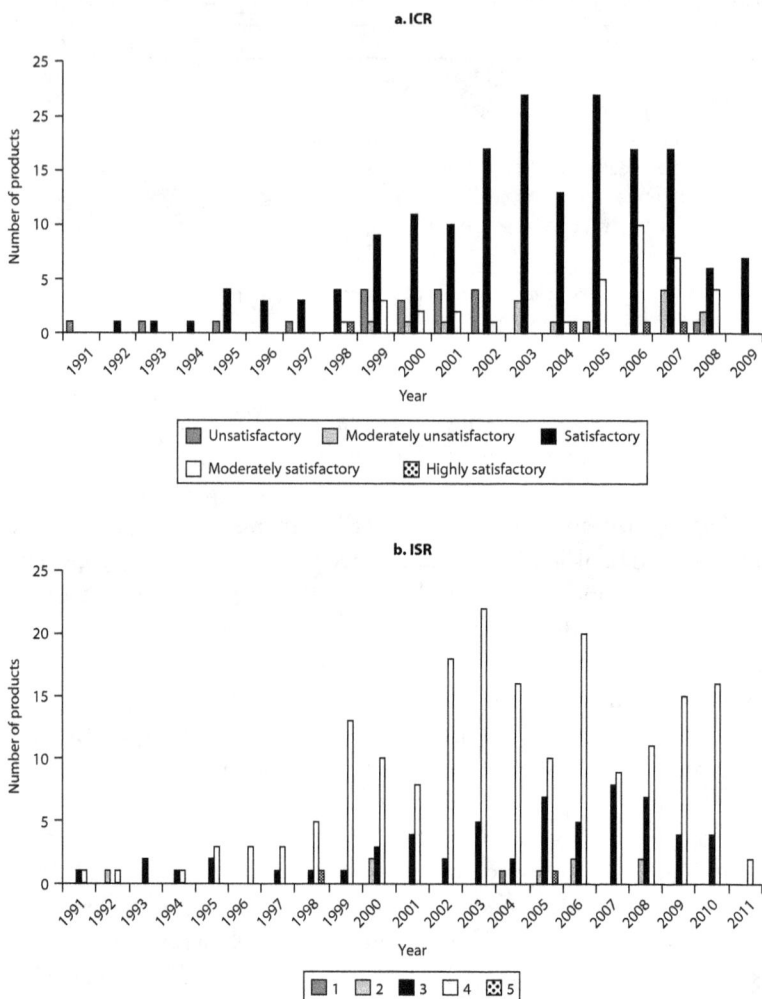

a. ICR

b. ISR

Source: World Bank data.
Note: ICR = Implementation Completion Report; ISR = Implementation Status Report; MTEF = medium-term expenditure framework.

encompassed all regions, with the largest number of operations being in Africa and in Europe and Central Asia, and given priority to low-income countries, followed by lower- and upper-middle-income countries.

Bank products usually combine initial implementation objectives with more ambitious MTEF goals. Given the data limitations, it proved difficult to determine the extent to which these objectives were achieved.

However, the qualitative analysis indicates that Bank advice and support, particularly in the context of MTEF-related lending operations, were conducive to achieving fiscal stability and allocative and technical efficiency. The most common objectives pursued in MTEF-related Bank loans were fiscal discipline and allocative efficiency, although some products also sought to improve technical efficiency. Furthermore, the existing Bank evaluations (ICRs and ISRs) show that a majority of MTEF-related lending products were rated satisfactory (70 percent). In addition, the number of these products rated as less than satisfactory has declined since 2002, indicating better design and implementation of more recent Bank lending operations supporting MTEFs.

Note

1. Technical efficiency as a desired goal was mentioned in several documents, although no MTPFs were found in the analysis.

MTEF Multicountry Studies

This appendix presents the main findings of five cross-country studies examining the performance of medium-term expenditure frameworks (MTEFs): Le Houerou and Taliercio (2002), Holmes and Evans (2003), Filc and Scartascini (2010), Kasek and Webber (2009), and Oyugi (2008).

Le Houerou and Taliercio (2002), in a World Bank study using information on Ghana, Guinea, Kenya, Malawi, Mozambique, Rwanda, South Africa, Tanzania, and Uganda, explore in more detail the impact of MTEFs in Ghana, South Africa, Tanzania, and Uganda. The following are the main findings:

- *Fiscal discipline.* Only small improvement is evident in the fiscal balance in South Africa and Tanzania, although other studies report improved macroeconomic outcomes (Bevan and Palomba 2000).
- *Resource allocation.* Some evidence is found of reallocation to social spending (linked to poverty reduction strategies) in South Africa, Tanzania, and Uganda, but the pattern is not consistent.
- *Budget predictability.* No improvement is found in the budget deviation index.
- *Political accountability.* MTEFs are published in all four countries (and others), and civil society involvement has increased.

- *Budget credibility.* This is not examined because predictability is required for credibility.

Overall, the efficiency gains from MTEFs are yet to emerge, but MTEFs in Africa are still young.

Based on experience to date, Le Houerou and Taliercio (2002) recommend the following:

- MTEFs should complement basic budget reform, be integrated with the budget process, and be based on sector expenditure frameworks.
- They should be implemented governmentwide, taking into account country capacity and political and institutional constraints.

Holmes and Evans (2003), in an Overseas Development Institute study, focus on links between MTEFs and the Poverty Reduction Strategy Paper (PRSP) process in Albania, Benin, Burkina Faso, Cameroon, Ghana, Rwanda, South Africa, Tanzania, and Uganda. Detailed case studies are prepared for each of these countries.

The main lessons from the study are the following:

- Recognize that initial conditions matter (Albania paid attention to this, MTEF played a catalytic role in Tanzania, but excessive "projectization" in Ghana was problemmatic).
- Integrate various phases of the budget cycle (Albania, South Africa, and Uganda—countries with maturing MTEFs—did this).
- Pay early attention to fiscal stability and sustainability (doing so lent credibility to the aggregate resource constraint in South Africa, Tanzania, and Uganda, while not doing so had the opposite effect in Burkina Faso, Cameroon, and Ghana).
- Foster political engagement (Albania, South Africa, and Uganda engaged politicians in setting priorities, but focused more on new than on existing policies).
- Allow for a strategic phase in budget preparation (most countries are developing sector expenditure frameworks).
- Engage sector and line ministries (the quality of budget execution distinguishes different groups of countries, especially struggling countries such as Burkina Faso, Cameroon, and Ghana).
- Sequence the introduction of a performance focus (important given that PRSPs are about outcomes, but only South Africa made significant progress in this regard).

The study finds a strong link to the PRSP process that increased the legitimacy of out-year estimates and led to a sustained increase in pro-poor spending, but separating the responsibilities for budgeting, finance, and planning limited the comprehensiveness of MTEFs and tended to be a centralizing force that ran counter to decentralization.

Based on these findings, the recommendations focus on the following:

- Build the budget basics, make MTEFs comprehensive, and assign a single agency overall responsibility for the MTEF.
- Use reliable macroeconomic and fiscal projections and impose top-down ceilings.
- Create sector working groups, include a strategic phase in budget preparation, and develop a more performance-oriented budget system.
- Implement MTEFs in a way that supports decentralization.

Filc and Scartascini (2010) study MTEFs in Latin America, focusing on Argentina, Colombia, and Peru. In general, MTEFs in the region have been introduced in connection with fiscal responsibility legislation and therefore emphasize fiscal discipline. The country case studies reveal the following:

- Colombia combines a 10-year medium-term fiscal framework (MTFF) and a three-year medium-term budgetary framework (MTBF), guided by a plan setting sector goals. The legislature cannot modify the MTFF or the MTBF, and the annual budget is adapted to the MTBF. Budgets have become more predictable, and fiscal discipline has improved, but tensions between central and subnational governments limit the reach of the MTEF. Results-based budgeting has yet to have much effect.

- Peru's medium-term macroeconomic framework provides an overall spending envelope (effectively an MTFF), which is adjusted annually. It is sent to the legislature but is not discussed, and it has little impact on the budget process. While sector plans are geared to resource availability, sector allocations are based on historical data. An initiative is seeking to establish multiyear budgets for investment, but coordination between the central and subnational governments is weak.

- Argentina implemented a well-designed MTEF, but failed to deliver budget discipline. The MTEF was suspended in 2002–04 due to crisis volatility. It was then extended to subnational governments, but is poorly connected with sector policies. The current aim is to use the MTEF to achieve better fiscal discipline.

Kasek and Webber (2009), in a World Bank study of emerging Europe, focus on Bulgaria, Croatia, Latvia, Poland, the Slovak Republic, and Turkey, all countries where European Union convergence programs and multiyear investment planning require a medium-term perspective. The Slovak Republic integrates planning and budgeting well, with a beneficial impact on budget predictability and credibility, fiscal discipline, overall fiscal performance, and borrowing costs. An unallocated reserve (to meet political priorities), the need to improve strategic planning, and reform fatigue are concerns. Elsewhere, MTEFs are still being developed, with an emphasis on improving strategic planning, linking the MTEF more closely with the annual budget, and developing capacity. Budgeting in these countries remains mainly incremental, while the MTEF is a guideline.

Oyugi (2008), in a study for the Southern and Eastern Africa Policy Research Network, covers Botswana, Kenya, Namibia, Tanzania, and Zambia, although Botswana has a national development plan rather than an MTEF. Kenya, Namibia, and Tanzania are found to have comprehensive MTEFs that successfully link planning with budgeting and shift resources to priority areas. Botswana's plan has all the characteristics of a good MTEF, and the MTEF in Namibia has been instrumental in improving transparency and accountability. However, problems cast doubt on these conclusions. Large budget deviations have compromised fiscal discipline in Botswana and Namibia, annual budgets in Tanzania are unrealistic, budget reallocation has proved difficult in Kenya, and sector advisory groups rarely meet in Zambia.

References

Bevan, D., and G. Palomba. 2000. "Uganda: The Budget and Medium-Term Expenditure Framework Set in a Wider Context." Background Paper for Poverty Reduction Support Credit with DFID Finance, London.

Filc, G., and C. Scartascini. 2010. "Is Latin America on the Right Track? An Analysis of Medium-Term Frameworks and the Budget Process." IDB Working Paper IDB-WP_160, Inter-American Development Bank, Department of Research and Chief Economist, Washington, DC.

Holmes, M., and A. Evans. 2003. "A Review of Experience in Implementing Medium-Term Expenditure Frameworks in a PRSP Context: A Synthesis of Eight Country Studies." Overseas Development Institute, London.

Kasek, L., and D. Webber, eds. 2009. *Performance-Based Budgeting and Medium-Term Expenditure Frameworks in Emerging Europe.* Washington, DC: World Bank.

Le Houerou, P., and R. Taliercio. 2002. "Medium-Term Expenditure Frameworks: From Concept to Practice (Preliminary Lessons from Africa)." Africa Region Working Paper 28, World Bank, Washington, DC.

Oyugi, L. 2008. "Experiences with Medium-Term Expenditure Framework in Selected Southern and Eastern African Countries." SEAPREN Working Paper 7, Southern and Eastern Africa Policy Research Network.

MTEF Country Coding

The data on medium-term expenditure frameworks (MTEFs) were compiled from a large number of sources, both primary as well as secondary. To the extent that the information was available, the MTEF series represent de facto implementation of MTEFs. International Monetary Fund (IMF) Article IV country reports, IMF Reports on the Observance of Standards and Codes, fiscal transparency modules, World Bank Public Expenditure Reviews, World Bank country financial accountability assessments, country budget documents, as well as assessments provided by the World Bank, IMF, country public financial management experts, and country economists were the main sources of information. Other sources included Organisation for Economic Co-operation and Development documents, case studies conducted by development partners, a European Commission survey of medium-term budgetary frameworks, and country websites. For the majority of countries, several sources were cross-checked to ensure the objectivity and validity of information. The use of multiple sources gives a more comprehensive picture of MTEF implementation across countries, but it may be associated with risks concerning the reliability and consistency of data.

MTEF scores are based on an ordinal scale from 0 to 3, as indicated in tables C.1 and C.2. A country with a medium-term fiscal framework

(MTFF) imposed in the context of an IMF program without evidence that it provides a basis for budget formulation is coded as having no MTEF. A country with a piloted medium-term budgetary framework (MTBF) is coded as having an MTFF because an MTEF that is applied in only a few sectors is unlikely to ensure strategic reallocation of resources. The coding describes the highest MTEF stage attained—no MTEF, an MTFF, an MTBF, and a medium-term performance framework (MTPF).

Table C.1   Scoring System

Score	Explanation
0	No MTFF (also IMF program without country-driven MTFF)
1	MTFF (also piloted MTBF in some sectors)
2	MTBF
3	MTPF

Note: MTBF = medium-term budgetary framework; MTEF = medium-term expenditure framework; MTFF = medium-term fiscal framework; MTPF = medium-term performance framework.

Table C.2 MTEF Coding, 1990–2008

Economy	1990	1991	1992	1993	1994	1995	1996	1997	1998	1999	2000	2001	2002	2003	2004	2005	2006	2007	2008
Afghanistan	0	0	0	0	0	0	0	0	0	0	0	0	0	0	0	1	1	1	1
Albania	0	0	0	0	0	0	0	0	0	0	0	1	1	1	1	1	2	2	2
Algeria	0	0	0	0	0	0	0	0	0	0	0	0	0	0	0	0	0	1	2
Angola	0	0	0	0	0	0	0	0	0	0	0	0	0	0	0	0	0	0	0
Antigua and Barbuda	0	0	0	0	0	0	0	0	0	0	0	0	0	0	0	0	0	0	0
Argentina	0	0	0	0	0	0	0	0	2	2	2	2	0	0	0	2	2	2	2
Armenia	0	0	0	0	0	0	0	0	0	0	0	0	2	2	2	2	2	2	3
Australia	3	3	3	3	3	3	3	3	3	3	3	3	3	3	3	3	3	3	3
Austria	0	0	0	0	0	0	0	0	1	1	1	1	1	1	1	1	1	1	3
Azerbaijan	0	0	0	0	0	0	0	0	0	0	0	0	0	0	0	0	0	0	0
Bahrain	0	0	0	0	0	0	0	0	0	0	0	0	0	0	0	0	1	1	1
Bangladesh	0	0	0	0	0	0	0	0	0	0	0	0	0	0	0	1	1	1	1
Barbados	0	0	0	0	0	0	0	0	0	0	0	0	0	0	0	0	0	0	0
Belarus	0	0	0	0	0	0	0	0	0	0	0	0	0	0	0	0	0	0	0
Belgium	0	0	0	0	0	0	0	0	0	1	1	1	1	1	1	1	1	1	1
Belize	0	0	0	0	0	0	0	0	0	0	0	0	0	0	0	0	0	0	0
Benin	0	0	0	0	0	0	0	0	0	0	0	0	0	0	0	1	2	2	2
Bhutan	0	0	0	0	0	0	0	0	0	0	0	0	0	0	0	0	0	1	1
Bolivia	0	0	0	0	0	0	0	0	0	0	0	0	0	0	0	0	0	0	0
Bosnia and Herzegovina	0	0	0	0	0	0	0	0	0	0	0	0	0	0	2	2	2	2	2
Botswana	1	1	1	1	1	1	1	1	1	1	1	1	1	1	1	1	1	1	1
Brazil	0	0	0	0	0	0	0	0	0	0	0	1	1	1	1	1	1	1	1
Bulgaria	0	0	0	0	0	0	0	0	0	0	1	1	2	2	1	1	2	3	3
Burkina Faso	0	0	0	0	0	0	0	0	0	0	0	1	2	2	2	2	2	2	3

(continued next page)

135

Table C.2 (continued)

Economy	1990	1991	1992	1993	1994	1995	1996	1997	1998	1999	2000	2001	2002	2003	2004	2005	2006	2007	2008
Burundi	0	0	0	0	0	0	0	0	0	0	0	0	0	0	0	0	0	0	1
Cambodia	0	0	0	0	0	0	0	0	0	0	0	0	0	1	1	1	1	2	2
Cameroon	0	0	0	0	0	0	0	0	0	0	0	1	1	1	1	1	1	1	1
Canada	1	2	2	2	2	3	3	3	3	3	3	3	3	3	3	3	3	3	3
Cape Verde	0	0	0	0	0	0	0	0	0	0	0	0	0	0	1	2	2	2	2
Central African Republic	0	0	0	0	0	0	0	0	0	0	0	0	0	0	0	0	0	0	0
Chad	0	0	0	0	0	0	0	0	0	0	0	0	0	0	0	1	2	2	2
Chile	0	0	0	0	0	0	0	0	0	0	1	1	1	1	1	1	1	1	1
China	0	0	0	0	0	0	0	0	0	0	0	0	0	0	0	0	0	0	0
Colombia	0	0	0	0	0	0	0	0	0	0	0	0	0	1	1	1	2	2	2
Comoros	0	0	0	0	0	0	0	0	0	0	0	0	0	0	0	0	1	1	1
Congo, Dem. Rep.	0	0	0	0	0	0	0	0	0	0	0	0	0	0	0	0	1	1	1
Congo, Rep.	0	0	0	0	0	0	0	0	0	0	0	0	0	0	0	0	0	1	1
Costa Rica	0	0	0	0	0	0	0	0	0	0	0	0	0	0	0	0	0	0	0
Côte d'Ivoire	0	0	0	0	0	0	0	0	0	0	0	0	0	0	0	0	0	0	0
Croatia	0	0	0	0	0	0	0	0	0	0	0	0	0	0	0	1	1	2	2
Cyprus	0	0	0	0	0	0	0	0	0	0	0	0	0	0	0	0	0	0	0
Czech Republic	0	0	0	0	0	0	0	0	0	0	0	1	1	1	2	2	2	2	2
Denmark	2	2	2	2	2	2	2	3	3	3	3	3	3	3	3	3	3	3	3
Djibouti	0	0	0	0	0	0	0	0	0	0	0	0	0	0	0	0	0	0	0
Dominica	0	0	0	0	0	0	0	0	0	0	0	0	0	0	0	1	1	1	1
Dominican Republic	0	0	0	0	0	0	0	0	0	0	0	0	0	0	0	0	0	0	0
Ecuador	0	0	0	0	0	0	0	0	0	0	0	0	0	0	0	0	0	0	0

Egypt, Arab Rep.	0	0	0	0	0	0	0	0	0	0	0	0	0	0	0	0
El Salvador	0	0	0	0	0	0	0	0	0	0	0	0	0	0	0	0
Equatorial Guinea	0	0	0	0	0	0	0	0	0	0	0	0	0	0	0	0
Eritrea	0	0	0	0	0	0	0	0	0	0	0	0	0	0	1	1
Estonia	0	0	0	0	0	0	0	0	1	1	2	2	1	2	2	0
Ethiopia	0	0	0	0	0	0	0	0	0	1	1	1	1	1	1	1
Fiji	0	0	0	0	0	1	0	0	0	0	0	0	0	0	0	0
Finland	0	0	0	1	1	1	1	1	1	1	3	3	3	3	3	3
France	0	0	0	0	0	1	1	1	1	1	1	1	3	3	3	3
Gabon	0	0	0	0	0	0	0	0	0	0	0	0	0	0	0	0
Gambia, The	0	0	0	0	0	0	0	0	0	0	0	0	0	0	0	0
Georgia	0	0	0	0	0	0	0	0	0	1	1	1	2	2	2	2
Germany	0	0	0	0	0	0	1	1	1	1	1	1	1	1	1	1
Ghana	0	0	0	0	0	0	2	2	2	2	2	2	2	2	2	2
Greece	0	0	0	0	0	1	1	1	1	1	1	1	1	1	1	1
Grenada	0	0	0	0	0	0	0	0	0	0	0	0	0	0	0	0
Guatemala	0	0	0	0	0	0	0	0	0	0	0	0	0	0	0	0
Guinea	0	0	0	0	0	1	2	2	2	2	2	2	2	2	2	2
Guinea-Bissau	0	0	0	0	0	0	0	0	0	0	0	0	0	0	0	0
Guyana	0	0	0	0	0	0	0	0	0	0	0	0	0	0	0	0
Haiti	0	0	0	0	0	0	0	0	0	0	0	0	0	0	0	0
Honduras	0	0	0	0	0	0	0	0	0	1	1	1	1	1	1	1
Hong Kong SAR, China	0	0	0	0	0	0	0	0	0	0	0	0	1	1	1	1
Hungary	0	0	0	0	0	1	1	1	0	1	1	1	1	1	1	1
Iceland	0	0	0	0	0	0	0	0	0	0	1	1	1	1	1	1

(continued next page)

Table C.2 (continued)

Economy	1990	1991	1992	1993	1994	1995	1996	1997	1998	1999	2000	2001	2002	2003	2004	2005	2006	2007	2008
India	0	0	0	0	0	0	0	0	0	0	0	0	0	1	1	1	1	1	1
Indonesia	0	0	0	0	0	0	0	0	0	0	0	0	0	0	0	0	0	0	1
Iran, Islamic Rep.	0	0	0	0	0	0	0	0	0	0	0	0	0	0	0	0	0	0	0
Iraq	0	0	0	0	0	0	0	0	0	0	0	0	0	0	0	0	1	1	1
Ireland	0	0	0	0	0	0	0	0	1	1	1	1	1	1	1	1	1	1	1
Israel	0	0	0	0	0	0	0	0	0	1	0	1	1	1	1	1	1	1	1
Italy	0	0	0	0	0	0	0	0	1	1	1	1	1	1	1	1	1	1	2
Jamaica	0	0	0	0	0	0	0	0	0	0	0	0	0	0	0	0	0	0	0
Japan	0	0	0	0	0	0	0	0	0	0	1	1	1	1	1	1	1	1	1
Jordan	0	0	0	0	0	0	0	0	0	0	0	0	0	0	0	1	1	1	2
Kazakhstan	0	0	0	0	0	0	0	0	0	0	0	0	1	1	1	1	1	1	1
Kenya	0	0	0	0	0	0	0	0	0	0	2	2	2	2	2	2	2	2	2
Korea, Rep.	1	1	1	1	1	1	1	1	1	1	1	1	1	1	1	3	3	3	3
Kosovo	0	0	0	0	0	0	0	0	0	0	0	0	0	0	0	0	2	2	2
Kuwait	0	0	0	0	0	0	0	0	0	0	0	0	0	0	0	0	0	0	1
Kyrgyz Republic	0	0	0	0	0	0	0	0	1	1	1	1	1	1	1	1	1	1	1
Lao PDR	0	0	0	0	0	0	0	0	0	0	0	0	0	0	0	0	0	0	0
Latvia	0	0	0	0	0	0	0	0	0	0	0	1	1	1	1	1	1	1	2
Lebanon	0	0	0	0	0	0	0	0	0	0	0	0	0	0	0	0	0	0	1
Lesotho	0	0	0	0	0	0	0	0	0	0	0	0	0	0	0	1	1	1	1
Liberia	0	0	0	0	0	0	0	0	0	0	0	0	0	0	0	0	0	0	1
Lithuania	0	0	0	0	0	0	0	0	0	0	0	0	1	1	1	1	1	1	1
Luxembourg	0	0	0	0	0	0	0	0	1	1	1	1	1	1	1	1	1	1	1
Macedonia, FYR	0	0	0	0	0	0	0	0	0	0	0	0	0	0	1	1	1	1	1
Madagascar	0	0	0	0	0	0	0	2	2	2	2	2	2	2	2	2	2	2	2
Malawi	0	0	0	0	0	1	1	2	2	2	2	2	2	2	2	2	2	2	2

Country																	
Malaysia	0	0	0	0	0	0	0	0	0	0	0	0	0	0	0	1	1
Maldives	0	0	0	0	0	0	0	0	0	0	0	0	0	0	0	1	0
Mali	0	0	1	1	1	1	1	1	1	1	1	1	1	1	1	1	1
Malta	0	0	0	0	0	1	1	1	1	1	1	1	1	1	1	1	2
Marshall Islands	0	0	0	0	0	0	0	0	0	1	1	1	1	1	1	1	1
Mauritania	0	0	0	0	0	1	1	1	1	1	1	2	2	2	2	2	2
Mauritius	0	0	0	0	0	0	0	0	1	1	1	1	2	2	2	2	3
Mexico	0	0	0	0	0	0	0	0	0	1	1	1	1	2	2	1	1
Moldova	0	0	0	0	0	0	1	1	1	1	2	2	2	2	2	2	2
Mongolia	0	0	0	0	0	0	0	0	0	0	0	0	0	0	1	1	1
Montenegro	0	0	0	0	0	0	0	0	0	0	0	0	0	0	1	0	0
Morocco	0	0	0	0	0	2	2	2	2	2	0	1	1	1	1	1	1
Mozambique	0	0	0	0	2	2	2	2	2	2	2	2	2	2	2	2	2
Myanmar	0	0	0	0	0	0	0	0	0	0	0	0	0	0	0	0	0
Namibia	0	0	0	0	0	2	2	0	2	2	2	2	3	3	3	3	3
Nepal	0	0	0	0	0	2	2	2	2	2	2	2	3	2	3	3	3
Netherlands	1	1	3	3	3	3	3	3	3	3	3	3	3	2	2	2	2
New Zealand	1	1	3	3	3	3	3	3	3	3	3	3	3	3	3	3	3
Nicaragua	0	0	0	0	0	0	0	0	0	1	1	1	1	1	1	1	1
Niger	0	0	0	0	0	0	0	0	0	0	0	1	1	1	1	1	1
Nigeria	0	0	0	0	0	0	0	1	0	0	0	0	0	0	0	1	1
Norway	1	1	1	1	2	2	2	2	2	2	2	3	3	3	3	3	3
Oman	0	0	0	0	0	0	0	0	0	0	0	0	0	0	0	0	0
Pakistan	0	0	0	0	0	0	0	0	0	0	0	1	1	1	1	1	1
Panama	0	0	0	0	0	0	0	0	0	1	0	0	0	0	0	0	1
Papua New Guinea	0	0	0	0	0	0	0	0	0	0	0	0	0	1	1	1	1
Paraguay	0	0	0	0	0	0	0	0	0	0	0	0	1	1	1	1	1

(continued next page)

Table C.2 *(continued)*

Economy	1990	1991	1992	1993	1994	1995	1996	1997	1998	1999	2000	2001	2002	2003	2004	2005	2006	2007	2008
Peru	0	0	0	0	0	0	0	0	0	0	1	1	1	1	1	1	1	1	1
Philippines	0	0	0	0	0	0	0	0	0	0	0	1	1	1	1	1	1	1	1
Poland	0	0	0	0	0	0	0	0	0	0	0	0	0	0	1	1	1	1	1
Portugal	0	0	0	0	0	0	0	0	1	1	1	1	1	1	1	1	1	1	1
Qatar	0	0	0	0	0	0	0	0	0	0	0	0	0	0	0	0	0	0	0
Romania	0	0	0	0	0	0	0	0	0	0	0	0	1	1	1	1	1	1	1
Russian Federation	0	0	0	0	0	0	0	0	0	0	0	0	0	0	0	0	0	0	0
Rwanda	0	0	0	0	0	0	0	0	0	0	2	2	2	2	2	2	2	2	2
Samoa	0	0	0	0	0	0	0	0	0	0	0	0	0	0	0	0	0	0	0
São Tomé and Príncipe	0	0	0	0	0	0	0	0	0	0	0	0	0	0	0	0	0	0	0
Saudi Arabia	0	0	0	0	0	0	0	0	0	0	0	0	0	0	0	0	0	0	0
Senegal	0	0	0	0	0	0	0	0	0	0	0	0	0	0	1	1	1	1	1
Serbia	0	0	0	0	0	0	0	0	0	0	0	0	0	1	1	1	1	1	1
Seychelles	0	0	0	0	0	0	0	0	0	0	0	0	0	0	0	0	0	0	0
Sierra Leone	0	0	0	0	0	0	1	1	1	1	0	0	0	0	0	0	1	1	1
Singapore	1	1	1	1	1	1	1	1	1	1	3	3	3	3	3	3	3	3	3
Slovak Republic	0	0	0	0	0	0	0	0	0	0	1	1	1	1	1	2	2	2	2
Slovenia	0	0	0	0	0	0	0	0	0	2	1	1	2	2	2	2	2	2	2
Solomon Islands	0	0	0	0	0	0	0	0	0	0	0	0	0	0	0	0	1	1	1
South Africa	0	0	0	0	0	0	0	0	2	2	2	2	3	3	3	3	3	3	3
Spain	0	0	0	0	0	0	0	0	1	1	1	1	1	1	1	1	2	2	2
Sri Lanka	0	0	0	0	0	0	0	0	1	1	1	1	0	1	1	2	2	2	2
St. Kitts and Nevis	0	0	0	0	0	0	0	0	0	0	0	0	0	0	0	0	0	0	0

St. Lucia	0	0	0	0	0	0	0	0	0	0	0	2	2	2	2	2	2	2
St. Vincent and the Grenadines	0	0	0	0	0	0	0	0	0	0	0	0	0	0	0	0	0	0
Sudan	0	0	0	0	0	0	0	0	0	0	0	0	0	0	0	0	0	0
Suriname	0	0	0	0	0	0	0	0	0	0	0	2	2	2	2	2	0	0
Swaziland	0	0	1	1	1	1	1	0	0	2	2	2	2	2	2	2	2	2
Sweden	1	1	1	3	3	3	3	3	3	3	3	3	3	3	3	3	3	3
Switzerland	0	0	0	1	0	1	1	1	1	1	1	1	1	1	1	1	1	1
Syrian Arab Republic	0	0	0	0	0	0	0	0	0	0	0	0	0	0	0	0	0	0
Tajikistan	0	0	0	0	0	0	0	0	0	1	0	1	1	1	1	1	1	1
Tanzania	0	0	0	0	2	2	2	2	2	2	2	2	2	2	2	2	2	2
Thailand	0	0	0	0	1	1	1	1	1	1	1	1	1	2	1	2	2	2
Timor-Leste	0	0	0	0	0	0	0	0	0	0	0	0	0	0	0	0	0	0
Togo	0	0	0	0	0	0	0	0	0	0	0	0	0	0	0	0	0	0
Tonga	0	0	0	0	0	0	0	0	0	0	0	0	0	0	0	0	1	1
Trinidad and Tobago	0	0	0	0	0	0	0	0	0	0	0	0	0	0	0	0	0	0
Tunisia	0	0	0	0	0	0	0	0	0	0	0	0	1	0	1	1	1	1
Turkey	0	0	0	0	0	0	0	0	0	0	0	0	0	0	2	2	2	2
Turkmenistan	0	0	0	0	0	0	0	0	0	0	0	0	0	0	0	0	0	0
Tuvalu	0	0	0	0	1	1	1	1	2	2	2	2	2	2	2	2	2	0
Uganda	0	0	1	1	1	1	2	2	2	2	2	2	2	2	2	2	2	2
Ukraine	0	0	0	0	0	0	0	0	0	0	0	0	0	0	0	0	0	1
United Arab Emirates	0	0	0	0	0	0	0	0	0	0	0	0	0	0	0	0	0	0
United Kingdom	1	1	1	1	1	1	3	3	3	3	3	3	3	3	3	3	3	3

(continued next page)

Table C.2 *(continued)*

Economy	1990	1991	1992	1993	1994	1995	1996	1997	1998	1999	2000	2001	2002	2003	2004	2005	2006	2007	2008
United States	1	2	2	2	2	2	2	2	2	2	2	2	2	1	1	1	1	1	1
Uruguay	0	0	0	0	0	0	0	0	0	0	0	0	0	0	0	1	1	1	1
Uzbekistan	0	0	0	0	0	0	0	0	0	0	0	0	0	0	0	0	0	0	1
Vanuatu	0	0	0	0	0	0	0	0	0	0	0	0	0	0	0	0	2	2	2
Venezuela, RB	0	0	0	0	0	0	0	0	0	1	1	1	1	1	1	1	1	1	1
Vietnam	0	0	0	0	0	0	0	0	0	0	0	0	0	0	1	1	1	1	1
West Bank and Gaza	0	0	0	0	0	0	0	0	0	0	0	0	0	0	0	0	0	0	1
Yemen, Rep.	0	0	0	0	0	0	0	0	0	0	0	0	0	0	0	0	0	1	1
Zambia	0	0	0	0	0	0	0	0	0	0	0	0	0	2	2	2	2	2	2
Zimbabwe	0	0	0	0	0	0	0	0	0	0	0	0	0	0	0	0	0	0	0

Source: World Bank.

Note: MTBF = medium-term budgetary framework; MTEF = medium-term expenditure framework; MTFF = medium-term fiscal framework; MTPF = medium-term performance framework. 0 = no MTEF; 1 = MTFF; 2 = MTBF; 3 = MTPF. A country's MTEF status is defined by the highest MTEF stage achieved. These data are maintained and updated on an annual cycle. Some proposed revisions have been received. These will be reviewed further and contained in the next substantive update of the entire data set.

APPENDIX D

Variables and Data Sources

Table D.1 Variables and Data Sources

Variable	Source	Definition
Fiscal balance	WEO	Ratio of the overall central government fiscal balance to GDP
Total expenditure volatility	WEO	Absolute value of the % change in the deviation of the ratio of total central government expenditure to GDP from the trend component extrapolated using the HP filter, minus the same deviation at time $t-1$, normalized by the trend at time $t-1$
Health expenditure share	WHO	General government expenditure on health as a % of total government expenditure
Health expenditure volatility	WHO	Absolute value of the % change in the deviation of the ratio of health expenditure to total expenditure from the trend component extrapolated using the HP filter, minus the same deviation at time $t-1$, normalized by the trend at time $t-1$
Cost-effectiveness of health expenditure	WDI	Estimates of the efficiency scores from a stochastic frontier model that shows life expectancy as output and health spending per capita in PPP terms as input (along

(continued next page)

143

Table D.1 *(continued)*

Variable	Source	Definition
		with population density, years of schooling, a government indicator for voice and accountability and one for government effectiveness, a dummy variable for OECD countries, and year effects)
MTFF	World Bank and IMF documents; case studies	Dummy variable that takes the value 1 if the MTFF is the highest framework adopted, 0 otherwise
MTBF	World Bank and IMF documents; case studies	Dummy variable that takes the value 1 if the MTBF is the highest framework adopted, 0 otherwise
MTPF	World Bank and IMF documents; case studies	Dummy variable that takes the value 1 if the MTPF is the highest framework adopted, 0 otherwise
MTFF diffusion	World Bank and IMF documents; case studies; UN data	Ratio of countries in the same UN region adopting an MTFF to the number of countries in the UN region, excluding the country itself
MTBF diffusion	World Bank and IMF documents; case studies; UN data	Ratio of countries in the same UN region adopting an MTBF to the number of countries in the UN region, excluding the country itself
MTPF diffusion	World Bank and IMF documents; case studies; UN data	Ratio of countries in the same UN region adopting an MTPF to the number of countries in the UN region, excluding the country itself
Health spending per capita (PPP)	WHO	Current health expenditure per capita in PPP terms
GDP per capita (PPP)	WEO	Current GDP per capita in PPP terms
Population density	WDI	People per square kilometer
Years of schooling	WDI	Number of years of primary and secondary education completed
Government voice and accountability	WGI	Index capturing perceptions of the extent to which a country's citizens are able to participate in selecting their government, as well as freedom of expression, freedom of association, and a free media
Government effectiveness	WGI	Index capturing perceptions of the quality of public services, the quality of the civil service, and the degree of its independence from political pressures; the quality of policy formulation and implementation; and the credibility of the government's commitment to such policies

Table D.1   *(continued)*

Variable	Source	Definition
OECD	OECD	Dummy variable that takes the value 1 if the country belongs to the OECD, 0 otherwise
Fiscal rule	FAD fiscal rules database	Dummy variable that takes the value 1 if a debt rule, budget balance rule, revenue rule, or expenditure rule is adopted, 0 otherwise
Political cohesion	DPI	Dummy variable that takes the value 1 if the fraction of seats held by the government (calculated by dividing the number of government seats by the total number of seats) is higher than 50%, 0 otherwise
Democracy	Cheibub, Gandhi, and Vreeland (2010)	Democracy-dictatorship dummy variable that takes the value 1 if a regime meets the following requirements: (1) the chief executive must be chosen by popular election or by a body that was itself popularly elected, (2) the legislature must be popularly elected, (3) more than one party competes in elections, (4) power has alternated under electoral rules identical to the ones that brought the incumbent to office, 0 otherwise
IMF missions	IMF	Number of IMF FAD technical assistance missions per year
GDP growth	WDI	Real GDP growth rate
Trade openness	WDI	Trade openness measured as the ratio of the sum of imports plus exports to GDP
Inflation	WEO	Inflation rate
HIPC Initiative	World Bank	Dummy variable that takes the value 1 if the country is in the period between the decision point and the completion point, 0 otherwise
Aid	OECD	Overseas development assistance net disbursements as a % of GDP
Oil exporter	WEO	Dummy variable that takes the value 1 if the ratio of oil exports to GDP is higher or equal to 30%
Conflict	CSCW	Dummy variable that takes the value 1 if there are at least 1,000 battle-related deaths, 0 otherwise
IMF program	IMF	Dummy variable that takes the value 1 if the country has an IMF program, 0 otherwise
Population	WDI	Population in millions

(continued next page)

Table D.1   *(continued)*

Variable	Source	Definition
Credit market access	S&P	Dummy variable that takes the value 1 if the country has an investment-grade sovereign risk rating from Standard and Poor's, 0 otherwise

Note: CSCW = Centre for the Study of Civil War; DPI = Database of Political Institutions; FAD = Fiscal Affairs Department; GDP = gross domestic product; HIPC = Heavily Indebted Poor Country; HP = Hodrick-Presscott; IMF = International Monetary Fund; MTBF = medium-term budgetary framework; MTEF = medium-term expenditure framework; MTFF = medium-term fiscal framework; MTPF = medium-term performance framework; OECD = Organisation for Economic Co-operation and Development; PPP = purchasing power parity; S&P = Standard and Poor's; UN = United Nations; WDI = World Development Indicators; WEO = World Economic Outlook; WGI = World Governance Indicators; WHO = World Health Organization.

Reference

Cheibub, J., J. Gandhi, and J. Vreeland. 2010. "Democracy and Dictatorship Revisited." *Public Choice* 143 (1–2): 67–101.

Event Studies Figures

Figure E.1   Total Expenditure Volatility

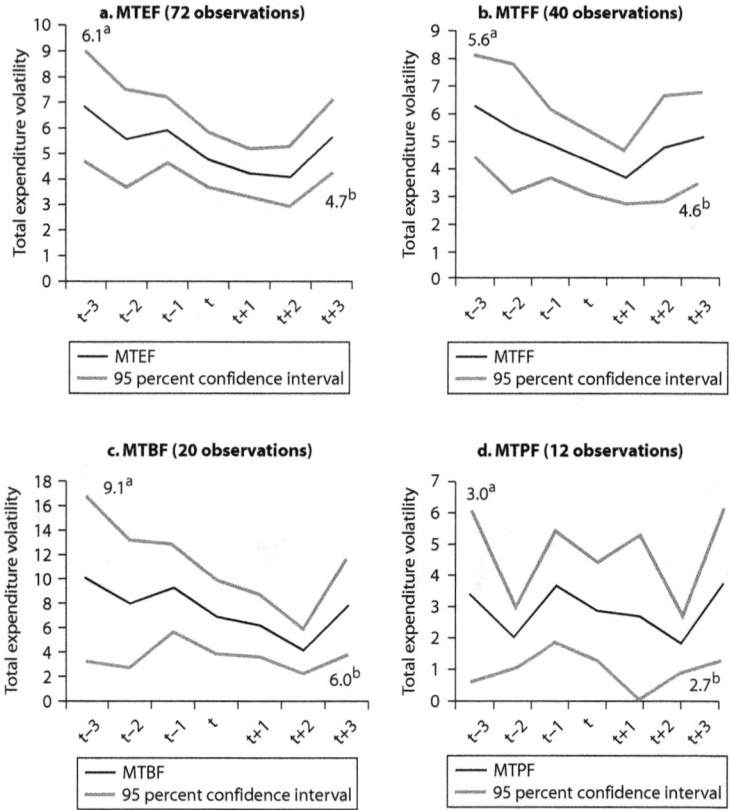

a. MTEF (72 observations)

b. MTFF (40 observations)

c. MTBF (20 observations)

d. MTPF (12 observations)

Source: Authors' analysis of World Bank data.
Note: MTBF = medium-term budgetary framework; MTEF=medium-term expenditure framework; MTFF = medium-term fiscal framework; MTPF = medium-term performance framework.
a. Pre-MTEF mean.
b. Post-MTEF mean.

Figure E.2   Health Expenditure Share

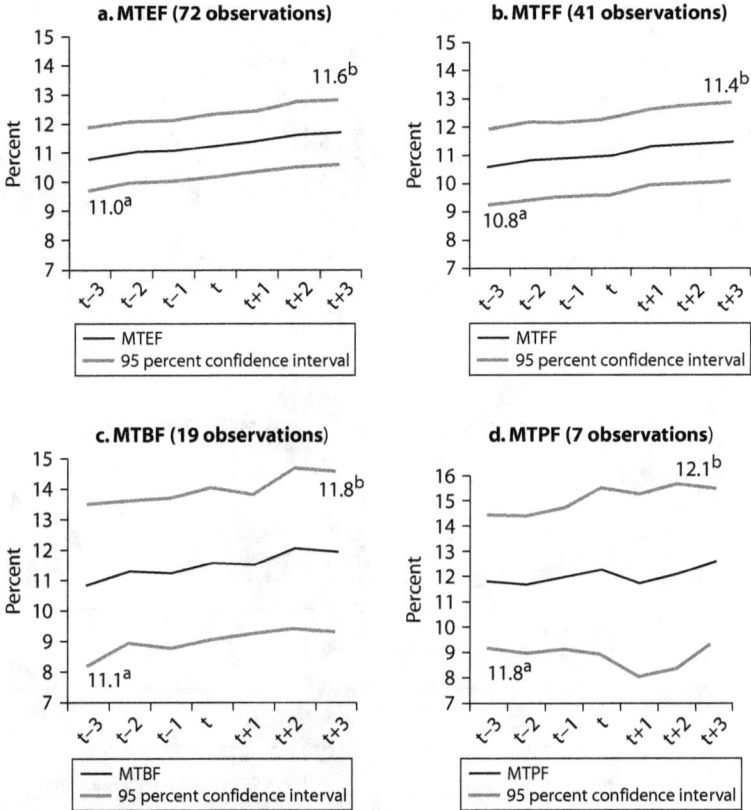

a. MTEF (72 observations)

11.6[b]

11.0[a]

— MTEF
— 95 percent confidence interval

b. MTFF (41 observations)

11.4[b]

10.8[a]

— MTFF
— 95 percent confidence interval

c. MTBF (19 observations)

11.8[b]

11.1[a]

— MTBF
— 95 percent confidence interval

d. MTPF (7 observations)

12.1[b]

11.8[a]

— MTPF
— 95 percent confidence interval

Source: Authors' analysis of World Bank data.
Note: MTBF = medium-term budgetary framework; MTEF = medium-term expenditure framework;
MTFF = medium-term fiscal framework; MTPF = medium-term performance framework.
a. Pre-MTEF mean.
b. Post-MTEF mean.

Figure E.3   Health Expenditure Volatility

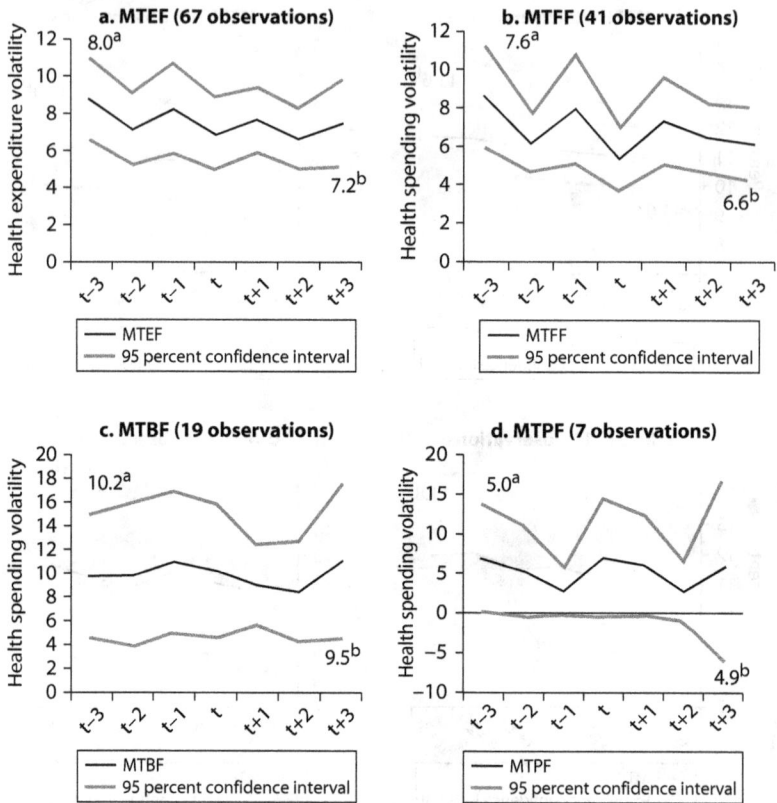

a. MTEF (67 observations)

8.0[a]

7.2[b]

Health expenditure volatility

— MTEF
— 95 percent confidence interval

b. MTFF (41 observations)

7.6[a]

6.6[b]

Health spending volatility

— MTFF
— 95 percent confidence interval

c. MTBF (19 observations)

10.2[a]

9.5[b]

Health spending volatility

— MTBF
— 95 percent confidence interval

d. MTPF (7 observations)

5.0[a]

4.9[b]

Health spending volatility

— MTPF
— 95 percent confidence interval

Source: Authors' analysis of World Bank data.
Note: MTBF = medium-term budgetary framework; MTEF = medium-term expenditure framework; MTFF = medium-term fiscal framework; MTPF = medium-term performance framework.
a. Pre-MTEF mean.
b. Post-MTEF mean.

Figure E.4   Cost-Effectiveness of Health Expenditure

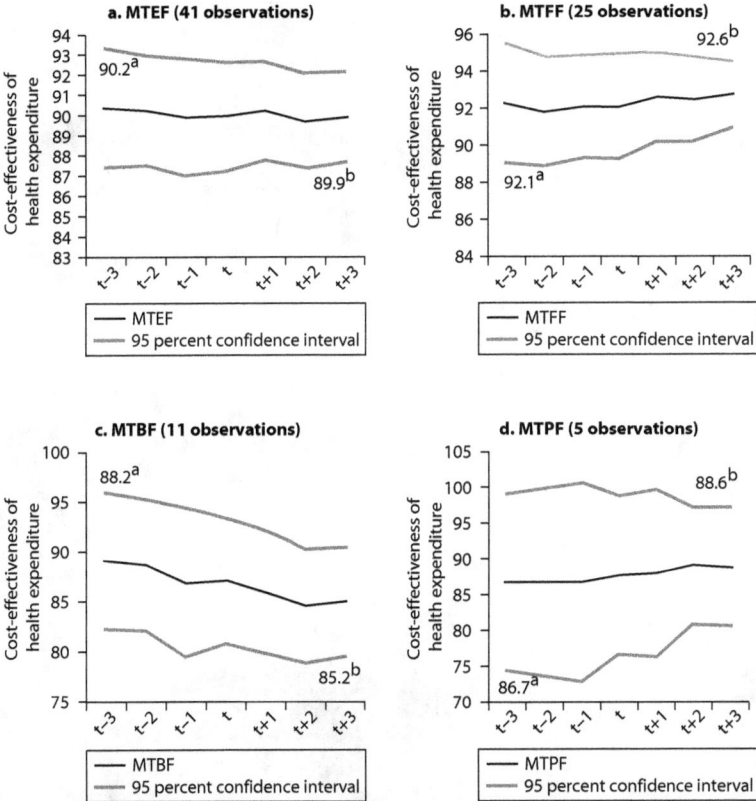

a. MTEF (41 observations)

b. MTFF (25 observations)

c. MTBF (11 observations)

d. MTPF (5 observations)

Source: Authors' analysis of World Bank data.
Note: MTBF = medium-term budgetary framework; MTEF = medium-term expenditure framework; MTFF = medium-term fiscal framework; MTPF = medium-term performance framework. A lower value of the index means an improvement in cost-effectiveness, as defined in chapter 4.
a. Pre-MTEF mean.
b. Post-MTEF mean.

Econometric Results

This appendix provides a detailed description of the data definitions and the econometric strategy adopted to analyze the impact of medium-term expenditure frameworks (MTEFs) on fiscal discipine, allocative efficiency, and technical efficiency. It also presents the complete set of econometric results.

Data

To exploit both cross-sectional and time-series variation, a panel data set is constructed of MTEF stages for 181 countries over the period 1990–2008. A brief description of the variables used in the analysis is provided below, while appendix D contains a comprehensive list of variables and sources.

Fiscal discipline is measured by the *fiscal balance* and, more specifically, by the central government's overall balance. Although the literature commonly uses the primary balance as an indicator of macro-fiscal performance, this information is only available for a limited sample of countries. However, the primary balance is used as a robustness check. General government data also provide better coverage of fiscal activity, but only central government data are available for a large number of countries.

One measure of allocative efficiency is *total expenditure volatility*, which is measured by the volatility of total central government expenditure as a share of gross domestic product (GDP). This should decline as overall spending becomes more stable because it is determined by medium-term objectives and resource availability. It would also be useful to look at the volatility of budget composition, since an MTEF should help to protect high-priority spending and therefore make it less volatile. However, health care is the only category of spending for which good cross-sectional and time-series data are available. Allocative efficiency is therefore also measured by the *health expenditure share*, which is the ratio of general government health expenditure to total expenditure, and by *health expenditure volatility*, which is the volatility of the health expenditure share.

Both measures of volatility are defined as the absolute value of the percentage change in the deviation of the ratio of total expenditure to GDP or health expenditure to total expenditure, x_{it}, from the trend component extrapolated using the Hodrick-Prescott (HP) filter, $\tau_{x,it}$, minus the same deviation at time $t-1$, normalized by the trend at time $t-1$:[1]

$$Volatility_{it} = \left| \frac{[(x_{it} - \tau_{x,it}) - (x_{it-2} - \tau_{x,it-1})]}{\tau_{x,it-1}} * 100 \right|. \qquad (F.1)$$

Stochastic frontier analysis is used to obtain a measure for technical efficiency, the *cost-effectiveness of health expenditure*. This technique is inspired by Farrell (1957), who defines technical efficiency as the ability to produce the maximum possible output from a given set of inputs and measures it in terms of the relationship between observed output and the maximum attainable output given observed inputs. The country with the highest health output after controlling for inputs is the most efficient, and the efficiency of other countries is measured with respect to that country.

The frontier is defined as a function of efficient production to which two disturbances are added: v_{it}, a symmetrical disturbance that includes random noise, and u_{it}, a biased strictly non-negative disturbance that reflects technical inefficiencies.[2] The problem that arises with these methods is that the u_{it} component cannot be observed and must be inferred from the composite error term, $\varepsilon_{it} = v_{it} + u_{it}$. The noise and inefficiency components are separated using the conditional expectation of u_{it} given ε_{it} (see Jondrow et al. 1982). Thus a production function that shows how level of health, proxied by life expectancy, varies with inputs, such as health spending per capita in purchasing power parity (PPP) terms, is estimated as follows:

$$LifeExpectancy_{it} = \alpha + \beta\, HealthSpending\_pc\_PPP_{it} + \gamma\, Covariates_{it}$$
$$+ \tau_t + v_{it} - u_{it}, \tag{F.2}$$

where the group of covariates is the same as the one used in Greene (2005), when data are available.[3] This group includes population density, years of schooling, an indicator of voice and accountability, an indicator of government effectiveness, a dummy variable for Organisation for Economic Co-operation and Development (OECD) countries, and year effects.[4] All input variables, as well as the output variable, enter the production function in log form. Technical efficiency scores are obtained as a transformation of the non-negative disturbance:

$$TechnicalEfficiencyScores_{it} = e^{-v_{it}}. \tag{F.3}$$

The MTEF variables used in the regressions consist of three mutually exclusive dummies[5]—medium-term fiscal framework (MTFF), mediumterm budgetary framework (MTBF), and medium-term performance framework (MTPF). MTEF country coding is explained and shown in appendix C.

To test whether the MTEF impact is enhanced by factors that the literature has suggested have an influence on fiscal performance, several conditioning variables are included in the regressions. To test the impact of fiscal rules, a dummy variable is constructed and given the value 1 when an expenditure rule, a revenue rule, a debt rule, or a budget balance rule (or a combination of them) is operational and the value 0 otherwise. Along the same lines, political cohesion is measured through a dummy variable that takes the value 1 if the fraction of seats held by the government (calculated by dividing the number of government seats by the total number of seats) is higher than 50 percent and the value 0 otherwise. Many indicators have been used to measure democracy, such as those produced by Freedom House, Polity IV, and so forth. Cheibub, Gandhi, and Vreeland (2010) address the strengths and weaknesses of the main indicators of democracy, concluding that they are not interchangeable. However, they also argue that a measure of democracy based on a minimalist conception is compatible with most of the theoretical issues that inform empirical research. Thus in their extension of the data set first published in Alvarez et al. (1996), they include the variable democracy-dictatorship, which is adopted in this analysis. OECD membership is added to test for any specific country group effects, and the number of International Monetary Fund (IMF) technical assistance missions is introduced to test for an enhanced MTEF impact. Basic descriptive statistics for the data used in the analysis are reported in table F.1.

Econometric Strategy

Three well-known methodological challenges must be overcome to identify the impact of an MTEF on fiscal performance: reverse causality, omitted-variable, and errors-in-variables biases.

First, reverse causality arises because fiscal performance may prompt a country to adopt an MTEF. This type of problem is discussed extensively in the literature, where the focus is on the link between fiscal stress and budgetary reform (see Alesina and Perotti 1999; Stein, Talvi, and Grisanti 1999; Knight and Levinson 2000; Perotti and Kontopoulos 2002; Fabrizio and Mody 2006). There are two dimensions to reverse causality. In the case of an MTEF, one possibility is that *poor* fiscal performance increases the chance that a country will adopt an MTEF, in which case ordinary least squares (OLS) estimates suggesting that an MTEF improves fiscal performance would suffer from a reverse causality bias that is negative. If this were the case, the estimates would still be useful as a lower bound for the actual effect. The other possibility is that MTEF adoption is a response to *good* fiscal performance, in which case OLS estimates suggesting that an MTEF improves fiscal performance would suffer from a reverse causality bias that is positive. In this case, the estimates are less informative. The use of instrumental variables is the usual response to reverse causality bias, but the literature does not find an instrument that influences the probability of a budgetary reform (or a change in fiscal institutions in general) and is not itself affected by fiscal performance. Because of this, past papers assume that fiscal performance cannot quickly feed back into budgetary reforms.

Second, omitted-variable bias arises due to the failure to account for a factor that affects both the adoption of an MTEF and fiscal performance. For instance, strong economic growth may reduce the pressure on a government to reform fiscal institutions and, at the same time, improve the government's fiscal outcomes, thus leading to negative omitted-variable bias. In general, the risk of attributing the effect of omitted variables to the regressors will generate an overstatement of the MTEF effect. As suggested by Fabrizio and Mody (2006), a partial solution to this problem is to disregard the variation across countries and analyze only the within-country variation. This approach, in effect, eliminates the country-specific fixed

Table F.1   Descriptive Statistics

Variable	Observations	Mean	Standard deviation Across	Within	Minimum	Maximum
Fiscal balance	2,991	−2.24	9.40	9.59	−151.33	384.15
Total expenditure volatility	2,826	7.53	5.30	8.43	0.00	132.84
Health expenditure share	2,471	10.64	4.18	1.93	0.00	41.33
Health expenditure volatility	2,293	8.88	6.92	10.45	0.00	188.74
Cost-effectiveness of health expenditure	1,434	90.82	7.58	1.20	61.51	99.21
MTFF	3,378	0.17	0.20	0.32	0.00	1.00
MTBF	3,378	0.07	0.15	0.22	0.00	1.00
MTPF	3,378	0.04	0.15	0.13	0.00	1.00
MTFF diffusion	3,359	0.17	0.12	0.18	0.00	1.00
MTBF diffusion	3,359	0.07	0.09	0.12	0.00	1.00
MTPF diffusion	3,359	0.04	0.12	0.08	0.00	1.00
Health spending per capita (PPP)	2,465	667.68	939.93	284.37	0.00	7,536.27
GDP per capita (PPP)	3,140	8,735.82	10,464.41	3,428.78	122.88	79,485.46
Population density	3,304	188.89	638.90	60.86	1.43	6,943.19
Years of schooling	1,435	10.50	2.29	0.56	2.10	16.67
Government voice and accountability	1,798	47.78	27.92	5.26	0.00	100.00
Government effectiveness	1,756	48.18	27.96	6.59	0.00	100.00
OECD	3,439	0.16	0.36	0.08	0.00	1.00
Fiscal rule	3,439	0.25	0.32	0.29	0.00	1.00
Political cohesion	2,798	0.82	0.25	0.29	0.00	1.00
Democracy	3,325	0.56	0.46	0.18	0.00	1.00
IMF missions	3,439	0.51	0.75	1.64	0.00	32.00
GDP growth	3,250	3.74	2.63	6.18	−51.03	106.28
Trade openness	3,069	85.28	49.14	16.89	0.31	456.65
Inflation	3,202	47.39	164.88	477.52	−26.32	23,773.10
HIPC Initiative	3,439	0.04	0.10	0.17	0.00	1.00
Aid	3,233	3.67	6.88	3.81	−2.96	96.42
Oil exporter	3,233	0.07	0.24	0.11	0.00	1.00
Conflict	3,439	0.05	0.14	0.17	0.00	1.00
IMF program	3,378	0.33	0.35	0.32	0.00	1.00
Population	3,426	32.86	122.00	8.64	0.01	1,324.66
Life expectancy	3,331	66.09	10.13	2.13	26.41	82.59

Note: GDP = gross domestic product; HIPC = Heavily Indebted Poor Country; IMF = International Monetary Fund; MTBF = medium-term budgetary framework; MTEF = medium-term expenditure framework; MTFF = medium-term fiscal framework; MTPF = medium-term performance framework; PPP = purchasing power parity. The sample consists of 181 countries during 1990–2008. Data sources and units of measurement are presented in appendix D.

effects that may influence budget deficits but may not be observed. Thus, by focusing on variations within a country over time, the problem of omitted variables is alleviated but not eliminated. Most studies have not been able to adopt this method either because budget institutions do not change much over time or because changes are difficult to measure. Where it has been implemented, Knight and Levinson (2000) suggest that the results are typically different from those obtained in cross-country analysis, indicating that the problem of omitted variables is relevant.

Finally, if some of the variables in the analysis are not measured accurately, there is the potential for errors-in-variables bias, which usually dampens the effect of interest.

To address the reverse causality problem, an instrument for MTEF adoption is defined as the geographic diffusion of a given MTEF stage. As mentioned, MTEFs have, to a certain extent, spread geographically among close countries. Countries in the same region adopt MTEFs at around the same time. That said, there is little reason to expect that a neighbor's fiscal institutions directly affect a country's fiscal performance, which means that instrument exogeneity is assured. Regional MTEF diffusion is defined as follows:

$$Diffusion_{i,t}^{MTEF} = reformers_{r,t} - i \ / \ r - i, \qquad \text{(F.4)}$$

where i is the observed country, t is the total number of countries in the geographic region,[6] and *reformers* is the number of countries in the region that introduced the MTEF.

Unfortunately, only two of the three instruments pass the relevance test: MTPF diffusion is not strong enough to serve as a valid instrument jointly with the other two. To overcome the strength issue, the three static instruments are augmented with dynamic instruments, as suggested by Arellano and Bond (1991).[7] This strategy allows us to account for possible persistence in fiscal outcomes, by using a lagged dependent variable.[8] The Arellano and Bond estimation, also known as "difference generalized method of moments (GMM)," transforms all regressors by differencing and uses the generalized method of moments (Hansen 1982).[9] However, the lagged levels of the regressors might be poor instruments for the first-differenced regressors. If this is the case, the Arellano and Bover (1995) or Blundell and Bond (1998) estimator, also known as "system GMM," should be used. This estimator uses the levels equation to obtain a system of two equations: one differenced and one in levels. By adding the second equation, additional instruments can be obtained. Thus, the variables in levels in the second equation are instrumented with their own first differences. The underlying additional assumption is that the first differences of instrumented variables are uncorrelated with the fixed effects. This technique allows the introduction of more instruments and can dramatically improve estimator efficiency.

To deal with the omitted-variable bias, both country and time variation in the data are exploited by controlling for (a) long-term country characteristics, such as culture and norms (using country fixed effects) and (b) global factors that affect all countries, such as resource prices (using year fixed effects). A possible concern about the exogeneity of neighbors' MTEF adoption status is that it is driven by regional shocks that affect countries located in the same geographic region. To control for this, region-year interactions (or region-specific time trends) are included.

The measurement error problem is only partially solved. More specifically, although in the empirical model the primary explanatory variable, MTEF status, can be observed with a reasonably high degree of precision, there is still scope for measurement error in the other explanatory variables.

An empirical model relating fiscal performance to the introduction of an MTEF and a set of covariates is estimated for each measure of performance:

$$FiscalPerformance_{it} = \alpha + \beta_1\, MTFF_{it} + \beta_2\, MTBF_{it} + \beta_3\, MTPF_{it}$$
$$+ \gamma\, Covariates_{it} + v_i + \tau_t + u_{it}, \qquad (F.5)$$

where the dependent variable $FiscalPerformance_{it}$ is the fiscal balance, total expenditure volatility, health expenditure share, health expenditure volatility, and cost-effectiveness of health expenditure; $MTFF_{it}$, $MTBF_{it}$, and $MTPF_{it}$ are mutually exclusive dummy variables for the presence of the frameworks; $Covariates_{it}$ includes a set of controls commonly used in the literature, such as GDP growth, trade openness, population, inflation, aid, and dummies for oil exporters, conflicts, Heavily Indebted Poor Countries (HIPC) Initiative, IMF program, and credit market access; v_{it} is a set of unchanging country-specific effects (proxied by country dummies); τ_t are effects common to all countries in period t (time dummies); and u_{it} is the error term. Errors are robust to heteroskedasticity and, following Bertrand, Duflo, and Mullainathan (2004), are clustered at the country level to correct for possible serial correlation within countries.

To test the conditional-effects hypotheses, a second set of regressions is estimated with the addition of interaction terms. This studies the conditional effects on MTFFs:

$$FiscalPerformance_{it} = \alpha + \theta_0 \, c_{it} + \beta_1 \, MTFF_{it} + \theta_1 \, (MTFF_{it} \, {}^*c_{it})$$
$$+ \beta_2 \, MTBF_{it} + \beta_3 \, MTPF_{it}$$
$$+ \gamma \, Covariates_{it} + v_i + \tau_t + u_{it}, \qquad (F.6)$$

where c_{it} is one of the conditioning variables identified above.

To check the sensitivity of the results to alternative specifications, the model is estimated with alternative sets of covariates and instruments. Furthermore, the robustness of the results is checked by using pooled OLS and by introducing fixed effects, year effects, and regional trends. In these models, identification is based on uninstrumented difference-in-differences comparisons.

Another relevant concern is the robustness of the results to possible outliers. In particular, because of the large changes in fiscal balance in some countries or changes in fiscal institutions that are not well documented, the question arises as to whether the results are driven by these countries. The approach proposed by Milesi-Ferretti, Perotti, and Rostagno (2002) is followed, excluding one region at a time to test for the possibility of influential observations.

Econometric Results

The results for the fiscal balance are presented in table F.2. From column 1 to column 8, the same specification is estimated using different techniques. Endogeneity is best handled when the Arellano-Bond system GMM estimator is adopted (columns 5 to 8), and the results overall confirm a strong and positive contribution of all the stages of the MTEF on fiscal discipline. It is shown that the higher the level of MTEF sophistication—from an MTFF to an MTBF and finally to an MTPF—the bigger the magnitude of the impact. In column 8, the preferred specification, the adoption of an MTFF increases the fiscal balance by 0.85 percentage points, the MTBF by 0.99 percentage points, and the MTPF by 2.82 percentage points. The relatively large and implausible effect of MTPF implementation might be due to the small number of observations in the data set.

Among the controls, the coefficient for oil exporters has an important impact on fiscal discipline. It has a positive and significant sign of fairly large magnitude. At the same time, armed conflicts worsen the fiscal

Table F.2 MTEF Effects on Fiscal Discipline

dependent variable = fiscal balance = central government balance as % of GDP

Variable	Pooled OLS (1)	FE (2)	DID (3)	DID with regional trends (4)	AB system GMM (5)	AB system GMM with IV (6)	AB system GMM with year effects (7)	AB system GMM with IV and with year effects (8)	AB system GMM with IV and with year effects (9)
MTFF	1.94***	1.46***	0.09	0.46	1.16***	1.61***	0.58	0.85**	0.86*
	(0.43)	(0.44)	(0.52)	(0.48)	(0.37)	(0.42)	(0.44)	(0.42)	(0.49)
MTBF	1.65***	2.24***	0.22	0.64	1.56***	1.95***	0.82	0.99*	1.17*
	(0.54)	(0.55)	(0.70)	(0.66)	(0.50)	(0.54)	(0.56)	(0.52)	(0.60)
MTPF	3.95***	5.67***	2.47**	2.97***	2.57***	3.83***	1.82**	2.82***	3.00**
	(0.63)	(0.86)	(1.06)	(0.84)	(0.92)	(0.99)	(0.93)	(0.96)	(1.25)
Lag GDP growth	0.08***	0.11***	0.08***	0.07***	-0.03	-0.03	-0.03	-0.03	-0.01
	(0.03)	(0.03)	(0.02)	(0.02)	(0.02)	(0.02)	(0.02)	(0.02)	(0.02)
Trade openness	0.01	0.01	0.00	0.00	0.00	0.00	0.00	0.00	0.00
	(0.00)	(0.01)	(0.01)	(0.01)	(0.00)	(0.00)	(0.00)	(0.00)	(0.00)
Oil exporter	6.08***	4.37***	3.52***	3.20***	4.08***	4.17***	3.84***	3.89***	5.09***
	(1.68)	(0.96)	(0.97)	(0.92)	(1.03)	(1.04)	(1.04)	(1.04)	(1.18)
Conflict	-3.04**	-2.56**	-2.05**	-2.00*	-1.61**	-1.58**	-1.60**	-1.56**	-1.64*
	(1.23)	(1.11)	(1.03)	(1.10)	(0.66)	(0.65)	(0.65)	(0.64)	(0.88)
Lag IMF program	0.08	0.25	0.49	0.32	-0.25	0.23	-0.22	-0.20	-0.41
	(0.44)	(0.37)	(0.36)	(0.38)	(0.29)	(0.30)	(0.30)	(0.30)	(0.41)
Population	0.00	0.02	-0.07*	-0.06	0.00	0.00	0.00	0.00	0.00
	(0.01)	(0.04)	(0.04)	(0.06)	(0.00)	(0.00)	(0.00)	(0.00)	(0.00)
Population squared	0.00	0.00	0.00	0.00	0.00	0.00	0.00	0.00	0.00
	(0.00)	(0.00)	(0.00)	(0.00)	(0.00)	(0.00)	(0.00)	(0.00)	(0.00)

(continued next page)

Table F.2 (continued)

Variable	Pooled OLS (1)	FE (2)	DID (3)	DID with regional trends (4)	AB system GMM (5)	AB system GMM with IV (6)	AB system GMM with year effects (7)	AB system GMM with IV and with year effects (8)	AB system GMM with IV and with year effects (9)
Inflation	0.00**	0.00**	0.00**	0.00	0.00	0.00	0.00	0.00	0.01***
	(0.00)	(0.00)	(0.00)	(0.00)	(0.00)	(0.00)	(0.00)	(0.00)	(0.00)
HIPC	-0.13	-0.46	-0.62	-2.03***	0.15	0.08	-0.10	-0.13	-0.05
	(0.77)	(0.76)	(0.80)	(0.72)	(0.76)	(0.75)	(0.78)	(0.77)	(0.80)
Aid	-0.11**	-0.06	-0.05	-0.02	-0.05*	-0.05	-0.06*	-0.05*	-0.04
	(0.05)	(0.05)	(0.04)	(0.04)	(0.03)	(0.03)	(0.03)	(0.03)	(0.04)
Lag fiscal discipline					0.37***	0.37***	0.33***	0.35***	0.31***
					(0.08)	(0.08)	(0.08)	(0.08)	(0.09)
Lag credit market access									0.70
									(0.53)
Fixed effects	N	Y	Y	Y					
Year effects	N	N	Y	N	N	N	Y	Y	Y
Countries	162	162	162	162	162	162	162	162	162
Instruments					27	30	44	47	43
AR(2) test [p-value]					0.171	0.168	0.134	0.126	0.255
Hansen J [p-value]					0.605	0.58	0.468	0.315	0.398
Observations	2,613	2,613	2,613	2,613	2,605	2,605	2,605	2,605	1,914
R-squared	0.16	0.49	0.53	0.55					

Note: AB = Arellano-Bond; DID = difference-in-differences; FE = fixed effects; GDP = gross domestic product; GMM = generalized method of moments; HIPC = Heavily Indebted Poor Country; IMF = International Monetary Fund; IV = Instrumental Variables; MTBF = medium-term budgetary framework; MTEF = medium-term expenditure framework; MTFF = medium-term fiscal framework; MTPF = medium- term performance framework; OECD = Organisation for Economic Co-operation and Development; OLS = ordinary least squares. Robust standard errors are in parentheses, clustered by country. GMM specifications use lags 1–3 of the endogenous variables with collapsed instrument matrix. Three additional instruments based on MTEF diffusion in the neighboring area are used as indicated. The constant term is included in all the regressions. * = significant at 10%; ** = significant at 5%; *** = significant at 1%.

balance. Likewise, the aid variable presents a small, significant, and negative coefficient. In column 9, a control for credit market access is included, but the estimated coefficient on this variable is not significant. Both the magnitude and the statistical significance of the three main coefficients remain robust, despite the large number of missing observations for this variable.

Estimates remain statistically strong and qualitatively similar across all specifications in table F.2. Although estimated coefficients for MTEF dummies are higher in magnitude, they are positive, significant, and almost always scaled from MTFFs to MTPFs. Significance is only lost for MTFFs and MTBFs when the uninstrumented difference-in-differences approach is used.

In table F.3, the conditioning variables that may potentially influence MTEF effectiveness are considered. Column 1 measures how the impact of MTFFs depends on the presence of fiscal rules. The estimates suggest that a fiscal rule does not significantly improve the effect of MTFF. Column 2 suggests that an MTFF's impact does not depend on whether the ruling government has a majority, while column 3 finds no support for the notion that MTEFs have different effects in democracies and autocracies. Column 4 finds no evidence that IMF technical assistance missions influence the effectiveness of an MTFF. Finally, column 5 suggests that MTPFs are significantly more effective in OECD countries.

Tables F.4, F.5, and F.6 show the empirical findings for the MTEF impact on allocative efficiency. Column 8 of table F.4 provides the results for the specification that best handles endogeneity issues. As shown in the results of column 8, the impact of MTEF on the volatility of total expenditures is negative and significant for all the MTEF stages. Moreover, the effects

Table F.3   MTEF Conditional Effects on Fiscal Discipline
dependent variable = fiscal balance = central government balance as % of GDP

Variable	AB system GMM with IV and with year effects (1)	AB system GMM with IV and with year effects (2)	AB system GMM with IV and with year effects (3)	AB system GMM with IV and with year effects (4)	AB system GMM with IV and with year effects (5)
MTFF	0.72	0.80	−0.08	0.88*	0.82*
	(0.55)	(0.75)	(1.12)	(0.46)	(0.43)
MTBF	1.08**	0.84*	2.05	0.91*	0.88*
	(0.51)	(0.50)	(1.36)	(0.53)	(0.52)
MTPF	3.08***	2.69***	0.75	0.59	2.77***
	(0.94)	(0.88)	(1.38)	(0.95)	(0.96)

(continued next page)

Table F.3   *(continued)*

Variable	AB system GMM with IV and with year effects (1)	AB system GMM with IV and with year effects (2)	AB system GMM with IV and with year effects (3)	AB system GMM with IV and with year effects (4)	AB system GMM with IV and with year effects (5)
MTFF x fiscal rule	0.60				
	(0.67)				
Fiscal rule	−0.53				
	(0.53)				
MTFF x political cohesion		0.03			
		(0.70)			
Political cohesion		−0.53			
		(0.43)			
Democracy			−1.27		
			(2.15)		
MTFF x democracy			1.63		
			(2.17)		
MTBF x democracy			−1.69		
			(2.47)		
MTPF x democracy			2.69		
			(2.37)		
MTPF x OECD				2.97**	
				(1.47)	
OECD				−0.39	
				(0.83)	
MTFF x IMF missions					−0.03
					(0.11)
IMF missions					−0.03
					(0.08)
Year effects	Y	Y	Y	Y	Y
Countries	162	148	161	162	162
Instruments	57	53	62	53	52
AR(2) test [*p*-value]	0.128	0.438	0.133	0.134	0.127
Hansen J [*p*-value]	0.251	0.203	0.511	0.362	0.544
Observations	2,605	2,254	2,587	2,605	2,605

Note: AB = Arellano-Bond; GDP = gross domestic product; GMM = generalized method of moments; IMF = International Monetary Fund; IV = Instrumental Variables; MTBF = medium-term budgetary framework; MTEF = medium-term expenditure framework; MTFF = medium-term fiscal framework; MTPF = medium-term performance framework; OECD = Organisation for Economic Co-operation and Development. Robust standard errors are in parentheses, clustered by country. GMM specifications use lags 1–3 of the endogenous variables with collapsed instrument matrix. Three additional instruments based on MTEF diffusion in the neighboring area are used as indicated. The constant term, lag of GDP growth, trade openness, oil exporter, conflict, lag IMF program, population, population squared, inflation, HIPC, aid, lag of fiscal discipline, and the constant term are included in all the regressions. * = significant at 10%; ** = significant at 5%; *** = significant at 1%.

Table F.4 MTEF Effects on Allocative Efficiency

dependent variable = total expenditure volatility = absolute value of the % change in the deviation of the ratio of total central government expenditure to GDP from the trend component, normalized by the trend at time t−1

Variable	Pooled OLS (1)	FE (2)	DID (3)	DID with regional trends (4)	AB system GMM (5)	AB system GMM with IV (6)	AB system GMM with year effects (7)	AB system GMM with IV and with year effects (8)	AB system GMM with IV and with year effects (9)
MTFF	-2.85***	-1.11*	0.36	0.26	-1.43***	-1.76***	-1.29***	-1.74***	-1.04*
	(0.45)	(0.58)	(0.74)	(0.71)	(0.42)	(0.38)	(0.48)	(0.43)	(0.55)
MTBF	-2.80***	-2.81***	-0.86	-0.81	-2.30***	-2.34***	-2.17***	-2.38***	-1.81***
	(0.57)	(1.01)	(1.21)	(1.11)	(0.47)	(0.43)	(0.56)	(0.51)	(0.59)
MTPF	-4.20***	-1.54**	1.71	-0.36	-2.50***	-3.40***	-2.44***	-3.42***	-1.76**
	(0.72)	(0.75)	(1.22)	(1.08)	(0.65)	(0.65)	(0.72)	(0.70)	(0.86)
Lag GDP growth	-0.17**	-0.22***	-0.20***	-0.19***	-0.05	-0.05	-0.05	-0.04	-0.04
	(0.06)	(0.08)	(0.07)	(0.06)	(0.06)	(0.06)	(0.06)	(0.06)	(0.07)
Trade openness	0.00	0.01	0.03	0.03	0.00	0.00	0.00	0.00	0.00
	(0.01)	(0.02)	(0.02)	(0.02)	(0.00)	(0.01)	(0.01)	(0.01)	(0.01)
Oil exporter	3.44***	2.42	3.24	3.39	1.77**	1.70**	2.04**	1.95**	2.52***
	(1.30)	(2.04)	(2.03)	(2.32)	(0.83)	(0.83)	(0.81)	(0.81)	(0.89)
Conflict	1.54	0.34	-0.11	-0.32	-0.66	-0.69	-0.82	-0.84	-1.11
	(1.16)	(1.06)	(1.01)	(1.06)	(0.73)	(0.73)	(0.74)	(0.74)	(0.95)
Lag IMF program	0.32	0.16	0.02	-0.34	-0.45	-0.49	-0.43	-0.47	-0.62
	(0.51)	(0.76)	(0.76)	(0.72)	(0.64)	(0.64)	(0.63)	(0.64)	(0.57)
Population	-0.01	-0.10	0.01	-0.03	0.00	0.00	0.00	0.00	0.00
	(0.01)	(0.06)	(0.06)	(0.06)	(0.01)	(0.01)	(0.01)	(0.01)	(0.00)
Population squared	0.00	0.00*	0.00	0.00	0.00	0.00	0.00	0.00	0.00
	(0.00)	(0.00)	(0.00)	(0.00)	(0.00)	(0.00)	(0.00)	(0.00)	(0.00)

(continued next page)

Table F.4 *(continued)*

Variable	Pooled OLS (1)	FE (2)	DID (3)	DID with regional trends (4)	AB system GMM (5)	AB system GMM with IV (6)	AB system GMM with year effects (7)	AB system GMM with IV and with year effects (8)	AB system GMM with IV and with year effects (9)
Inflation	0.01***	0.01**	0.01*	0.00	0.00**	0.00**	0.00**	0.00**	0.01***
	(0.00)	(0.00)	(0.00)	(0.00)	(0.00)	(0.00)	(0.00)	(0.00)	(0.00)
HIPC	0.15	−0.88	−0.38	−0.32	0.62	0.71	0.56	0.64	0.87
	(1.15)	(1.39)	(1.44)	(1.39)	(1.07)	(1.06)	(1.07)	(1.06)	(1.03)
Aid	0.31***	0.16	0.12	0.11	0.20***	0.20***	0.21***	0.20***	0.09**
	(0.07)	(0.11)	(0.10)	(0.11)	(0.06)	(0.06)	(0.06)	(0.06)	(0.04)
Lag volatility					0.35***	0.35***	0.36***	0.36***	0.29***
					(0.06)	(0.06)	(0.06)	(0.06)	(0.06)
Lag credit market access									−2.11***
									(0.55)
Fixed effects	N	Y	Y	Y					
Year effects	N	N	Y	N	N	N	Y	Y	Y
Countries	162	162	162	162	162	162	162	162	162
Instruments					55	58	71	74	71
AR(2) test [p-value]					0.421	0.422	0.436	0.439	0.861
Hansen J [p-value]					0.307	0.139	0.195	0.145	0.225
Observations	2,605	2,605	2,605	2,605	2,456	2,456	2,456	2,456	1,909
R-square	0.13	0.30	0.31	0.32					

Note: AB = Arellano-Bond; DID = difference-in-differences; FE = fixed effects; GMM = generalized method of moments; HIPC = Heavily Indebted Poor Country; IMF = International Monetary Fund; IV = Instrumental Variables; MTBF = medium-term budgetary framework; MTEF = medium-term expenditure framework; MTFF = medium-term fiscal framework; MTPF = medium-term performance framework; OECD = Organisation for Economic Co-operation and Development; OLS = ordinary least squares. Robust standard errors are in parentheses, clustered by country. GMM specifications use lags 1–3 of the endogenous variables with collapsed instrument matrix. Three additional instruments based on MTEF diffusion in the neighboring area are used as indicated. The constant term is included in all the regressions. * = significant at 10%; ** = significant at 5%; *** = significant at 1%.

Table F.5 MTEF Effects on Allocative Efficiency

dependent variable = health expenditure volatility + the absolute value of the % change in the deviation of the ratio of health expenditure to total expenditure from the trend component, normalized by the trend at time t−1

Variable	Pooled OLS (1)	FE (2)	DID (3)	DID with regional trends (4)	AB system GMM (5)	AB system GMM with IV (6)	AB system GMM with year effects (7)	AB system GMM with IV and with year effects (8)	AB system GMM with IV and with year effects (9)
MTFF	-2.88***	-1.56*	-0.60	-0.87	-1.90**	-3.06***	-1.62	-2.66***	-2.01*
	(0.59)	(0.90)	(0.99)	(0.90)	(0.96)	(0.87)	(1.04)	(0.91)	(1.06)
MTBF	-2.27*	-2.21*	-0.50	-0.75	-2.82***	-3.58***	-2.24**	-2.95***	-2.51**
	(1.08)	(1.19)	(1.19)	(1.17)	(0.88)	(0.92)	(0.96)	(0.97)	(1.03)
MTPF	-4.16***	-2.20	0.65	-1.58	-0.09	-2.84*	0.48	-2.19	-0.38
	(0.77)	(1.53)	(1.86)	(1.73)	(2.25)	(1.48)	(2.33)	(1.55)	(1.73)
Lag GDP growth	0.09	-0.02	0.02	-0.01	0.14	0.15	0.16	0.16	0.15
	(0.13)	(0.12)	(0.11)	(0.11)	(0.13)	(0.13)	(0.13)	(0.13)	(0.13)
Trade openness	0.00	-0.04*	-0.03	-0.05	0.00	0.00	0.00	0.00	0.00
	(0.01)	(0.02)	(0.02)	(0.03)	(0.01)	(0.01)	(0.01)	(0.01)	(0.01)
Oil exporter	2.43*	0.73	1.45	1.68	1.56	1.28	1.91*	1.61	1.80*
	(1.25)	(2.24)	(2.16)	(2.29)	(1.01)	(1.01)	(1.05)	(1.05)	(1.01)
Conflict	1.28	2.47	1.76	1.62	1.71	1.65	1.47	1.43	1.17
	(2.40)	(2.56)	(2.59)	(2.24)	(1.74)	(1.76)	(1.71)	(1.72)	(1.79)
Lag IMF program	1.55	0.76	0.32	0.53	1.00	0.92	1.01	0.93	0.55
	(1.04)	(1.04)	(0.99)	(1.11)	(0.91)	(0.89)	(0.90)	(0.88)	(0.79)

(continued next page)

167

Table F.5 *(continued)*

Variable	Pooled OLS (1)	FE (2)	DiD (3)	DiD with regional trends (4)	AB system GMM (5)	AB system GMM with IV (6)	AB system GMM with year effects (7)	AB system GMM with IV and with year effects (8)	AB system GMM with IV and with year effects (9)
Population	−0.01	−0.04	0.07	0.04	0.00	0.00	0.00	0.00	0.00
	(0.01)	(0.13)	(0.14)	(0.18)	(0.01)	(0.01)	(0.01)	(0.01)	(0.01)
Population squared	0.00	0.00	0.00	0.00	0.00	0.00	0.00	0.00	0.00
	(0.00)	(0.00)	(0.00)	(0.00)	(0.00)	(0.00)	(0.00)	(0.00)	(0.00)
Inflation	0.01***	0.01***	0.01***	0.01*	0.01	0.00	0.01	0.01	0.01
	(0.00)	(0.00)	(0.00)	(0.00)	(0.01)	(0.01)	(0.01)	(0.01)	(0.01)
HIPC	−0.63	−0.55	−1.34	0.89	−0.51	−0.35	−0.93	−0.79	−0.88
	(1.58)	(1.87)	(1.92)	(1.71)	(1.45)	(1.45)	(1.43)	(1.45)	(1.42)
Aid	0.58***	0.49	0.47	0.49	0.50*	0.49*	0.52*	0.51*	0.48*
	(0.22)	(0.41)	(0.41)	(0.43)	(0.28)	(0.28)	(0.28)	(0.28)	(0.29)
Lag volatility					0.28***	0.28***	0.26***	0.27***	0.26***
					(0.07)	(0.06)	(0.06)	(0.06)	(0.06)

	(1)	(2)	(3)	(4)	(5)	(6)	(7)	(8)	(9)
Lag credit market access									−1.64 (1.11)
Fixed effects	N	Y	Y	Y	N	N	Y	Y	Y
Year effects	N	N	Y	Y	N	N	Y	Y	Y
Countries	172	172	172	172	172	172	172	172	172
Instruments					27	30	38	41	42
AR(2) test [p-value]					0.723	0.734	0.786	0.761	0.777
Hansen J [p-value]					0.646	0.301	0.455	0.214	0.271
Observations	2,047	2,047	2,047	2,047	1,882	1,882	1,882	1,882	1,882
R-squared	0.13	0.33	0.34	0.35					

Note: AB = Arellano-Bond; DID = difference-in-differences; FE = fixed effects; GDP = gross domestic product; GMM = generalized method of moments; HIPC = Heavily Indebted Poor Country; IMF = International Monetary Fund; IV = Instrumental Variables; MTBF = medium-term budgetary framework; MTEF = medium-term expenditure framework; MTFF = medium-term fiscal framework; MTPF = medium-term performance framework; N = no; OECD = Organisation for Economic Co-operation and Development; OLS = ordinary least squares; Y = yes. Robust standard errors are in parentheses, clustered by country. GMM specifications use lags 1–3 of the endogenous variables with collapsed instrument matrix. Three additional instruments based on MTEF diffusion in the neighboring area are used as indicated. The constant term is included in all the regressions. * = significant at 10%; ** = significant at 5%; *** = significant at 1%.

Table F.6 MTEF Effects on Allocative Efficiency

dependent variable = health expenditure share = general government expenditure on health as a % of total government expenditure

Variable	Pooled OLS (1)	FE (2)	DID (3)	DID with regional trends (4)	AB system GMM (5)	AB system GMM with IV (6)	AB system GMM with year effects (7)	AB system GMM with IV and with year effects (8)	AB system GMM with IV and with year effects (9)
MTFF	1.81***	0.39*	0.06	−0.04	0.17	0.26**	0.14	0.40***	0.20
	(0.40)	(0.24)	(0.28)	(0.24)	(0.15)	(0.12)	(0.17)	(0.13)	(0.14)
MTBF	2.20***	1.02***	0.58	0.30	0.38*	0.33**	0.36	0.48***	0.39**
	(0.75)	(0.32)	(0.36)	(0.32)	(0.21)	(0.14)	(0.24)	(0.16)	(0.19)
MTPF	2.82***	1.56***	0.84	0.10	0.28	0.85**	0.25	1.04***	0.51
	(0.68)	(0.48)	(0.56)	(0.64)	(0.43)	(0.37)	(0.42)	(0.37)	(0.38)
Lag GDP growth	−0.05	−0.01	−0.02	0.00	0.02	0.03**	0.02	0.03**	0.03*
	(0.03)	(0.02)	(0.02)	(0.02)	(0.01)	(0.01)	(0.01)	(0.01)	(0.01)
Trade openness	−0.01	0.00	0.00	0.00	0.00	0.00	0.00	0.00	0.00
	(0.01)	(0.01)	(0.01)	(0.01)	(0.00)	(0.00)	(0.00)	(0.00)	(0.00)
Oil exporter	−2.59***	−0.17	−0.29	0.02	−0.89***	−0.53***	−0.87***	−0.52**	−0.70***
	(0.68)	(0.30)	(0.33)	(0.41)	(0.26)	(0.20)	(0.26)	(0.21)	(0.25)
Conflict	−1.42*	−0.20	−0.09	−0.03	−0.28	−0.12	−0.27	−0.14	−0.07
	(0.74)	(0.32)	(0.33)	(0.29)	(0.22)	(0.20)	(0.22)	(0.20)	(0.20)
Lag IMF program	−0.59	−0.18	−0.14	−0.12	−0.24*	−0.14	−0.23*	−0.15	0.00
	(0.46)	(0.25)	(0.26)	(0.24)	(0.14)	(0.11)	(0.14)	(0.11)	(0.12)
Population	−0.02*	0.03	0.00	−0.03	0.00	0.00	0.00	0.00	0.00
	(0.01)	(0.03)	(0.03)	(0.03)	(0.00)	(0.00)	(0.00)	(0.00)	(0.00)

	(1)	(2)	(3)	(4)	(5)	(6)	(7)	(8)	(9)
Population squared	0.00*	0.00*	0.00	0.00	0.00	0.00	0.00	0.00	0.00
	(0.00)	(0.00)	(0.00)	(0.00)	(0.00)	(0.00)	(0.00)	(0.00)	(0.00)
Inflation	0.00**	0.00**	0.00	0.00	0.00	0.00	0.00	0.00	0.00
	(0.00)	(0.00)	(0.00)	(0.00)	(0.00)	(0.00)	(0.00)	(0.00)	(0.00)
HIPC	1.06	0.64	0.56	0.35	0.29	0.16	0.24	0.12	0.19
	(0.78)	(0.63)	(0.62)	(0.62)	(0.29)	(0.26)	(0.28)	(0.26)	(0.27)
Aid	-0.10*	0.01	0.02	0.02	-0.01	0.01	-0.01	0.01	0.01
	(0.05)	(0.02)	(0.02)	(0.02)	(0.02)	(0.02)	(0.02)	(0.02)	(0.01)
Lag productive spending					0.72***	0.85***	0.73***	0.84***	0.79***
					(0.04)	(0.03)	(0.04)	(0.04)	(0.04)
Lag credit market access									0.74***
									(0.19)
Fixed effects	N	Y	Y	Y	N	N	Y	Y	Y
Year effects	N	N	Y	Y	N	N	Y	Y	Y
Countries	172	172	172	172	172	172	172	172	172
Instruments					55	58	67	70	71
AR(2) test [p-value]					0.635	0.600	0.702	0.680	0.691
Hansen J [p-value]					0.384	0.173	0.667	0.204	0.253
Observations	2,209	2,209	2,209	2,209	2,047	2,047	2,047	2,047	2,047
R-squared	0.14	0.84	0.85	0.86					

Note: AB = Arellano-Bond; DID = difference-in-differences; FE = fixed effects; GDP = gross domestic product; GMM = generalized method of moments; HIPC = Heavily Indebted Poor Country; IMF = International Monetary Fund; IV = Instrumental Variables; MTBF = medium-term budgetary framework; MTEF = medium-term expenditure framework; MTFF = medium-term fiscal framework; MTPF = medium-term performance framework; N = no; OECD = Organisation for Economic Co-operation and Development; OLS = ordinary least squares; Y = yes. Robust standard errors are in parentheses, clustered by country. GMM specifications use lags 1–10 of the endogenous variables with collapsed instrument matrix. Three additional instruments based on MTEF diffusion in the neighboring area are used as indicated. The constant term is included in all the regressions. * = significant at 10%; ** = significant at 5%; *** = significant at 1%.

become bigger moving from an MTFF to an MTPF. A country adopting an MTFF experiences a reduction in total expenditure volatility of 1.74 percentage points, compared to a country adopting an MTBF, which experiences a reduction of 2.38 percentage points. The MTPF implementation shows the stronger effect, with a reduction of 3.42 percentage points.

Being an oil exporter significantly increases the volatility of total expenditure. Likewise, inflation has a positive, albeit small, effect. Finally, aid flows exert a positive and significant effect on the variation of total expenditures. The magnitude of the coefficients is reduced for the specification in column 9, which includes credit market access, but this implies the loss of more than 20 percent of the observations.

Table F.5 presents the results for the health expenditure share. Column 8 shows a positive and significant effect for all the MTEF phases, with the magnitude scaled from MTFF to MTPF. More specifically, MTFF adoption increases expenditure on health as a percentage of total expenditure by 0.40 percentage points, MTBFs by 0.48 percentage points, and MTPFs by 1.04 percentage points. Only MTBFs are significant once the credit market access variable is introduced, which also has a positive and strongly significant effect.

GDP growth increases the health expenditure share. At the same time, being an oil exporter negatively affects it. The use of other techniques generates positive signs on the MTEF dummies, but the results are not always significant.

The dependent variable in table F.6 is health expenditure volatility. Column 8 shows that MTBFs reduce health expenditure volatility by 2.95 percentage points and a non-negligible negative and that a significant effect comes from implementation of the MTFF, which reduces health expenditure volatility by 2.66 percentage points. Finally, countries that have an MTPF do not experience a significant reduction in health expenditure volatility.

The only covariate that presents a significant coefficient is the aid variable. In column 9, the credit market access variable is once again added to the specification, and, although the coefficient has the expected negative sign, it is not significant. In the same specification, being an oil exporter significantly increases health expenditure volatility.

Overall, tables F.4–F.6 provide evidence that MTEF adoption exerts a positive effect on allocative efficiency. The results are quite robust to the employment of other techniques, although significance is lost when the difference-in-differences approach is used.

Finally, table F.7 presents estimates of the MTEF's impact on the cost-effectiveness of health expenditure. Column 8 shows a positive and

Table F.7 MTEF Effects on Technical Efficiency

dependent variable = cost-effectiveness of health expenditure = efficiency scores estimated from a stochastic frontier model showing life expectancy as output

Variable	Pooled OLS (1)	FE (2)	DID (3)	DID with regional trends (4)	AB system GMM (5)	AB system GMM with IV (6)	AB system GMM with year effects (7)	AB system GMM with IV and with year effects (8)	AB system GMM with IV and with year effects (9)
MTFF	-0.13	-0.37	-0.54**	-0.25	-0.12	-0.02	0.10	0.11	0.03
	(0.96)	(0.25)	(0.26)	(0.21)	(0.13)	(0.11)	(0.16)	(0.13)	(0.14)
MTBF	-5.29***	-0.54	-0.77*	-0.56	-0.19	-0.10	0.07	0.07	0.01
	(1.50)	(0.42)	(0.45)	(0.36)	(0.18)	(0.15)	(0.21)	(0.17)	(0.18)
MTPF	-1.28	-0.10	-0.45	0.41	0.28	0.42**	0.61**	0.51***	0.38*
	(1.93)	(0.83)	(0.86)	(0.85)	(0.27)	(0.20)	(0.25)	(0.19)	(0.23)
Lag GDP growth	-0.11	-0.05***	-0.06***	-0.06***	0.00	-0.01	0.00	0.00	0.00
	(0.08)	(0.01)	(0.01)	(0.01)	(0.01)	(0.01)	(0.01)	(0.01)	(0.01)
Trade openness	-0.02	0.00	0.00	-0.01	0.00	0.00	0.00	0.00	0.00
	(0.01)	(0.01)	(0.01)	(0.01)	(0.00)	(0.00)	(0.00)	(0.00)	(0.00)
Oil exporter	-6.95***	-1.50***	-1.61***	-0.96***	0.11	0.04	0.17	0.06	0.02
	(2.15)	(0.58)	(0.56)	(0.22)	(0.17)	(0.15)	(0.17)	(0.15)	(0.15)
Conflict	-0.00	0.37	0.40	0.30	0.11	0.13	0.03	0.04	0.06
	(1.34)	(0.30)	(0.29)	(0.27)	(0.33)	(0.31)	(0.31)	(0.30)	(0.30)
Lag IMF program	-0.21	0.13	0.09	0.15	-0.01	-0.03	-0.04	-0.07	-0.04
	(0.89)	(0.24)	(0.25)	(0.21)	(0.08)	(0.07)	(0.08)	(0.07)	(0.07)
Population	-0.01	0.03	0.00	-0.01	0.00	0.00	0.00	0.00	0.00
	(0.01)	(0.07)	(0.07)	(0.07)	(0.00)	(0.00)	(0.00)	(0.00)	(0.00)
Population squared	0.00	0.00	0.00	0.00	0.00	0.00	0.00	0.00	0.00
	(0.00)	(0.00)	(0.00)	(0.00)	(0.00)	(0.00)	(0.00)	(0.00)	(0.00)
Inflation	-0.01***	0.00	0.00**	0.00	0.00	0.00	0.00**	0.00*	0.00*
	(0.01)	(0.00)	(0.00)	(0.00)	(0.00)	(0.00)	(0.00)	(0.00)	(0.00)

(continued next page)

Table F.7 *(continued)*

Variable	Pooled OLS (1)	FE (2)	DID (3)	DID with regional trends (4)	AB system GMM (5)	AB system GMM with IV (6)	AB system GMM with year effects (7)	AB system GMM with IV and with year effects (8)	AB system GMM with IV and with year effects (9)
HIPC	-6.80***	-0.12	-0.07	0.09	0.28*	0.16	0.20	0.09	0.08
	(1.57)	(0.34)	(0.34)	(0.25)	(0.15)	(0.15)	(0.14)	(0.15)	(0.15)
Aid	-0.14	0.05*	0.05*	0.05	0.01	0.01	0.02	0.02	0.02
	(0.09)	(0.03)	(0.03)	(0.03)	(0.01)	(0.01)	(0.01)	(0.01)	(0.01)
Lag technical efficiency					1.06***	1.04***	1.06***	1.04***	1.04***
					(0.01)	(0.01)	(0.01)	(0.01)	(0.01)
Lag credit market access									0.10
									(0.10)
Fixed effects	N	Y	Y	Y	N	N	Y	Y	Y
Year effects	N	N	Y	N	N	N	Y	Y	Y
Countries	164	164	164	164	161	161	161	161	161
Instruments					103	106	111	114	115
AR(2) test [p-value]					0.522	0.459	0.628	0.592	0.644
Hansen J [p-value]					0.057	0.051	0.176	0.164	0.155
Observations	1,317	1,317	1,317	1,317	1,157	1,157	1,157	1,157	1,157
R-squared	0.21	0.98	0.98	0.98					

Note: AB = Arellano-Bond; DID = difference-in-differences; FE = fixed effects; GDP = gross domestic product; GMM = generalized method of moments; HIPC = Heavily Indebted Poor Country; IMF = International Monetary Fund; IV = Instrumental Variables; MTBF = medium-term budgetary framework; MTEF = medium-term expenditure framework; MTFF = medium-term fiscal framework; MTPF = medium-term performance framework; N = no; OECD = Organisation for Economic Co-operation and Development; OLS = ordinary least squares; Y = yes. The technical efficiency scores are based on estimating the production function $(LifeExpectancy)\_it = \alpha + \beta(HealthSpending\_pc\_PPP)\_it + \gamma(Covariates)\_it + \tau_t + v\_it - u\_it$, where the group of covariates includes population density, years of schooling, a government indicator for voice and accountability, and one for government effectiveness; a dummy variable for OECD countries, and year effects. Robust standard errors are in parentheses, clustered by country. GMM specifications use lags 1–2 of the endogenous variables with collapsed instrument matrix. Three additional instruments based on MTEF diffusion in the neighboring area are used as indicated. The constant term is included in all the regressions. * = significant at 10%; ** =significant at 5%; *** = significant at 1%.

significant effect from MTPF adoption. This is the only stage of MTEF that has a significant effect for technical efficiency. The results are quite robust for all the specifications employing the GMM estimator. The findings from the application of other estimation techniques show mixed results.

Overall these results provide strong evidence that MTEF adoption improves fiscal discipline and that more advanced stages yield a greater impact. At the same time, allocative efficiency is improved, and, again, the effect is larger moving from an MTFF, to an MTBF, and finally to an MTPF; productive spending is enhanced in MTEF countries, and MTBF (and MTFF to a lesser extent) adoption decreases the volatility of health spending as a ratio of total spending, thus improving allocative efficiency. Finally, the MTPF is the only MTEF phase that exerts a significant effect on technical efficiency in the health sector, although results are not always robust.

Furthermore, Grigoli et al. (2012) take another approach but arrive at very similar findings for the impact of MTEFs on fiscal performance. To address possible endogeneity bias resulting from adding covariates that may depend on the measures of fiscal performance, their paper uses Difference (or D-) GMM rather than System GMM and limits covariates (to only external openness and conflict). As shown in table F.8, the results for the MTEF impact on fiscal performance are similar in significance and magnitude to the preferred specification in this study, which has a wider set of covariates to reduce bias from omitted variables. The congruence of the two studies provides further evidence for the robustness of this study's results.

Table F.8   MTEF Effects on Fiscal Discipline, Allocative Efficiency, and Technical Efficiency

dependent variable = fiscal balance = central government balance as % of GDP
dependent variable = total expenditure volatility = absolute value of the % change in the deviation of the ratio of total central government expenditure to GDP from the trend component, normalized by the trend at time t−1
dependent variable = cost-effectiveness of health expenditure = efficiency scores estimated from a stochastic frontier model showing life expectancy as output

Indicator	D-GMM-IV (1)	D-GMM-IV (2)	D-GMM-IV (3)
Fiscal balance i,t−1	0.423*** (0.040)		
Fiscal balance i,t−2	0.101*** (0.038)		

(continued next page)

Table F.8   *(continued)*

Indicator	D-GMM-IV (1)	D-GMM-IV (2)	D-GMM-IV (3)
Total expenditure volatility $i,t-1$		0.105	
		(0.065)	
Technical efficiency $i,t-1$			0.934***
			-0.047
MTFFi,t	1.305**	-0.092	0.009
	(0.605)	(1.889)	-0.119
MTBFi,t	2.427**	-5.823**	0.427
	(1.147)	(2.415)	-0.281
MTPFi,t	3.375**	-10.530	1.015*
	(1.359)	(6.699)	-0.588
Openness i,t	0.009	0.005	-0.001
	(0.008)	(0.013)	-0.001
Conflict i,t	-1.055	-0.918	0.000
	(0.670)	(1.492)	-0.048
Year effects	Y	Y	Y
Internal instruments	Y	Y	Y
External instruments	Y	Y	Y
AR(1) test [p-value]	0.000	0.000	0.039
AR(2) test [p-value]	0.911	0.769	0.384
Hansen J [p-value]	0.792	0.582	0.647
Sample period	1990–2008	1996–2008	1995–2008
Countries	161	170	169
Observations	2,316	1,698	1,801

Source: Grigoli et al. 2012.
Note: D = Difference; GDP = gross domestic product; GMM = generalized method of moments; IV = Instrumental Variables; MTBF = medium-term budgetary framework; MTEF = medium-term expenditure framework; MTFF = medium-term fiscal framework; MTPF = medium-term performance framework; N = no; Y = yes. Columns 1, 2, and 3 report two-step estimates and standard errors with the Windmeijer correction. GMM models use the orthogonal deviations transform. The internal instruments are the second and third lags of fiscal balance i,t, and of MTFF i,t, MTBF i,t, MTPF i,t. The external instruments are based on MTEF diffusion in the neighboring area. * significant at 10%; ** significant at 5%; *** significant at 1%.

Notes

1. For the HP filter, the smoothing parameter, λ, is set to 6.25.
2. In this manner, external events that affect the production function are normally distributed; however, for v_{it}, the inefficiency term, various distributions have been proposed: normal mean distribution, exponential distribution, normal truncated distribution, and Gamma distribution. There is no a priori reason to prefer any specific type of distribution on the errors.

3. As a backup strategy, the same production function is also estimated with immunizations (measles) as the output of the health sector. Child mortality also is used as an alternative, but this indicator is a "reverse" output in which a lower value is better, requiring a slight modification to the model. Thus, it is adjusted by using the reciprocal of child mortality, but this modification is a nonlinear transformation and causes the results to be non-equivalent (in general, any nonlinear transformation of input or output data leads to differences in inefficiency estimation results, including the ordering of production units, or countries in this case).

4. As in Greene (2005), some of the data series are incomplete and have to be linearly interpolated.

5. The value 1 is given in the years in which the country adopted its highest MTEF phase, the value 0 otherwise. Thus if a country has an MTPF, the other dummies are coded as 0 to isolate the impact on the dependent variables and to compare the coefficients for the different MTEF phases in the same regression.

6. The United Nations classification of subregions has been adopted to calculate the diffusion instrument.

7. The Arellano and Bond (1991) and Arellano and Bover (1995) or Blundell and Bond (1998) dynamic panel estimators have become increasingly popular. As Roodman (2006) notes, both are general estimators designed for situations with "small T, large N" panels, a linear functional relationship, a single left-hand-side variable that is dynamic, independent variables that are not strictly exogenous (correlated with past and possibly current realizations of the error), fixed individual effects, and heteroskedasticity and autocorrelation within individuals but not across them.

8. Lagging the dependent variable might alleviate the reverse causality problem as well, if fiscal reforms respond to fiscal crises with a lag.

9. Sometimes, the forward orthogonal deviations transform, proposed by Arellano and Bover (1995), is performed instead of differencing.

References

Alesina, A., and R. Perotti. 1999. "Budget Deficits and Budget Institutions." In *Fiscal Institutions and Fiscal Performance,* ed. J. Poterba and J. von Hagen, 13–36. Chicago, IL: University of Chicago Press.

Alvarez, M., J. A. Cheibub, F. Limongi, and A. Przeworski. 1996. "Classifying Political Regimes." *Studies in Comparative International Development* 31 (2): 1–37.

Arellano, M., and S. Bond. 1991. "Some Tests of Specification for Panel Data: Monte Carlo Evidence and an Application to Employment Equations." *Review of Economic Studies* 58 (2): 277–97.

Arellano, M., and O. Bover. 1995. "Another Look at the Instrumental Variables Estimation of Error Components Models." *Journal of Econometrics* 68 (1): 29–51.

Bertrand, M., E. Duflo, and S. Mullainathan. 2004. "How Much Should We Trust Difference-in-Differences Estimates." *Quarterly Journal of Economics* 119 (1): 249–75.

Blundell, R., and S. Bond. 1998. "Initial Conditions and Moment Restrictions in Dynamic Panel Data Models." *Journal of Econometrics* 87 (1): 11–43.

Cheibub, J., J. Gandhi, and J. Vreeland. 2010. "Democracy and Dictatorship Revisited." *Public Choice* 143 (1–2): 67–101.

Fabrizio, S., and A. Mody. 2006. "Can Budget Institutions Counteract Political Indiscipline?" *Economic Policy* 21 (48): 689–739.

Farrell, M. J. 1957. "The Measurement of Productive Efficiency." *Journal of the Royal Statistical Society*, Series A. General, 120 (3): 253–82.

Greene, W. H. 2005. "Reconsidering Heterogeneity in Panel Data Estimators of the Stochastic Frontier Model." *Journal of Econometrics* 126 (2): 269–303.

Grigoli, F., Z. Mills, M. Verhoeven, and R. Vlaicu. 2012. "MTEFs and Fiscal Performance: Panel Data Evidence." Policy Research Working Paper. World Bank, Washington, DC.

Hansen, L. 1982. "Large Sample Properties of Generalized Method of Moments Estimators." *Econometrica* 50 (3): 1029–54.

Jondrow, J., C. A. K. Lovell, I. Materov, and P. Schmidt. 1982. "On the Estimation of Technical Inefficiency in the Stochastic Frontier Production Function Model." *Journal of Econometrics* 19 (2/3): 233–38.

Knight, B., and A. Levinson. 2000. "Fiscal Institutions in US States." In *Institutions, Politics, and Fiscal Policy*, ed. R. Strauch and J. von Hagen. Boston: Kluwer Academic.

Milesi-Ferretti, G. M., R. Perotti, and M. Rostagno. 2002. "Electoral Systems and Public Spending." *Quarterly Journal of Economics* 117 (2): 609–57.

Perotti, R., and Y. Kontopoulos. 2002. "Fragmented Fiscal Policy." *Journal of Public Economics* 86 (2): 191–222.

Roodman, D. 2006. "How to Do xtabond2: An Introduction to 'Difference' and 'System' GMM in Stata." CGD Working Paper 103, Center for Global Development, Washington, DC.

Stein, E., E. Talvi, and A. Grisanti. 1999. "Institutional Arrangements and Fiscal Performance: The Latin American Experience." In *Fiscal Institutions and Fiscal Performance*, ed. J. Poterba and J. von Hagen. Chicago, IL: University of Chicago Press.

APPENDIX G

MTEF Case Studies

This appendix presents country case studies pertaining to the implementation of different stages of a medium-term expenditure framework (MTEF)—medium-term fiscal, budgetary, or performance framework (MTFF, MTBF, or MTPF). It revisits the case studies of four countries investigated by Holmes and Evans (2003)—Albania, Ghana, South Africa, and Uganda—and adds six more that were selected based on their potential interest and the aim of achieving broader regional coverage. The additional countries are Armenia, Brazil, Jordan, the Republic of Korea, Nicaragua, and the Russian Federation. The case studies are based on existing ones, including those written as background for the Holmes and Evans study, public expenditure and financial accountability (PEFA) reports, International Monetary Fund (IMF) Reports on the Observance of Standards and Codes (ROSCs), and, in each case, input from country experts, with information organized in the form of responses to the questionnaire in box G.1. In some cases, the information available from existing sources and responses to the questionnaire were incomplete. However, for one country, Russia, the case study goes well beyond what was requested.

Box G.1

Case Study Questionnaire

Origins

- When was the MTEF introduced? Was it piloted in selected spending agencies? If so, how was it phased in?
- What stage MTEF is now in place? When did the transition(s) between stages occur?
- What motivated the MTEF? Who were its advocates? Did it have opponents?

Design

- How many years are covered by the MTEF? Is it a fixed or rolling framework? What is the status of out-year ceilings?
- Which spending agencies are covered? Are categories of spending excluded? What proportion of central or general government spending is covered?
- How disaggregated is the MTEF by agency and program?
- Does the MTEF coexist with other medium-term planning instruments, such as a development or public investment plan?

Implementation

- Who takes the lead in MTEF preparation? How are bottom-up budget requests reconciled with top-down resource constraints?
- How are MTEF and budget decisions sequenced and coordinated? Are MTEF ceilings published? Are ceilings approved by parliament?
- For MTFFs, who is responsible for revenue forecasting, and how accurate are forecasts? Who prepares the macro-fiscal framework? Are there fiscal rules? Does the government publish medium-term macro-fiscal targets?
- For MTBFs, do spending agencies prepare strategic plans? If so, how are these used to inform spending priorities? Are programs systematically costed? If there is a public investment plan, how is this integrated with the MTEF? Are stakeholders involved in setting priorities?
- For MTPFs, is agency or program performance assessed using relevant indicators? Who specifies the indicators? Is funding linked to results? If so, in what way?
- If there are subnational MTEFs, how are these coordinated with the central MTEF?

(continued next page)

Box G.1 *(continued)*

Impact

- Is there a perception that the government has become more fiscally responsible, the quality of budgeting has improved, or spending is better prioritized as a result of the MTEF?
- Are budgets more realistic, in the sense that they are being executed as planned and expenditure ceilings effectively restrain spending? Are spending agencies able to plan better?

Influences

- What are the key factors that have determined the success or failure of the MTEF? (Only comment on the most relevant): the economic situation, especially the soundness of public finances; political support for fiscal reform in general and the MTEF in particular; the quality of public financial management, especially the budget process and procedures; past experience with medium-term planning; civil service and broader government capacity; external influence and support; regional and international trends and experience; and appropriateness of MTEF design and implementation given country characteristics.

Note: MTBF = medium-term budgetary framework; MTEF = medium-term expenditure framework; MTFF = medium-term fiscal framework; MTPF = medium-term performance framework.

Albania

Table G.1 summarizes the case study for Albania, which reflects the information on MTEF implementation up to 2011.

Origins

Albania's first MTEF—a piloted MTBF, also known as the medium-term budget plan—covered the 2001–03 period. Revisions were initially made in parallel with preparing and updating the Government Poverty Reduction Strategy (GPRS) and later in line with National Strategies for Development and Integration (NSDI). Due to capacity constraints, the MTEF initially covered five pilot sectors—education, health, infrastructure, labor and social affairs, and transport; it was extended to all sectors in 2006. The 2008 Organic Budget Law gives legal backing to the central role of the MTEF.

The MTEF was introduced to provide a mechanism for translating policy priorities of the GPRS and NSDI into budgetary policy and actions, to provide a realistic macro-fiscal framework for developing

Table G.1   Summary of Case Study of Albania

Issue	Details
Implementation	An MTBF was implemented on a pilot basis in 2001 and was fully implemented in 2006. The U.K. Department for International Development and the World Bank provided support.
Basic features	The three-year rolling framework has fixed expenditure ceilings. All spending agencies and categories of spending are covered, including externally financed public investment. Program allocations can be changed by up to 10 percent within a given year.
Macro-fiscal framework	The resource envelope is routinely overestimated due to optimistic revenue forecasts. This results in large within-year cuts in expenditure ceilings. Revenue shortfalls due to the global financial crisis were not properly acknowledged.
Strategic objectives	Budget allocations are intended to support national development and poverty reduction objectives. Spending agencies prepare sector strategies and expenditure plans. The MTEF is formally coordinated with the Public Investment Program, but the latter is not resource constrained. In general, budgets, policies, and objectives are not yet well aligned.
Link to budget	MTEF preparation is the first stage in the annual budget cycle.
Participants and support	The Ministry of Finance is in the lead, guided by an MTEF steering committee and in consultation with interministerial and sector working groups. Parliament does not approve the MTEF. A lack of sustained political support has impaired effectiveness.
Institutional capacity	The Ministry of Finance exercises strong leadership and has developed the necessary capacity over time, but spending agencies do not possess the required skills.
Performance focus	There is limited use of performance indicators, and performance has little influence on budget allocations.
Quality of budgeting	Budgets are more strategic, budget preparation is cooperative, and fiscal discipline and spending composition have improved. Overly optimistic revenue forecasts remain a problem. Public expenditure and financial accountability scores suggest that budget credibility remains an issue.
Other issues	More attention needs to be paid to complementary budgetary and public financial management reforms, especially cash management, procurement, audit, and parliamentary oversight.

Note: MTBF = medium-term budgetary framework; MTEF = medium-term expenditure framework.

GPRS proposals, and to promote budget transparency and accountability. Subsequent rolling forward of the MTEF sought to address some of the weaknesses in the initial MTEF and enable the framework to provide more effective support for preparation of the annual budget. The Ministry of Finance (MoF) has been the primary advocate of the MTEF. While the

MoF used to be responsible for developing sector strategies and expenditure plans, this role is now shared with the Department of Strategy and Donor Coordination in the Council of Ministers.

Design

The MTEF is fully integrated with the budget cycle and covers a three-year period. The rolling framework is revised and updated annually during the first half of each year as an integral part of the annual budget planning cycle. Expenditure ceilings are fixed for three years. The MTEF covers both current and capital expenditure, including public investment projects financed from external sources.

The MTEF now covers all spending agencies and is disaggregated by sector. A revised budget calendar was developed to emphasize the role of spending agencies in preparing the MTEF. The MTEF includes the macro-fiscal framework, sector expenditure strategies, and three-year central and sector expenditure plans. The introduction of the MTEF signaled the government's intention to move toward a more comprehensive approach to public expenditure planning, in which public investment requirements are considered part of broader sector and ministry expenditure programs.

The MoF sets sector and program ceilings, and spending agencies prepare detailed budget estimates in line with program ceilings. In-year reallocation between programs is possible up to 10 percent of annual program allocations. Reallocations must be approved by the Council of Ministers, except in the case of capital projects, for which approval of the minister of finance is required. Reallocations are reconciled when medium-term plans are revised as part of the annual budget process. A contingency reserve of up to 3 percent of the total value of approved funds can only be used for financing unusual expenditures not foreseen in the budget preparation phase, and expenditures must be approved by the Council of Ministers. Budget allocations do not carry over from one year to the next, unless specifically stipulated in advance.

Implementation

The MoF takes the lead in preparing the MTEF. The policies and strategies identified in the GPRS and NSDI influence expenditure priorities identified in the MTEF as well as the choice of sectors for more detailed expenditure analysis in future cycles. Bottom-up budget requests are coordinated through a participatory process involving an MTEF steering committee and working group as well as sector technical working groups.

After some initial missteps, which meant that the MTEF and budget were not well coordinated and the annual budget was not properly anchored by medium-term fiscal targets (see the 2003 ROSC), the MTEF is now well integrated into the budget cycle, and the annual budget and the MTEF are more consistent. The Budget and Treasury Departments of the MoF play a central role in managing the budget and in formulating budget policies, planning, and the allocation of resources consistent with a macroeconomic framework. The MTEF is prepared during February to May. It is approved by the Council of Ministers in June and incorporated into the budget preparation guidelines that are issued by mid-July. An interministerial working group monitors the preparation of both the MTEF and the NSDI. The general secretary of the MoF exercises day-to-day management of the MTEF process and coordinates with spending agencies.

The MTEF process involves preparing an MTEF issues paper that provides initial estimates and policy guidelines; preparing and developing analysis that elaborates the macro-fiscal framework, analyzes sector expenditure strategies, and develops expenditure plans; holding a budget options workshop to review MTEF recommendations, resource allocations, and expenditure plans; finalizing and approving the MTEF document (by the Council of Ministers); preparing the budget and presenting the draft budget to parliament; presenting the MTEF to parliament for information; and publishing MTEF ceilings.

The MoF is responsible for setting indicative resource guidelines that give the expected order of magnitude of future public spending in the sector and show how existing resources are allocated between key program areas within the sector. Revenue forecasts are generally overestimates. The MoF prepares the macro-fiscal framework, which includes (a) analysis of trends and developments in the real economy and their implications for public sector revenues and public expenditure demands; (b) analysis of domestic revenue trends and issues, assessment of the likely impact of new revenue initiatives and measures, and preparation of revenue projections; (c) assessment of trends and issues in external project financing and projections of commitments and disbursements; (d) projections of external budgetary support and domestic borrowing; (e) assessment of foreign and domestic borrowing projections in the context of overall fiscal sustainability; and (f) setting of the consolidated budget resource framework for the coming three-year period.

Spending agencies prepare strategic plans in line with policy priorities as outlined by the NSDI. Deeper reforms of medium-term budget planning were initiated in 2000. However, aligning MTEF sector proposals with development priorities has been difficult. The introduction of the Integrated Planning System in 2005 aimed to align the national policy processes of the NSDI more closely with the MTEF process. The NSDI provides a single comprehensive strategy covering all sectors. Spending agencies are then required to elaborate their medium-term expenditure plans so as to deliver their policy objectives and goals. Implementation of the system was undertaken in phases. The initial focus during 2006 was on establishing central structures and developing the basic methodologies and processes of the system; spending agencies began using the system in 2007.

The monitoring of agency and program performance is still weak. A few indicators at the activity level are defined in the process of preparing the MTEF, which are monitored and reviewed during the midyear budget review and during the negotiation of each new MTEF. Underperformance is sometimes reflected in the funding of the next budget plan, but the links are not always clear, given the influence of many factors on budget allocations, including political agendas in some sensitive sectors.

There are no MTEFs at the subnational level. While the 2008 Organic Budget Law provides for MTEFs at the subnational level, the MoF does not have the resources to provide training and oversight of MTEF implementation at the subnational levels.

Impact
The MTEF brought into much sharper focus the preparation of annual budgets and heightened the level of analysis in budget preparation. There was strong political endorsement of the proposals to increase spending on education, transport, and infrastructure maintenance. The MTEF opened the budget process to a broader constituency within the government, increased cooperation between the MoF and spending agencies, and provided a systematic approach to budget prioritization, expenditure classification, and costing of GPRS programs. However, spending patterns have been slow to adjust to new policy and program priorities. Revenue forecasts continue to be overly optimistic: Albania scores a B for PEFA indicator PI-3, revenue out-turns compared to budgets, while nearly three-quarters of the assessed countries score an A. This has resulted in significant in-year spending cutbacks in some years. Substantial inefficiencies persist in the delivery of public programs. Weaknesses in budget execution and procurement continue to undermine the integrity of the budget, while accountability is weak. The coverage and quality of budget reports also need to be improved.

Efforts to link policy and program development to resource allocation and management through the MTEF have achieved only limited success. Strategies and plans have been developed without adequately taking into account resource constraints. New policy priorities have not been reflected in the budget planning process. Over time, the MoF has increased the pressure on spending agencies to ensure meaningful compliance with the requirements of the MTEF process. However, the results of budget reforms have been mixed, and the improvements in quality have not always been sustained. In education, transport, and public works, the quality of the budget presentations has improved considerably. However, since 2008 and the global economic crisis, the reluctance of government to accept the slowdown of the Albanian economy has led to even more optimistic revenue forecasts, and budget ceilings subsequently have had to be cut heavily in the middle of budget implementation, undermining the process of MTBF preparation.

Influences

The economic transition in Albania was characterized by short-lived economic collapse followed by sustained economic recovery. In the aftermath of the 1997 crisis, several governments initiated a recovery program of structural and fiscal reforms. Implementation of the program facilitated strong economic performance until 2008. However, the failure to acknowledge the impact of the global economic slowdown on macroeconomic projections is putting at risk the positive achievements of the past.

With regard to political support for fiscal reform in general and the MTEF in particular, the strong commitment and active involvement of the minister of finance has facilitated implementation of the MTEF and coordination with spending agencies. However, political support for the MTEF has been inconsistent and fragmented.

The MTEF and budget planning processes have not effectively linked resource allocations to strategic policy and program priorities. Significant weaknesses remain in budget execution, especially in cash management and procurement. Substantial budgetary reallocation and underexecution during implementation have undercut the government's efforts to consolidate the budget as a predictable tool for policy implementation and seriously undermined the integrity of the budget and the efficiency of public spending. In addition, audit and parliamentary oversight have been severely limited by capacity constraints. PEFA scores suggest that budget credibility remains an issue.

The MTEF consolidated two previous initiatives in Albania: (a) the experience, since 1993, with sector policy and program development under the Public Investment Program, and (b) an integrated exercise that was initiated on a small scale during the Kosovo refugee crisis in 1999 to allocate additional budgetary support to priority areas.

With regard to capacity of the civil service and broader government, establishing the analytical capacities required within the MoF to implement an effective MTEF took time, but has been achieved. However, strengthening capacity in the relevant budget and planning units of spending agencies has proved difficult.

The MTEF has been supported by two major programs of the U.K. Department for International Development (DFID) and recently by a trust fund managed by the World Bank. The MTEF has also drawn on international experience with the introduction of strategic expenditure planning in both advanced and developing countries.

Finally, even though Albania's MTEF is considered a success, it has been challenging to implement. Piloting the MTBF was appropriate given capacity constraints.

Armenia

Table G.2 summarizes the case study of Armenia, which reflects the information on MTEF implementation up to 2011.

Origins

While an MTEF was announced in 1999 as part of the Medium-Term Strategy on the Use of Privatization Proceeds (2000–02), the initial focus was on managing within an aggregate resource envelope consistent with IMF program targets. An MTBF was formally in place for 2003. While adoption of an MTEF was a condition of the Bank's Structural Adjustment Credit III Program in 1999, the idea was owned by the government and had no opponents. This is because it was seen as an integral part of the response to the macroeconomic and microeconomic challenges facing the government at the time—external vulnerability and domestic volatility, debt sustainability, large infrastructure and social needs, and inefficient subsidization of utilities.

Design

The MTEF covers three years, and it is a rolling framework (table G.3 provides a snapshot of an MTEF for education). Ceilings for the first

Table G.2   Summary of Case Study of Armenia

Issue	Details
Implementation	An MTBF has been in place since 2003. The transition to an MTPF began in 2008. There has been good donor coordination.
Basic features	The three-year rolling framework has indicative out-year expenditure ceilings. All spending agencies and categories of spending are covered.
Macro-fiscal framework	High growth, revenue overperformance, and debt restructuring have eased the resource constraints. MTEF was suspended in 2009 due to uncertainties created by the global financial crisis.
Strategic objectives	The principal objective is to increase budget credibility and predictability. A high score for PEFA budget credibility suggests success in this regard. Budget allocations are guided by Public Expenditure Reviews and Poverty Reduction Strategy Papers. Links among the MTEF, the annual budget, and the Sustainable Development Plan are to be strengthened.
Link to budget	MTEF preparation is the first stage in the annual budget cycle.
Participants and support	A ministerial steering committee provides MTEF strategy, while a Ministry of Finance–led working group oversees implementation. Parliament does not approve the MTEF.
Institutional capacity	The Ministry of Finance has spearheaded the training effort on MTEF and broader reform of public financial management.
Performance focus	Performance budgeting is being introduced, although a shift in focus from inputs to outputs and outcomes has yet to be achieved.
Quality of budgeting	Spending agencies now recognize resource constraints, and fiscal discipline has improved as a result. Efficiency has been slow to improve, but budgeting is becoming increasingly strategic in focus.
Other issues	The government's ongoing strategy for public financial management reform targets areas that will strengthen the MTEF (for example, fiscal forecasting capability).

Note: MTBF = medium-term budgetary framework; MTEF = medium-term expenditure framework.

year—the budget year—are binding. Those for the second and third years are flexible, but they provide the starting point for the next year's budget. All budget agencies (around 70) and all budget spending are covered. The MTEF is integrated with the annual budget under the Budget System Law, and it is the only comprehensive multiyear financial planning instrument in the country.

Implementation
MTEF preparation begins in January, when the Budget Directorate of the MoF prepares and circulates the macro-fiscal framework comprising the

Table G.3   Public Expenditure on Education in Armenia, by Area, 2009–13
drams, millions

			As per 2011–13 MTEF		
Type of expenditure	2009 actual	2010 adopted budget	2011	2012	2013
Total expenditures	106,947.8	99,294.6	108,318.5	106,706.5	111,765.5
01., 02. Preschool, elementary general, and secondary general education	71,573.3	70,300.5	73,431.0	77,026.3	80,959.9
03. Initial vocational (technical) and secondary vocational education	4,679.1	4,881.2	5,013.4	5,040.0	5,293.5
04. Higher education	7,469.6	7,522.6	7,724.8	7,710.1	8,137.9
05. Education not classified by levels	3,119.5	3,265.9	3,591.2	3,579.9	3,770.6
06. Auxiliary educational services	20,106.3	13,324.4	18,558.1	13,350.2	13,603.6

Source: Government of Armenia 2011.

aggregate resource envelope and top-down expenditure allocations. Spending agencies then prepare sector expenditure frameworks in April to June, in consultation with the MoF. The cabinet adopts the MTEF in late June; it is sent to the national assembly for information and published by July 1. The MoF then issues the budget circular in July–August, budget submissions are made and reviewed in October–November, budget and expenditure ceilings are approved by the cabinet by end-November, the budget is reviewed and, if necessary, amended by the Parliamentary Budget Commission in December, and the final budget is approved by the national assembly by end-December.

A ministerial steering committee headed by the prime minister provides strategic guidance on the MTEF, while a working group headed by the first deputy minister of finance in charge of the budget oversees its preparation. The former provides strong political leadership for the MTEF process, while the latter ensures that priorities and targets are set for each sector and that MTEF functional allocations are guided by these priorities and targets. However, this does not quite work as intended, mainly because the annual budget remains focused on inputs and because line items often lack significance in terms of program objectives.

Performance-based budgeting is being introduced in two stages. The first stage, for 2005–09, focused on improving the formulation of the budget, the definition of budget programs, the use of performance indicators, and the reporting on performance. The second stage is addressing linkages with other functional areas of public financial management (PFM) reform, including budget execution and treasury reforms, internal and external audit, and the development of management systems with a focus on outcomes and outputs.

Impact

There is evidence that the MTEF has contributed to greater fiscal discipline by changing the culture in line ministries to one where sector policies are implemented within given limits; allocative efficiency is fostered through high-level discussions by the steering committee, which has a broad vision; strategic planning and budgeting are strengthened through gradual alignment of MTEF and Poverty Reduction Strategy Paper (PRSP) processes; and policy formulation is improved by generating debate on the basis of aggregate macro-fiscal parameters. However, progress was not immediate; indeed, a 2003 critique claimed that the MTEF was not strategic or consequential in terms of annual budgets.

Moreover, there was a setback in 2009 when the global economic crisis resulted in a 14.5 percent reduction in GDP. This forced the fiscal balance from near 0 in 2008 to a deficit of 8 percent of GDP, exceeding the government's official deficit limit of 5 percent of GDP. With the temporary abandonment of this limit to avoid a procyclical fiscal stance and uncertainty about immediate economic prospects, the MTEF was suspended. It was reinstated in 2010, and maintaining the momentum of budget reform despite this interruption has been a key challenge.

For the future, priorities are to enhance linkages between the MTEF and the annual budget and between the MTEF and the successor to the PRSP—the Sustainable Development Plan—by strengthening macro-fiscal forecasting and investment appraisal and shifting the focus to accountability and value for money. These priorities are reflected in the government's 2010 PFM reform strategy.

Influences

MTEF implementation benefited from a favorable enabling environment. The economic situation during 2000–08 was characterized by sustained high growth, revenue overperformance, a successful debt restructuring, and improvement in the debt profile. Poverty rates fell due to high economic growth, increased remittances, and a well-funded social protection system. The political system was stable, with coalition governments that favored reforms.

There was a commitment to better-quality budget management and stronger fiscal institutions, building on the successful implementation of first-generation reforms during 1995–2000, which focused on the legal framework and basic budget systems. An overarching objective was to increase budget credibility and predictability, and a high PEFA score for budget credibility points to success in this regard. Reform was guided by experiences elsewhere, and the MoF provided training to MoF and line ministry staff on the MTEF and broader PFM methodologies and procedures.

Armenia also benefited from good donor coordination, with the Bank playing a lead role through Public Expenditure Reviews (PERs) and PRSPs and with the DFID, the German Agency for International Cooperation (GIZ), and the U.S. Agency for International Development (USAID) providing key support.

Brazil

Table G.4 summarizes the case study of Brazil, which reflects the information on MTEF implementation up to 2011.

Origins
Although Brazil does not have a formal MTEF, the building blocks are in place for its development. The constitution of 1988 created a new set of rules and processes for managing budget decision making at all levels of government.

The Plano Plurianual (PPA, the Multiyear Plan) is formulated in the first year of a government and defines the main strategic targets and programs of the incoming administration. It serves as the institutional framework for planning expenditure for the coming four years. The PPA must be analyzed, amended, and approved by congress by the last month of the first year of its mandate and is valid until the end of the first year of the next elected government. It cannot be classified as an MTBF because it is not based on a reconciliation of multiyear resource envelopes with bottom-up estimates of the needs of spending agencies. Moreover, the PPA can be altered on an annual basis, and therefore its indicative multiyear budget allocations are not binding,

Table G.4   Summary of Case Study of Brazil

Issue	Details
Implementation	There is no formal MTEF, although the equivalent of an MTFF has been in place since 2001.
Basic features	The Budget Guidelines Law (LDO) is in effect an MTFF. The Multiyear Plan (PPA) is a four-year plan meant to reflect strategic government priorities and to constrain annual budget laws. It is not binding in practice, as it is subject to annual changes. It cannot be classified as an MTBF. There is also, at least in practice, limited emphasis on performance measurement and evaluation. There are subnational LDOs and PPAs.
Macro-fiscal framework	The LDO is a comprehensive, three-year rolling projection of revenue, expenditure, and the fiscal balance. Short-term forecasting is quite accurate, but medium-term forecasting is less so. The LDO also specifies priority expenditures, which are protected from budget cuts.
Strategic objectives	The LDO and the PPA were meant (1) to introduce medium-term fiscal constraints and strategic government priorities into the budget process, (2) to increase transparency and accountability, and (3) to enhance fiscal controls. The system has achieved greater success on the third and, to some extent, the second objectives. However, strategic government objectives and resource allocation targets in the PPA have not necessarily been reflected in the annual budget because the PPA is subject to annual changes and has, in practice, a relatively limited impact on the budget preparation process (at least beyond the first year).
Link to budget	Annual budget laws are required to be consistent with the PPA and the LDO. In practice, the PPA is subject to change during preparation of the Budget Guidelines Law, when LDO revenue estimates can also be updated.
Participants and support	The Ministry of Planning and Budget oversees the PPA and shares responsibility for the LDO with the Ministry of Finance and the Presidency.
Institutional capacity	The Brazilian public service is highly capable overall, but could benefit from improved interagency coordination and specific MTEF-related training.
Performance focus	While the PPA emphasizes performance, in practice the quality of performance indicators is low, the overall monitoring and evaluation framework is weak, and funding is not linked to results. This is perhaps the weakest aspect of budget reform.
Quality of budgeting	Control over spending has increased significantly, especially given the close link between the LDO and the Fiscal Responsibility Law. Annual budgets still lack credibility because of significant carryover between years, and their link to strategic government priorities is weak.

Note: MTBF = medium-term budgetary framework; MTEF = medium-term expenditure framework; MTFF = medium-term fiscal framework; MTPF = medium-term performance framework; PEFA = public expenditure and financial accountability.

which weakens its effectiveness as an instrument for the strategic allocation of resources.

The Budget Guidelines Law (LDO) is formulated every year, around April. It defines revenue, expenditure, and fiscal balance targets in a three-year rolling framework, thus classifying it as an MTFF. While its purpose is to link the PPA with annual budgets, this integration has not been successful, and the prioritization and resource allocations defined in the PPA have not been reflected in the annual budgets. The importance of the LDO has grown as a consequence of the strong fiscal adjustment implemented since 1999 and enactment of the Fiscal Responsibility Law (LRF) in 2000 (as a result of which the MTFF became fully functional in 2001). The LDO presents fiscal targets in terms of primary surpluses for three years (including the current budget year). These targets are crucial in signaling the government's fiscal adjustment efforts.

The main goal behind the introduction of these instruments (PPA, LDO, and LRF) was to coordinate planning of the budget through a hier-archical structure that develops this process over a four-year period. Two additional motivations for this reform were, on the one hand, to intro-duce greater transparency and accountability to the process, given that Brazil was coming out of a military dictatorship, and, on the other hand, to introduce greater fiscal controls, given Brazil's previous history of poor fiscal control and macroeconomic instability, while allowing some fiscal policy flexibility.

Design
The LDO is a three-year rolling fiscal framework. Even though it sets out three-year rolling projections for the main macroeconomic and fiscal aggregates, including primary revenue and expenditure, these projections can be reviewed and changed during preparation of the annual budget. As a result, even the projections for the first of the three years may be ignored and new expenditure ceilings may be defined.

The coverage of the LDO macro-fiscal framework is comprehensive and includes all sources of funds and all government expenditure, includ-ing the net fiscal contribution of the state-owned enterprise sector (other than Petrobras, the state oil and gas corporation). Although the legislation allows for the interpretation that the PPA should cover only investment programs, coverage has been expanded since 2000 to include nearly all government expenditure. The PPA follows the same classification struc-ture as the budget and is presented by program and function; targets are associated with each program. The total cost of the program is presented and broken down by capital and current expenditure. While the PPA coexists with other planning instruments developed by spending agencies, the link between these instruments is not straightforward.

The PPA is evaluated and amended annually following approval of the annual budget, and changes can be made to both the PPA and the annual budget during the year. The executive can do this within certain limits (unless there is additional revenue), beyond which legislative approval is required. Brazil appropriates the budget on an expenditure authorization basis, and during budget execution the financial management system puts limits on agency commitments (*empenho*) and on cash payments (*pagamento*). At the end of each fiscal year, expenditures that have been committed but not yet paid may be carried over into the following year (*restos a pagar*). Residual expenditures carried forward are significant, particularly as a component of discretionary spending, and have increased rapidly as the budget has expanded in recent years.

Implementation

The macro-fiscal framework is prepared jointly by the MoF, the Ministry of Planning and Budget, and the chief of staff of the Presidency (*Casa Civil*). These same entities are responsible for agreeing on the revenue estimates that will be used for the budget process. Although the annual revenue estimates are accurate, the medium-term estimates are less so. The parameters for estimating revenue may be changed from the time that the LDO is submitted to the time that the budget proposal is presented; as a result, the estimates for year one of the LDO might change only six months after being approved by congress. The LDO provides budget execution information for the previous two fiscal years as well as fiscal targets, risks, and projections for the following two years in terms of primary balances, debt stock, and revenue and expenditure aggregates. All of this information is published on the website of the Ministry of Planning and Budget.

The PPA defines the overall government strategy as well as all programs and actions to be implemented in the period. However, it has lost much of its strategic content and has become an additional procedure in the budget process. The "government strategy" seems to be loosely defined and not properly costed. Nonetheless, the PPA highlights the government's political priorities—about one-quarter of the programs are designated as "priority," which means that they are protected from cuts during budget implementation. The LDO ensures this special treatment, which protects priority programs. An important caveat is that, despite the identification of priorities and special budgetary treatment, there are controversies over whether the process has indeed translated into prioritization of government spending. This is evidenced by the poor implementation of priority programs, partly due to cash rationing that diminishes the predictability of resource envelopes.

In addition to the PPA, some sectors have developed their own strategies. However, not all sector strategies are fully costed, nor are they broadly consistent with the projections in the PPA or LDO. This may be partly due to the relative political autonomy of some ministers, who do not necessarily come from within the president's party.

In theory, the PPA emphasizes performance by stating program objectives and performance indicators. However, as identified by an assessment conducted by the World Bank in 2006, several issues arise with regard to the monitoring and evaluation framework of the PPA. One of the obstacles is the technical difficulty in managing performance indicators. Even in spending agencies that embraced the idea of undertaking program budgeting and identifying performance indicators, problems of measurement (such as setting up useful indicators) are endemic. Indicators are defined jointly and negotiated between spending agencies and the Ministry of Planning and Budget during preparation of the PPA. Funding is not linked to results.

LDOs and PPAs also exist at the subnational level. There is little direct coordination, except to the extent that transfers between levels of government are generally rules based and predictable.

Impact

There is a perception that controls over government spending have improved as a result of the Fiscal Responsibility Law and the changes it introduced to the Budget Guidelines Law. At the same time, the PPA exercise does not ensure that strategic government priorities are reflected in the preparation of annual budget laws (other than in the year of its approval) or during budget execution. Moreover, performance indicators are usually insufficiently defined and do not inform budget allocation decisions. Recently, initiatives at the subnational level have been introduced to improve the strategic planning process, to associate it with the PPA, and to transform it into a tool for prioritizing government spending.

The credibility of the PPA and annual budget is compromised because they can be easily amended, as in the case of the Budget Guidelines Law. Moreover, the large amount of carryover allows for greater within-year budget flexibility for the executive, which can choose whether to execute the current year's planned expenditure or the expenditure planned for the previous years but carried forward. Nonetheless, the controls over aggregate spending are effective, and Brazil's fiscal management system, which has been highly regarded for many years (for example, see the 2001 ROSC), scores very highly in the recent PEFA report.

Ghana

Table G.5 summarizes the case study of Ghana, which reflects the information on MTEF implementation up to 2011.

Origins
The MTEF was introduced in 1999. The initial plan was to pilot the MTEF in three central government ministries, departments, and agencies (here called spending agencies), but it was instead introduced for all spending agencies to avoid having to work with two overlapping budget processes. Consulting Africa assisted the authorities with MTEF design and implementation, with the intention from the outset being to have an MTPF.

The MTEF was one of the two main components of the Public Financial Management Reform Program (PUFMARP), a five-year program initiated in 1996 and supported by the World Bank, DFID, the European Commission (EC), and the Canadian International Development Agency (CIDA). The other component was the Budgeting and Public Expenditure Management System (BPEMS). Specific objectives for the MTEF included improved fiscal discipline through realistic revenue projections and better expenditure prioritization. In addition to Ghana's development partners, the MTEF has been backed by the president, ministers, and other senior officials. However, because it was mainly consultant driven and senior officials had little input into its design, there was limited internal support of PUFMARP. Thus, although the Ministry of Finance and Economic Planning (MoFEP) has been a proponent of the MTEF, its Budget Division has not fully embraced it.

Design
While the MTEF is a three-year rolling framework, little attention is given to out-year estimates; indeed, the MoFEP does not even use the first out-year as a starting point for developing the following year's MTEF and budget. Out-year spending forecasts are not included in the budget estimates of spending agencies. Further, there are wide variations between

Table G.5   Summary of Case Study of Ghana

Issue	Details
Implementation	An MTPF has been in place since 1999. It was introduced as part of a broader consultant-driven initiative to reform public financial management.
Basic features	This three-year rolling framework has indicative out-year expenditure ceilings. It covers all spending agencies, but less than half of government spending because staff costs are excluded. While there is supposed to be limited flexibility for spending agencies to depart from budget allocations, expenditure ceilings are routinely ignored.
Macro-fiscal framework	Revenue forecasts are optimistic, and macro-fiscal planning is weak.
Strategic objectives	The MTEF is intended to be compatible with the Ghana Poverty Reduction Strategy, and spending agencies have mission statements emphasizing poverty reduction. However, too little information is available to make policy trade-offs.
Link to budget	The budget timetable is too tight to allow the MTEF to inform strategic spending decisions.
Participants and support	The MTEF has high-level support, but is widely viewed as a Ministry of Finance project. Being a consultant-driven rather than a homegrown MTEF has further undermined spending agency buy-in.
Institutional capacity	Civil service reform has lagged, and skill development has been slow.
Performance focus	Spending agencies report a large number of performance indicators, but performance is not a focus of public financial management.
Quality of budgeting	The MTEF has had little influence, and budgeting remains incremental and input oriented.
Other issues	Ghana would have been better served by first developing a good MTFF and then moving to an MTBF. Failure to put in place an appropriate information system was a major constraint, although this has been addressed recently.

Note: MTBF = medium-term budgetary framework; MTEF = medium-term expenditure framework; MTFF = medium-term fiscal framework; MTPF = medium-term performance framework.

indicative and final MTEF ceilings, across both agencies and spending categories.

While the macro-fiscal framework is reasonably comprehensive and includes all sources of funds, and all spending agencies are subject to MTEF ceilings, less than half of central government spending is subject to MTEF ceilings because staff costs are excluded. Since the budget in Ghana is classified by a mix of objectives, outputs, activities, and line items, and not by programs, ceilings on spending categories do not reflect systematic budget planning. Dual budgeting was abandoned when the MTEF was put in place.

Guidelines provide limited flexibility for spending agencies to change allocations across budget line items, after consultation with the Ministry of Finance and Economic Planning. In practice, spending agencies pay little attention to budget ceilings, which are routinely exceeded, especially when budgets are linked to specific financing sources. There is no contingency reserve, although part of the budget is appropriated as contingency to meet unforeseen expenditure demands. The unused part of the budget lapses at the end of the year, but it can be voted on again in the following year. Unused cash held by spending agencies at the close of the year is returned to the treasury.

Implementation

The MTEF is a project of the Budget Division of the Ministry of Finance and Economic Planning. The Budget Development Unit of the Budget Division coordinates the MTEF and budget preparation, starting with development of the top-down resource envelope. Spending agency budget committees prepare detailed bottom-up budget submissions. However, top-down ceilings are not approved by the cabinet, with the result that they are not taken seriously and budget submissions are not resource constrained. The budget timetable is too tight for spending strategies or intersector trade-offs to be considered seriously.

The MTEF and budget processes have been developed in parallel and are supposed to be fully compatible with and supportive of the Ghana Poverty Reduction Strategy. However, the MTEF was developed as a project rather than a budgeting or PFM reform, and information systems are geared to the requirements of the budget rather than the MTEF. The budget statement reports ceilings for spending agencies for the budget year and two out-years. The annual estimates of spending agencies include program and subprogram ceilings for the budget years, but not for the two out-years. MTEF ceilings are approved by parliament by virtue of their inclusion in the budget statement.

The Ministry of Finance and Economic Planning takes the lead in preparing revenue forecasts, which continue to be optimistic, as well as the macro-fiscal framework. Macroeconomic planning is a general weakness. Ghana does not have a fiscal rule, but it has been considering the introduction of a fiscal responsibility law since 2008. Medium-term debt, deficit, revenue, and expenditure targets are included in the budget statement.

Spending agencies have mission statements that specify their objectives and the resources allocated to specific outputs. The Ghana Poverty Reduction Strategy forces them to emphasize antipoverty programs, which are a spending priority. Beyond this, there is little linkage between their plans and budgets. The format of the current MTEF does not present strategic information in a way that enables the cabinet to understand and choose among relevant policy trade-offs. Spending agencies are not clear about the basis for the approved budget allocations. The creation of sector working groups, which include spending agencies, development partners, and other stakeholders, could give strategies greater traction. Spending agencies undertake activity-based costing using software developed by the MTEF consultants.

They also report a large number of self-selected input, output, and outcome indicators to the Budget Division, but these estimates are largely ignored, mainly because the budget structure is not geared to monitoring performance, the ministry does not focus on it, and, even if it did, the large amount of excessively detailed performance information sent to it would be difficult to understand.

Only transfers to districts are covered by the MTEF. The central government has deconcentrated some functions, but there is little decentralization. Where responsibilities have been decentralized, districts have not received additional funding.

Impact

The widely held view is that the MTEF has had little beneficial impact and the BPEMS has not achieved its objectives as designed. But the BPEMS has established the basic platform on which the current Government Integrated Financial Management Information System is building. Following initial reviews that were complimentary, subsequent reviews, including a periodic external review of public financial management by development partners, have highlighted numerous failings. Budgeting remains incremental and input focused, and the MTEF has not improved either budget realism or expenditure prioritization. The 2004 ROSC was highly critical, noting that the MTEF was largely a time-consuming, form-filling exercise and that budgeting remained incremental.

Influences

PUFMARP was a response to severe macroeconomic imbalances that had fiscal mismanagement as a root cause. While key macroeconomic aggregates have improved, this has reflected mainly a combination of sustained adjustment and structural reform under IMF and World Bank conditionality, debt relief, and the external environment. The quality of macroeconomic management has improved, but fiscal management remains weak, especially given the resources devoted to PFM reform.

Political support for fiscal and economic reform has tended to focus on form rather than substance. In the case of the MTEF, there was clear interest in modernizing budgeting but not enough commitment to the institutional changes needed to ensure that the MTEF worked well.

As designed, the MTPF was too ambitious, and the lack of progress with BPEMS had systemic implications. More attention should have been paid to ensuring that basic budget reforms were implemented to support an integrated budget or MTEF process. Fairly low PEFA scores point to limited payoff from many years of PFM reform.

Lack of progress with planned civil service reform has hampered progress with MTEF implementation, especially with regard to skills development. Technology has also been a constraint, including for BPEMS.

Development partners played a significant role in promoting and developing the MTEF. They should probably have curbed the enthusiasm of the MTEF consultants for an MTPF at the outset. However, their subsequent warning about MTEF design and implementation problems were well founded and timely, but were not acted upon by the government.

Even though Ghana is a leader in implementing an MTEF in Africa, the decision to introduce an MTPF was inappropriate given Ghana's starting point. Significant design failings have proved costly in terms of the misallocation of scarce human, physical, and financial resources. The MTEF should have been phased in, beginning with an MTFF that built on the medium-term frameworks used by the IMF and the World Bank. With a more measured strategy, by this time a well-functioning MTBF could have been in place and an MTPF planned for.

Jordan

Table G.6 summarizes the case study of Jordan, which reflects the information on MTEF implementation up to 2011.

Origins

An MTBF was introduced in 2008 and covered all spending agencies. It was part of a wide PFM reform initiated in 2004 to introduce an MTFF, which became effective in 2005, and to pave the way for results-oriented budgeting.

Table G.6   Summary of Case Study of Jordan

Issue	Details
Implementation	An MTFF was introduced in 2005, and an MTBF has been in place since 2008.
Basic features	The three-year rolling framework has indicative out-year expenditure ceilings. All spending agencies are covered. MTEF ceilings can be adjusted within-year, both through transfers of appropriations and supplementary budgets.
Macro-fiscal framework	Volatility in grants has been the main source of uncertainty in resource projections. The impact of commodity price developments and the global financial crisis were underestimated. A fiscal adjustment in 2010 in response to revenue shortfall and expenditure overruns in 2009 is being borne by capital spending.
Strategic objectives	A public financial management reform strategy is part of the National Agenda, which outlines Jordan's development strategy. The Executive Program translates objectives of the National Agenda into costed government programs to be funded through the MTEF.
Link to budget	Provisional ceilings in the budget circular are derived from the MTEF. The budget timetable is too compressed to accommodate recent delays in preparing the MTFF due to macroeconomic uncertainty. This has resulted in little bottom-up input into the budget.
Participants and support	The Ministry of Finance takes the lead. The Council of Ministers plays a central role in determining spending allocations that are consistent with the National Agenda, although the basis for setting priorities is unclear.
Institutional capacity	Implementing the MTEF has strained capacity at both the Ministry of Finance and spending agencies. The ministry is developing greater capacity to analyze spending choices.
Performance focus	Results-oriented budgeting is being planned. At present, spending agencies self-assess performance against key indicators for internal use.
Quality of budgeting	Medium-term planning has improved, despite a fragmented budget process where MTEF and annual budget preparation are inadequately coordinated. There has been some reallocation to targeted sectors.
Other issues	Given that the MTEF was introduced in the context of the global financial crisis, full benefits have yet to materialize. Other areas of PFM reform have to catch up, especially commitment control.

In 2004 Jordan initiated a major PFM reform (the Financial Management Reform Strategy, 2004–07) that sought to strengthen macro-fiscal capacity; this was followed by another strategy covering 2008–10. The MTEF component of the reform was financed by USAID and supported by the World Bank, DFID, GIZ, and the EC. Its specific objectives included improved fiscal discipline through realistic revenue projections, followed by better expenditure prioritization and the identification of fiscal space. The PFM reform strategy is part of the National Agenda, a document outlining Jordan's development strategy, based on a participatory approach by all stakeholders and endorsed by the highest levels of government and therefore benefiting from consensual support.

Design

The MTEF is a three-year rolling framework. The ceilings for years two and three are indicative and are used as a base for the following year's budget. It covers all spending agencies at the level of detail of account segments. It coexists with the Executive Program, a three-year program that translates the National Agenda into priorities and programs, including costing and phasing, and is coordinated by the Ministry of Planning. The MTEF has not been extended to local governments.

There is flexibility in the MTEF, with adjustments made during the year according to provisions of the annual General Budget Law at the level of items, projects, activities, or programs. Changes in the MTEF during the year can occur through a transfer made within a spending agency or through a supplementary budget. A contingency reserve in the MoF chapter of the budget can be used at the discretion of the Council of Ministers. The unused part of the budget at the end of the year is returned to the treasury. When the MTEF is rolled over, it uses the latest within-year changes as a base.

Implementation

The MTEF is prepared by the General Budget Department of the MoF. Earlier, spending agencies are required to prepare their forward estimates. This involves estimating expenditure requirements on approved programs and projects for the next three years (so-called unchanged policy forward estimates) and the costs of proposed new initiatives and projects to be started during the coming three years. Following finalization of the MTFF's aggregate resource envelope, the General Budget Department compares the unchanged policy forward estimates with the aggregate resource envelope. This indicates the scope for spending on new initiatives or projects without cutting existing spending or, alternatively, the magnitude of spending cuts needed to avoid exceeding the aggregate resource envelope. This information becomes the basis for preparing the MTEF.

The General Budget Department coordinates budget preparation, starting with development of the top-down resource envelope. Spending agencies prepare detailed bottom-up budget submissions, which are then studied and discussed with the General Budget Department. After that, the budget circular is issued, including provisional ceilings approved by the Council of Ministers, but not by parliament. The draft budget is prepared according to the ceilings provided to spending agencies and then approved by the Council of Ministers to be submitted to parliament.

Since the budget preparation timetable is overly compressed, finalization of the MTFF and budget ceilings has been delayed, due to considerable uncertainty regarding the macroeconomic environment in the past couple of years. This delay has not allowed sufficient time for spending agencies to prepare their budget proposals ahead of submission to the cabinet.

The MoF's Macro-Fiscal Unit takes the lead in preparing revenue forecasts and the macro-fiscal framework in cooperation with the General Budget Department and revenue collection departments. The main risks (downside but also upside) to revenue projections are related to foreign grants, which can be fairly sizable in Jordan but are highly volatile given regional political conditions. In addition, the impact of commodity price increases and the recent financial crisis were not well forecast. There are no fiscal rules, but the Public Debt Law sets a ceiling on total government debt, as well as subceilings on the split between domestic and external debt.

Spending agencies prepare their budget according to the results-oriented budgeting concept, including their strategic plans. They also prepare a list of capital projects arranged by priority. Since the 2010 budget, spending agencies must provide narratives for their respective chapters, describing and justifying their spending proposals at the program and project level and their associated expenditure forecasts. After studying the budget drafts of spending agencies and amending the MTEF and MTFF, the General Budget Department sends a paper to the Council of Ministers with policies, priorities, and sector distribution of capital expenditure within the medium-term framework. The paper also identifies fiscal space, and the Council of Ministers identifies sectors and projects that will get priority in new spending. In recent years, however, practically no fiscal space has been available. Investment spending is fully integrated in the MTEF. The MTEF takes into account the Executive Program prepared by the Ministry of Planning, with differences related mainly to the availability of financing in the budget.

Spending agencies provide the General Budget Department with performance indicators at the level of strategic objectives and programs. They also assess these indicators annually and provide the department with self-assessment for the year ended. Funding is not linked to results. Work is currently ongoing to improve the design of key performance indicators, with assistance from USAID.

Impact

Most recent evaluations of PFM reform in Jordan agree that there has been a marked improvement in the budget process, with the MTEF strengthening planning over the medium term. However, there is still some fragmentation in the budget planning process, with duplicate functions between the Ministry of Finance, the General Budget Department, and the Ministry of Planning, which hampers proper prioritization. Also, although each spending agency is able to prioritize its own projects, there are no tools for prioritizing projects across sectors and agencies.

The impact of the global financial crisis on Jordan has affected the smooth implementation of the newly adopted MTEF. In 2009, the deficit largely exceeded the budget target because of revenue shortfalls and expenditure overruns; as a result, administrative measures were used to tighten fiscal policy in 2010. The bulk of fiscal adjustment, as usual, fell on capital spending, as current spending is mostly considered nondiscretionary and therefore not subject to revaluation. Reductions in capital expenditure are usually borne by "new projects" without much prioritization. The share of public spending being prioritized through forward estimates is quite small. There has been little incentive for spending agencies to review ongoing activities and to identify how their existing resources can be better allocated and used.

The top-down approach to budgeting and the MTEF process have helped to allocate funds to targeted sectors, while taking into account the limited resources. Spending agencies prepare their budgets and reorder their priorities in accordance with the ceilings given to them. So far, however, out-year ceilings have not been very effective because exogenous factors (higher commodity prices, recession) have created pressures on the budget. Still, spending agencies consider that using the previous out-years as a basis for preparing the current-year budget facilitates the task of budget preparation and leads to more focused negotiations with the General Budget Department. It has also contributed to significant agency buy-in to the MTEF reforms.

In the past few years, there has been recourse to supplementary budgets due to unexpected factors such as revenue shortfalls as well as inadequate budgeting for certain items. In addition, some fundamental aspects of the PFM reforms are still lagging, in particular, a sound commitment control system. This loophole has resulted in the accumulation of a large float and payment arrears, which has hampered sound execution of the budget.

Influences

Up to 2008, with the debt target set by the Public Debt Law, important advances were made in the area of fiscal consolidation and reduction of public debt from high levels. However, Jordan was hit hard by the increases in oil and food prices in 2008 and the global financial crisis in 2009. As a result, fiscal performance has slipped relative to the budget. The launch of the MTBF in 2008 coincided with a period of heightened uncertainty, and it has therefore not yielded the expected positive impact.

There has been strong political support for PFM reform, supported by major donors. However, the MTEF process may have not been fully internalized beyond the MoF and main spending agencies. Also, the turnover of ministers of finance in Jordan is particularly high, and not all ministers have the same level of commitment to PFM reform and fiscal discipline. Finally, high-level political decisions sometimes override the MTEF, which hampers fiscal discipline.

The process of preparing the general budget is now subject to a legislative framework and specific timetable, bringing clarity to all stages of budget preparation. However, some weaknesses in the PFM system have adversely affected the success of the MTEF, especially the commitment control system and forward estimates for current spending.

There is a perception that the very ambitious PFM reform strategy has put a substantial burden on the General Budget Department, which does not have adequate human resource capacity. In addition, capacity in spending agencies varies greatly. As part of the ongoing reform, the General Budget Department recently created an Expenditure Policy Division to provide more in-depth analysis of expenditure policy options.

Development partners played a lead role in promoting and developing the MTEF, for which the government received intensive technical assistance. There is a need to improve coordination among providers and to design a well-defined framework with identified tasks and a clear division of labor.

Jordan was the first country to implement an MTEF in the Middle East. This has probably given the country an incentive to succeed and serve as a model in the region.

There is relatively strong ownership of the reform, which has taken into account the country's characteristics. However, in some areas of reform, implementation could be improved.

Korea

Table G.7 summarizes the case study of Korea, which reflects the information on MTEF implementation up to 2011.

Origins

The MTEF was formally introduced with the first National Fiscal Management Plan (NFMP), which covered the period 2004–08. An MTPF was piloted in four agencies (Public Procurement Service, National Tax Service, Korea Customs Service, and Korea Fair Trade Commission) in 2003 when preparing the 2004 budget and was extended to all spending agencies the next year. Prior to the MTPF, a medium-term macro-fiscal framework guided fiscal policy and budget formulation, but there was no formal MTFF (see the 2001 ROSC).

The vice minister at the Ministry of Planning and Budget (which was later merged with the Ministry of Finance to form the current Ministry of Strategy and Finance [MoSF]) championed comprehensive fiscal reform. The latter included not only the MTEF but also performance management and a financial management information system. The reform was conceived in response to several challenges: changing strategic priorities of the government (especially from economic growth to social welfare), increasing pension and health costs due to an aging population, growing complexity of ministerial programs and difficulty controlling spending on the part of the central Budget Office, and deteriorating fiscal sustainability after the Asian crisis. The government sought to establish a new institutional framework to cope with these challenges and to enhance the effectiveness and transparency of fiscal policy. There was little opposition to the reform because the vice minister and Budget Office assured the line ministries and parliament that the introduction of an MTEF would let the line ministries formulate their own budgets under the ceiling limit. This decentralization was aligned closely with the philosophy of the president and the ruling party, which is characterized as "participation government."

Table G.7   Summary of Case Study of Korea

Issue	Details
Implementation	An MTPF was piloted in 2004 and introduced in full in 2005.
Basic features	The MTPF is a five-year rolling framework. Out-year ceilings do not constrain successive MTEFs or budgets. All central government agencies and categories of spending are covered, broken down by sector or objective and major program.
Macro-fiscal framework	Even though growth forecasts are optimistic, the Tax Office in the Ministry of Strategy and Finance forecasts revenue conservatively.
Strategic objectives	Sector task forces review key policy issues. A few spending agencies prepare strategic plans, but programs are not systematically costed.
Link to budget	The Ministry of Finance sets program ceilings based on five-year cost estimates. Ceilings are not published and are not approved by parliament, but the Budget Office uses expenditures in the previous MTEF as a guideline for setting ceilings of the rolling MTEF.
Participants and support	The MTEF process is led by the Ministry of Finance, with strong senior ministerial support.
Institutional capacity	No issues reported.
Performance focus	There is a performance monitoring and review system, and funding is linked to results.
Quality of budgeting	The MTEF is believed to have improved fiscal responsibility, even though spending agencies have routinely exceeded the ceilings. The performance system has also increased spending efficiency.

Note: MTEF = medium-term expenditure framework; MTPF = medium-term performance framework.

Design

The MTEF covers five years, including the budget year. It is a rolling framework. Out-year ceilings have no binding force on future budgets or the NFMP and have changed significantly from one year to another. Many commentators and politicians have been quite critical on this point. Each year, when the Budget Office begins to formulate the next year's budget, budget and sector ceilings are set, taking into account the previous year's NFMP. But the former can deviate significantly from the latter. The final figures for total and sector spending can also deviate significantly from those set at the outset.

All central government and spending agencies are covered, including special accounts and public funds. The NFMP provides spending projections for 12–13 of 16 spending areas most directly related to people's lives and for the most important programs (for example, preschool, primary,

Table G.8   Government Expenditure on Education in Korea, 2010–14
won, billions, unless otherwise noted

Classification	2010	2011	2012	2013	2014	Annual growth rate (%)
Education sector	38,256	41,330	44,873	48,181	52,088	8.0
Primary and secondary	32,547	35,505	38,584	41,623	45,426	8.7
Tertiary	5,044	5,055	5,572	5,889	5,980	4.3
Lifelong and vocational	538	644	592	536	542	0.2
General	127	126	126	133	140	2.5

Source: Government of the Republic of Korea 2010.
Note: All the figures are planned in the budget, not actual.

secondary, and tertiary education in the case of education). A spending area can cover several ministries, which in turn can cover multiple programs and subprograms. Table G.8 provides an illustration of an MTEF in Korea. Medium- to long-term planning instruments do exist at the level of individual ministries (for example, the Comprehensive Territorial Development Plan of the Ministry of Construction and Transportation), but the NFMP takes precedence over them, as it is backed up by budget resources. There is no separate planning agency in Korea, and the MoSF does not have any other planning instruments.

While ceilings set at the beginning of budget preparation can be quite different from the ones finalized at the end, once the budget is approved by parliament and enters the implementation stage, ministries have to spend within the ceiling set for each program or subprogram. Spending ministries can reallocate spending across subdivisions of a program or subprogram, but reallocation across programs or subprograms requires prior approval by the MoSF and parliament. Each budget contains a contingency reserve, which can be used with the approval of the MoSF and the cabinet. All unused allocations are redeposited into the treasury single account managed by the central bank. There are exceptions, however, in the case of public funds (for example, the National Pension Fund) that manage their income independently.

Implementation

The Budget Office in the MoSF takes the lead. It first collects the five-year medium-term cost estimates for major programs and then sets program ceilings. Upon receiving their ceilings, spending ministries prepare their budget requests and send them to the MoSF. If the ministerial budget requests do not respect the ceilings, the MoSF will examine their requests more carefully and exercise more discretion. In particular, official expenses of each line ministry can reflect whether the ministry keeps its ceiling or not. Ceilings are not published, but they are provided to, but not approved by, parliament.

The Tax Office in the MoSF prepares revenue forecasts. Forecasts have been rather optimistic because the growth forecasts themselves have been optimistic. But optimism bias is not large and has been reduced recently. The MoSF also prepares the macro-fiscal framework. Korea does not have explicit fiscal rules, although the government feels politically responsible for containing deficits within the projections provided in the NFMP, and fiscal aggregates—spending, revenue, deficits, and debts—published in the NFMP serve as "targets" rather than "projections."

Spending ministries are not required to prepare strategic plans, and few of them do so. Programs are rarely costed systematically. Many investment plans have a far longer time horizon than the NFMP, and it is difficult to integrate them into the NFMP. When there is a conflict between investment plans and the NFMP, the latter takes precedence. Before preparing the NFMP, the MoSF, with the help of the Korea Development Institute, organizes sector task forces to review policy issues, and the MoSF incorporates these discussions into the NFMP. Public hearings are held to discuss proposals by the task forces.

The MoSF has introduced a performance monitoring system, a program review system (similar to the program assessment rating tool of the U.S. federal government), and a program evaluation system. Performance indicators are set by spending agencies and then reviewed by the MoSF. Program review and evaluation link funding to results. In particular, programs that receive low scores on the program review can have their funding cut by 10 percent.

Local governments are required to prepare medium-term plans, but, given the extreme uncertainly regarding the amount of grants available from the central government, their medium-term plans are not operationally significant.

Impact

There is much to be improved upon in the current MTEF, but it is generally believed to have been instrumental in improving fiscal responsibility and enhancing spending efficiency. Realism in budgeting has never been a serious problem in Korea. A more important benefit of the MTEF has been to strengthen the medium-term perspective in budgeting and the planning capacity of spending ministries. Moreover, the importance of the MTEF in maintaining fiscal soundness over the medium term is strongly emphasized. It is also recognized that parliament has to pay more attention to the MTEF, despite continuing to focus on the annual budget, and that ceilings need more binding force.

Influences

The role played by the vice minister and his political influence within the government was perhaps the most important factor behind the successful introduction of the MTEF in Korea. Much of the political support was motivated by experience following the Asian crisis and the need to prepare for upcoming fiscal challenges and to be able to respond to materializing risks. The fact that Korea was able to provide fiscal stimulus in response to the recent global economic and financial crisis is one payoff of the current approach.

Nicaragua

Table G.9 summarizes the case study of Nicaragua, which reflects the information on MTEF implementation up to 2011.

Origins

An MTBF was introduced through approval of the new financial management Law No. 550 of August 2005, although a medium-term macrofiscal framework had been in place since 2002. This law establishes that the general budget will include an annex describing the MTEF for at least the two following years, with nonbinding financial projections. The MTEF is mandatory for all public sector entities, although it was first piloted for the 2006 budget at three ministries of the central government (that is, education, infrastructure, and health). The pilot phase continued during 2007, with the three ministries introducing some improvements to the framework. In addition, the Information Technology Office of the Ministry of Finance completed development of SIGFA, the MTEF module of the information financial management system. The MTEF was extended to 21 central government entities for the 2008 budget, when the MTBF became operational. For the 2009 and 2010 budgets, it was extended to a further 10 spending agencies.

MTEF implementation forms part of a continuous PFM modernization process initiated in the mid-1990s. In principle, most stakeholders

Table G.9   Summary of Case Study of Nicaragua

Issue	Details
Implementation	Beginning with an MTFF in 2002, an MTBF has been piloted since 2006.
Basic features	The MTFF is a three-year rolling framework with indicative out-year expenditure ceilings.
Macro-fiscal framework	Revenue forecasts and the macro-fiscal framework are fully consistent with International Monetary Fund projections.
Strategic objectives	The Ministry of Finance produces a strategy document to support MTEF implementation. Sectors adapt their programs to the National Human Development Plan, but programs are not costed. The MTEF is coordinated with the Public Investment Plan.
Link to budget	No issues reported.
Participants and support	The Ministry of Finance led the effort, with limited buy-in at the sector level. Initially, the ministry was not able to provide an early indication of ceilings due to delays in setting social sector salaries.
Institutional capacity	Spending agencies have limited planning capacity, and some spending agencies have been reluctant to declare their true plans for fear of budget cuts if they fail to meet their targets.
Performance focus	Performance indicators play a limited role.
Quality of budgeting	MTEF is judged a success without any real evidence that it has contributed to better fiscal outcomes.
Other issues	MTEF remains the centerpiece of public financial management reform, and Nicaragua is seen as a regional leader in MTEF implementation.

Note: MTBF = medium-term budgetary framework; MTEF = medium-term expenditure framework; MTFF = medium-term fiscal framework.

supported the MTEF as a means of fostering expenditure discipline and getting better results from expenditure programs. But, in practice, the MTEF represents a huge challenge because the public sector is not used to working within medium-term budget constraints. It is more accustomed to asking for additional resources every year without considering the results or outcomes that might result from use of the requested funds. When the MTEF was introduced, some sectors were afraid that, should they reveal their true commitments and then underperform, the MoF would sanction them by reducing their next year's budget allocations.

Design
The MTEF covers a three-year period, including the budget year, and it is updated annually. Out-year ceilings are not binding and can be adjusted as macroeconomic assumptions and perspectives change. Although the

presentation of categories of spending is fairly aggregated, in principle no categories of spending are excluded from the review and adjustment under the MTEF. Table G.10 provides an illustration of an MTEF in Nicaragua. The MTEF is consistent with sector public investment programs under the National System for Public Investment (SNIP). SIGFA enables sectors and the MoF to review progress made with budget execution and to monitor results measured by a set of indicators. As a consequence, modifications to sector MTEFs can be made in parallel with mid-year budget modifications.

Implementation

Since the MTEF is relatively new, the MoF has been leading its preparation, which involves a series of meetings informing spending agencies about macroeconomic and fiscal constraints for upcoming years and about ceilings. However, during the pilot phase, information on ceilings was not provided at an early stage because social sector salary negotiations were not complete, and agencies were not in a position to discuss their program priorities and expected results. As a result, the allocation of resources across agencies and program structures remained practically unchanged. Since 2007, unions have agreed to advance salary negotiations, and the MoF has been able to generate MTEF ceilings earlier.

The Economic Affairs Analysis Office of the MoF is mainly responsible for revenue forecasting. Revenue forecasting is fully consistent with projections of the IMF as well as the central bank. The same office prepares the macro-fiscal framework, which forms part of the MTEF official documentation that is submitted to the national assembly, accompanying the draft annual budget law. Once the national assembly approves the budget law, the MoF publishes the budget, including the medium-term macro-fiscal targets. In addition, this information is available to the general public through the MoF website.

The learning-by-doing approach to the MTEF rollout has enabled sectors to improve the quality of their MTEFs. However, MTEF quality has been adversely influenced by political factors such as the national elections of 2006. In that year and in 2007, sector programs remained unchanged due to political uncertainty. But in 2008, with the first budget of the new administration, sectors adapted their programs to the priorities of the National Human Development Plan. In addition, the MoF received technical assistance to improve the quality of the MTEF rollout. The MoF could then provide manuals and specific training for officials to facilitate budget formulation and implementation of the MTEF.

Table G.10   MTEF for Secondary Education Sector in Nicaragua, by Program and Subprogram, 2009–14

C$, thousands

Program or subprogram	Actual 2009	Projected 2010	Assigned 2011	Projected 2012	Projected 2013	Projected 2014
Secondary education	617,679	580,018	791,692	100,707	194,657	213,856
Current expenses	468,160	508,729	661,758	4,753	104,753	120,467
Personnel	434,321	497,684	640,409	—	—	—
Nonpersonnel	11,212	7,480	12,736	4,224	104,224	119,858
Materials and supplies	2,343	645	5,013	529	529	609
Current transfers	20,284	2,920	3,600	—	—	—
Capital costs	149,519	71,289	129,934	95,954	89,904	93,389
Program activities	617,679	—	791,692	100,707	194,657	213,856
Current expenses	468,160	—	661,758	4,753	104,753	120,467
Personnel	434,321	—	640,409	—	—	—
Nonpersonnel	11,212	—	12,736	4,224	104,224	119,858
Materials and supplies	2,343	—	5,013	529	529	609
Current transfers	20,284	—	3,600	—	—	—
Capital expenses	149,519	—	129,934	95,954	89,904	93,389
Regular secondary education	—	548,497	—	—	—	—
Current expenses	—	490,438	—	—	—	—
Personnel	—	488,033	—	—	—	—
Nonpersonnel	—	2,051	—	—	—	—
Materials and supplies	—	354	—	—	—	—
Capital expenses	—	58,059	—	—	—	—
Nonregular secondary education	—	31,521	—	—	—	—
Current expenses	—	18,291	—	—	—	—
Personnel	—	9,651	—	—	—	—
Nonpersonnel	—	5,429	—	—	—	—
Materials and supplies	—	291	—	—	—	—
Current transfers	—	2,920	—	—	—	—

Source: Government of Nicaragua 2011.
Note: MTEF = medium-term expenditure framework; — = not available. Nicaragua's currency is the córdoba.

According to independent evaluations, the weak planning capabilities of public entities are a problem. For instance, agreeing to a set of indicators for preparing the MTEF is complicated because the sector strategic plans include different indicators. Although plans have been better aligned with the National Human Development Plan, and thus spending priorities are clearer, the SIGFA does not provide detailed information about factors that might affect the costs of programs and services. Thus, agencies are still unable to cost their programs.

A factor that might counterbalance this limitation is the integration of the Public Investment Plan into budget formulation, which goes some way toward ensuring ownership of the public investment programs. However, the 2006 SNIP misclassified some current expenditure as capital expenditure. Since then, it has applied good international practices to classifying public investment projects, which has improved the quality of the MTEF and its implementation.

The MoF has been producing a medium-term strategy document to support the MTEF rollout every year. However, funding of the MTEF is not linked to proposed results because of the uncertain macro-fiscal framework. In fact, in 2009 only some spending priorities and programs were protected, especially those related to poverty reduction.

No subnational MTEF is included in the overall MTEF yet. The MoF is planning to pilot a subnational MTEF in select municipal governments to strengthen sector MTEFs, especially for the social sectors.

Impact

According to Bank and IMF evaluations, Nicaragua has been able to maintain macroeconomic stability even under the difficult circumstances caused by the global financial crisis. How much of this can be attributed to implementation of the MTEF is debatable. However, the MTEF has forced sectors to recognize medium-term macro-fiscal constraints, and this recognition has supported the MoF in moderating sector expectations about the future availability of resources. Nevertheless, the lack of an updated PEFA report makes it difficult to assess whether the country's quality of budgeting has improved or spending is better prioritized as a result of the MTEF. However, the 2006 PEFA report suggests that budget credibility was a strong point in Nicaragua even before the rollout.

Further consolidation of the MTEF will demand that sectors be better able to plan and adjust their program structure to new priorities and the results achieved by programs. That said, the Swiss carried out three PERs for the education, health, and infrastructure sectors in Nicaragua between 2006 and 2008 that lacked counterpart ownership and therefore did not improve the quality of planning or contribute to discussions about the impact of programs and priorities. In this context, a new technical assistance program aims to train interested public officers to do quick PERs using good international practices.

Influences

The MTEF rollout in Nicaragua can be considered a success largely as a result of the continued political support for fiscal reform in general and the MTEF in particular. Consecutive administrations with different political views regarding economic and social development have promoted the introduction and consolidation of the MTEF. In addition, donors have selected the MTEF as a critical reform and a focus for technical assistance on PFM modernization and budget support. In fact, all budget support matrixes have included a set of indicators and actions to strengthen the MTEF and support implementation. Another positive point is that the Nicaraguan MTEF has been recognized as good regional PFM practice, and neighboring countries have asked Nicaragua to share its MTEF experience.

Russia

Table G.11 summarizes the case study of Russia, which reflects the information on MTEF implementation up to 2011.

Context

Multiyear budgeting in Russia is an important component of a larger PFM reform agenda that has been under way for more than a decade. The government has undertaken several far-reaching reforms aimed at improving the predictability, effectiveness, and transparency of public resource management. These reforms constitute a significant shift from centralized budget management and toward a modern, performance-based budget system with a strong medium-term focus. Initial reforms focused on fiscal discipline and resource allocation. The current agenda emphasizes performance budgeting and efficiency of spending. A chronology of key PFM milestones in Russia is presented in table G.12.

Origins

Budget Code amendments in 2007 introduced three-year budgets implementing part of the PFM reform strategy, Concept for Reforming the Budget Process in 2004–2006. Multiyear budgets were intended to improve fiscal planning and predictability of public spending and better align public spending with public policy priorities. The first multiyear budget covered 2008–10 at the federal level, including all federal ministries, agencies, and services. Since then, the federal budget and the budgets of extrabudgetary funds were authorized for the next budget year and a two-year planning period.

Table G.11   Summary of Case Study of Russia

Issue	Details
Implementation	An MTBF was implemented in 2007, with a shift to an MTPF and program budgeting in 2010. Multiyear budgeting is part of a longer-term agenda for public financial management reform.
Basic features	The three-year budget and appropriations are updated annually. All of federal government spending and two-thirds of general government spending are covered. Discretionary spending can be changed by 10 percent, and nondiscretionary spending can be changed by 5 percent for any line item, but changes must be offset by other spending changes or paid for from additional revenue. Unused budget allocations can be carried over to the next year. There is a contingency reserve.
Macro-fiscal framework	While the Ministry of Finance is responsible for revenue forecasting, the Ministry of Economic Development is responsible for macroeconomic forecasting, which includes oil and gas revenue forecasting. Forecasting is generally conservative, with unbudgeted revenue being added to reserves and used for debt reduction. The MTEF was suspended in 2008 due to the global financial crisis and was relaunched in 2010.
Strategic objectives	Sector development strategies cover 10–20 years, but do not focus on programs, and there is no costing. Strategies are discussed with stakeholders.
Link to budget	Three-year budgeting implies full integration.
Participants and support	The Budget Commission oversees budget formulation, while the Ministry of Finance is lead agency as far as most aspects of public financial management are concerned. The budget process is consultative, with input from think tanks and stakeholders. The government is fully committed to modernization, especially the minister of finance, who has held the post for 10 years.
Institutional capacity	No issues reported.
Performance focus	The performance management system has been piloted for several years, culminating in a new strategy for public financial management reform in 2010 that focuses on results-based management linking all spending to performance indicators.
Quality of budgeting	Fiscal discipline has improved since 2000 in the context of strong economic growth. Public expenditure and financial accountability indicators confirm that budgets are more realistic.
Other issues	The Budget Code addresses the relationship between the budget and the sovereign wealth funds set up to manage price volatility and ensure equity across generations.

Note: MTBF = medium-term budgetary framework; MTEF = medium-term expenditure framework; MTPF = medium-term performance framework.

Table G.12   Chronology of PFM Milestones in Russia, 2000–10

Year	Activity
2000–01	Budget Code (of 1998) entered into force, laying out the basic principles, including constraints on borrowing and deficits and a subnational fiscal rule.
2002	A treasury single account was introduced, transferring federal and regional budget execution to the federal treasury; fiscal decentralization was initiated to lower levels of government.
2003	A new federal law on local self-government was enacted, establishing a two-level system of local government throughout the country and laying the foundation for local self-governance reform.
2004	An Oil Stabilization Fund was established to improve management of oil revenues. The PFM reform strategy (Concept for Reforming the Budget Process in 2004–2006) was approved, simplifying budget classification, differentiating between new and existing expenditure commitments, and introducing performance budgeting instruments (performance reports).
2005	The Federal Law on the Distribution of Assignments between Levels of Government was adopted, delineating functions between federal, regional, and local governments and consistency in spending mandates. An Investment Fund was established to provide financial support and guarantees for public-private partnership projects in infrastructure.
2006	National priority projects were implemented to provide additional resources in the development of the public health, education, housing, and agriculture sectors. A new budget justification was introduced, linking the higher-level results data with inputs.
2007	Three-year budgeting and performance reports were introduced.
2008	The Oil Stabilization Fund was split into a Reserve Fund and a National Welfare Fund. A long-term government strategy was adopted (Concept of Long-Term Socio-Economic Development till 2020) and strategic public investments were identified (Key Areas of the Government Activities till 2012).
2009	A performance instrument for service delivery (public assignments) was introduced,
2010	A new PFM reform strategy was adopted (Concept for Raising the Efficiency of Public Spending till 2012), focusing on results-based management frameworks, linking all spending to performance indicators, efficiency, accountability, and performance, and shifting to program budgeting.

In June 2010, the government issued a new PFM reform strategy (Concept for Raising the Efficiency of Public Spending till 2012), emphasizing the efficiency of public spending and the gradual shift toward programmatic budgeting. The budgets of federal ministries and agencies will eventually be determined in state programs.

Design

Russia adopted a three-year rolling budget framework, updated annually (or as necessary). A unique feature of the Russian approach is that the out-year ministry ceilings are appropriated in the budget year, although the ceilings might be altered slightly during the next budget cycle. The out-year ceilings are less detailed than the budget-year ceilings and represent a spending floor for ministries to plan ahead, improving predictability and preserving some flexibility for sector ministries. The budget formulation procedure is divided into two parts. There is a technical update of the estimates for the upcoming budget year and the first out-year as contained in the previous year's budget (adjusted for inflation), with the addition of the second out-year (current policy estimates).

The three-year budget is the annual budget and therefore is fully integrated with the budget process. It covers 100 percent of the federal budget and 61 percent of the consolidated general government budget. It is disaggregated by line ministries and agencies or, more precisely, by main budget holders (directly translated as main budget fund administrators). With the introduction of program budgeting, the budget is expected to be disaggregated at the program and subprogram level.

Extrabudgetary funds, including the State Pension Fund, the Social Insurance Fund, and the Federal Mandatory Health Insurance Fund (social security funds) are not part of the federal budget. However, the budgets of these funds are considered by parliament together with the federal budget. Regional and local budgets are encouraged to cover three years but may cover one or three years, depending on the specifics of regional legislation. At the beginning of 2008, only about one-third of the regions managed to introduce three-year budgets.

The Budget Code has clear rules for reallocations during budget execution, and these differ for discretionary and mandatory spending:

- For discretionary spending, appropriations for each line item may be increased or decreased by up to 10 percent by the line ministry with approval of the Ministry of Finance.
- For mandatory spending, appropriations may be increased by up to 5 percent in response to underestimated demand under the current entitlement law. These increases must be offset by decreases in other appropriations or by revenue windfalls (revenues in excess of the budget estimates).
- The Budget Code allows the MoF to propose changes to the budget subject to legislative approval through a supplementary budget law

when revenues exceed or are less than budget targets by more than 10 percent.

In addition to the baseline budget allocated to spending units, separate provision is made for a contingency reserve (conditionally approved expenditures) that is unallocated by budget classification and can be used for funding new initiatives or adding funds to previously approved budget lines. The amount of contingency reserve is set at no less than 2.5 percent for the second year (budget year plus one) and 5 percent for the third year (budget year plus two). These contingency reserves are a major instrument providing flexibility for the three-year budgets. Further flexibility is provided by allowing spending unit budget allocations to be carried over to subsequent years with MoF approval. Any reallocations are reconciled when medium-term plans are revised as part of the annual budget process.

The Budget Code also contains three specific reserve funds: one for the president (a fairly discretionary fund), one for the government (also discretionary), and one for emergencies. The total appropriations for these funds cannot exceed 3 percent of the total budget expenditure. The reserve fund of the president cannot exceed 1 percent or one-third of the total amount allocated for all three reserve funds. The funds can be used discretionally through presidential decrees—for instance, to support organizations for disabled children, preserve historical and cultural monuments, and so on. The reserve fund of the government can be used for various purposes, such as top-level meetings, awards for state service, and others listed in the annual budget law. The emergency fund can be used to deal with disasters and emergencies and undertake preventive measures related to those events. The expenditures of these funds are recorded in budget reports by the treasury and the Ministry of Finance.

The Budget Code incorporates a set of fiscal rules:

- The federal budget deficit cannot exceed the total of capital expenditure and interest payments on the public debt (a golden rule).
- Targets are set for the non-oil and gas deficit and for the regular budget balance, and limits are placed on transfers from the Sovereign Wealth Fund to the budget. In 2008, the Oil Stabilization Fund was split into the Reserve Fund to manage revenue volatility and the National Welfare Fund to accumulate intergenerational equity. The assets of the Reserve Fund can be used to finance the federal budget deficit and service external debt. The nominal oil and gas transfer to finance federal

budget expenditure is defined in the three-year budget law. The Reserve Fund is capped at 10 percent of GDP. Revenues above the cap flow to the National Welfare Fund, which is used for transfers to the Pension Fund. Due to the economic crisis of 2009, the federal budget is expected to remain in deficit, which will be financed to a large extent by an extensive drawdown of the Reserve Fund and some external borrowing (see box G.2).

Implementation

The MoF is the core finance agency in charge of most aspects of public financial management. It leads in budget formulation. The budget process

---

Box G.2

Sovereign Wealth Fund

The Oil Stabilization Fund was established in 2004 and is managed by the Ministry of Finance. It was created to manage oil price volatility and foster fiscal discipline. The mineral extraction tax (95 percent of the total or the full amount of the federal share of the tax) and the export customs duty on oil (100 percent) go to the Oil Stabilization Fund. By law, the resources of the fund can be used to finance the federal budget deficit when the oil price exceeds the cut-off price. If the accumulated funds are above 2 percent of gross domestic product (GDP), they can be used to repay foreign debt.

In 2008, the Oil Stabilization Fund was split into the Reserve Fund to hedge against price volatility and the National Welfare Fund to accumulate intergenerational equity. The tax base of the funds was expanded to include the full proceeds of the mineral extraction tax and the export customs duty on gas flows. The nominal oil and gas transfer to finance federal budget expenditure is defined in the three-year budget law. The Reserve Fund is capped at 10 percent of GDP. Revenues above the cap flow to the National Welfare Fund, which is used for transfers to the Pension Fund in accordance with the federal budget law. From 2010 to 2014, oil and gas revenues of the federal budget will be used to finance federal budget expenditures instead of transfer due to the postcrisis fiscal stabilization efforts.

Sources: http://www.minfin.ru/ru/; Kraan et al. 2008.
Note: Oil and gas revenues consist of the oil and gas production tax and export customs duty on crude oil, natural gas, and oil products. In 2008, the total amount of the National Welfare Fund constituted US$32 billion, reaching about US$91 billion as of March 2011. The Reserve Fund was US$125 billion in 2008, but decreased almost fivefold by March 2011, as extensive resources were drawn down to finance anticrisis measures.

involves extensive consultations with the government, the Ministry of Economic Development, line ministries, think tanks, and other stakeholders in the course of policy design and formulation. Official involvement in budget formulation, especially in medium-term budget policy, centers on the Budget Commission, represented by the prime minister, the chair of the legislative budget committee, the ministers of finance and economic development, and line ministries. The line ministries are fully engaged in the process.

Budget formulation commences with circulation of the draft budget schedule, which sets the timetable for negotiations and meetings of the Budget Commission and the government. As noted earlier, the budget process has two stages: one for current or baseline spending and one for new initiatives. The MoF sends out the budget circular with baseline targets to line ministers (basically, total estimates for the first out-year adjusted for inflation). Line ministries, in turn, allocate their baseline three-year targets to budget holders. After final discussions and negotiations, the baseline targets of the federal budget are sent for approval to the Budget Commission and the government.

The process for allocating new funds starts when the Budget Commission and the government determine the size of the envelopes for new spending in the budget year and the size of unallocated envelopes in out-years. The Budget Commission and the government determine ministerial targets for new spending initiatives. Line ministers submit new spending proposals and start negotiations on the total amount and profile of new spending initiatives, amendment of expenditure limits (ministerial totals) for the budget year and the first out-year, expenditure limit (ministerial total) for the second out-year, and reserve funds for the national priority projects. The Budget Commission and the government make the final decision on ministerial budgets for three years. The draft federal budget law is published on the MoF website, and the approved federal budget is published both on the site and in the official newspaper of the government.

The MoF is responsible for revenue forecasting based on tax policies and macroeconomic forecasts. The Ministry of Economic Development prepares macroeconomic forecasts, including oil revenue forecasts. The assumptions underlying forecasts are agreed with the central bank and approved by the Budget Commission, which also resolves disputes between the ministries about the assumptions. The MoF also prepares macroeconomic forecasts, and this creates a certain degree of competition and tension between the ministries.

In recent years, Russia has taken a conservative approach to revenue estimation. The budget is based on conservative price assumptions of its key exports—oil and gas—which makes budget execution more stable in the face of fiscal volatility. Revenues have commonly been underestimated (with the exception of 2008–09, a year of economic crisis). Actual revenue receipts above the budgeted revenues have been used to build up cash reserves and reduce public debt.

Line ministries prepare sector development strategies, which cover a period of 10 to 20 years depending on the sector. The sector strategies sketch out key issues, priorities, and long-term objectives in general terms. They are not broken into programs and do not include costs. Most sector strategies are discussed in some way with key stakeholders. The Concept of Long-Term Socio-Economic Development till 2020 and the Key Areas of the Government Activities till 2012, adopted by the government in 2008, are considered significant steps toward formulating long- and medium-term socioeconomic objectives and priorities.

The performance management system has been evolving, with multiple instruments piloted at different stages of PFM reforms. Box G.3 lists the main instruments of performance management used in Russia. The government has experimented with various instruments, ranging from strategic planning and the use of programs to performance reporting and evaluation. The Program for Enhancing the Efficiency of Public Spending is the government's latest effort to strengthen performance by rationalizing performance instruments, better linking performance results with the budget process, and streamlining performance targets.

Impact and Influences

At the aggregate level, fiscal discipline has been good and budgets have been more realistic, as reflected in standard indicators of deficits and debt, However, this needs to be considered in the context of the overall PFM reform agenda and robust economic performance over the decade. Since 2000, the Russian economy has experienced strong economic growth and relatively favorable external market conditions (for the country's main export commodities), which has significantly improved Russia's fiscal position. The government has also consistently used conservative revenue forecasts and conservative approaches to managing oil revenues, resisting the temptation to overspend (commonly associated with sudden windfalls). The overall situation of Russian public finances has been substantially enhanced, with budget surpluses, lower public debt, and more fiscal reserves.

Box G.3

Key Performance Instruments and Measures in the Russian Federation

Strategic government priority setting (Key Areas of the Government Activities till 2012 or KAGA) contains activities and targets for each sector under broadly identified thematic areas. Most programs entail interministerial and interagency implementation and cover slightly more than one-third of budget expenditure. KAGA projects are planned in alignment with the budget. However, information on actual expenditures is not readily available. KAGA projects are prepared by line ministries.

In May 2004, the MoF issued a regulation on Reports on Results and Main Areas of Activity (DRONDs), obliging all federal ministries, services, and agencies to prepare performance reports with objectives, tasks, and targets for the next three years, including specific performance indicators and budget expenditures broken down by objectives, tasks, and programs. The DRONDs link federal budget expenditures to outcomes and outputs. The reports encompass all federal and departmental earmarked programs as well as nonprogram activities.

Improved budget justifications (justification of expenditure assignments) link budget appropriations by type (public services, earmarked programs, and interbudgetary transfers) with output and outcome indicators.

Improved policy costing (register of expenditure commitments) provides estimates of budget expenditures necessary to fulfill existing public commitments and government functions as specified in the legislation.

Federal earmarked programs are cross-ministerial programs that address complex issues of socioeconomic development and usually cover periods longer than three years. Annual performance reports focus on inputs and outputs rather than outcomes. The new programmatic instrument in Concept for Raising the Efficiency of Public Spending till 2012 intends to incorporate federal earmarked programs into state programs.

Source: World Bank 2011.

In the second half of 2008, like many other countries across the world, the Russian economy was hit hard by the global financial crisis. With the sudden fall in oil prices, reversal of capital flows, and disruption of access to external financing, real GDP dropped significantly. The fiscal surplus turned into a deficit for the first time in a decade. Thanks to the country's strong fiscal position and large reserves prior to the crisis, the government has managed to smooth the negative effects of the economic crisis. In the

Table G.13   Selected PEFA Indicators for the Russian Federation, 2000 and 2010

PEFA indicator and number	2000	2010
Aggregate expenditure out-turn compared to original approved budget (PI-1)	D	B–
Composition of expenditure out-turn compared to original approved budget (PI-2)	n.a.	A
Aggregate revenue out-turn compared to original approved budget (PI-3)	C	B
Multiyear perspective in fiscal planning, expenditure policy, and budgeting (PI-12)	D	A

Source: Estimates (not official PEFA scores) from World Bank 2011.
Note: PEFA = public expenditure and financial accountability; n.a. = not applicable.

medium term, the government is planning to implement a fiscal adjustment plan to reduce the budget deficit, which will take place in the context of efforts to increase the efficiency of budget spending and modernize the public administration.

Although medium-term budgeting in Russia was first introduced in 2007, that effort was suspended under the strains of the economic crisis. The current multiyear budget effort was restarted in the 2010–12 budget cycle. Only two budgets (2010–12 and 2011–13) have been adopted using the medium-term approach, not yet a full three-year cycle. So it is premature to assess the impact or influence of the multiyear innovation itself at this juncture. However, PEFA scores have improved (see table G.13).

At present, Russia would score an A on multiyear perspective in fiscal planning, expenditure policy, and budgeting (PEFA indicator 12). The introduction of multiyear budgets has improved the predictability of public spending, lengthening the fiscal planning horizon for ministries and enabling more robust medium-term planning. The budget is separated into current spending (baseline) and new initiatives, providing more stability and transparency within the medium-term framework. The Russian three-year budget approach also provides a foundation for macro-fiscal discipline by requiring and setting fiscal targets and using fiscal rules.

PEFA scores for aggregate expenditure deviation—deviation in the composition of spending and revenue deviation (PEFA indicators 1–3)— have improved in 2000–10. However, this improved performance reflects the fiscal policies pursued rather than the MTBF itself. In this context, the introduction of medium-term budgeting can be seen as an effort to institutionalize the prudent fiscal policies of the past decade. In Russia, prudent fiscal policies have resulted in the adoption of medium-term frameworks and fiscal rules that have grounded future public finances more firmly, rather than the reverse.

A key factor contributing to the past decade of good fiscal performance and continuous PFM reform has been the government's commitment to modernization and, more important, strong ownership by the MoF, which has been responsible for most aspects of PFM reforms since 2000. The fact that the current minister of finance has been holding the post for the last 10 years has contributed to the continuity and consistency of reform efforts.

South Africa

Table G.14 summarizes the case study of South Africa.

Origins

An MTBF was introduced in 1998. It was not piloted at the central and provincial levels, but it was recognized that the quality of implementation would vary across agencies. A pilot approach was planned for local

Table G.14   Summary of Case Study of South Africa

Issue	Details
Implementation	An MTBF was introduced in 1998, with an MTPF following in 2002.
Basic features	The three-year rolling framework has indicative out-year expenditure ceilings. The MTEF covers all categories of spending at both national and provincial levels.
Macro-fiscal framework	Revenue forecasting has been an area of significant improvement.
Strategic objectives	Sector strategic plans can be a largely pro forma effort to satisfy a formal requirement rather than to inform prioritization decisions. Parliament provides significant strategic guidance.
Link to budget	The MTEF is fully integrated into budget preparation.
Participants and support	The Ministry of Finance is in the lead, but the process is consultative, involving numerous bodies including national and provincial medium-term expenditure committees.
Institutional capacity	Technical capacity at the central level is high, especially at the National Treasury, but provincial governments are weaker.
Performance focus	The initial effort, in 2002, to introduce a performance element into the MTEF was premature, producing information of variable quality that was not used to inform spending decisions.
Quality of budgeting	Neither parliament nor provincial legislatures make full use of MTEF information.
Other issues	The 2011 MTEF is to be driven by activities and outputs specified in service delivery agreements.

Note: MTBF = medium-term budgetary framework; MTEF = medium-term expenditure framework; MTPF = medium-term performance framework.

government. Transition to an MTPF occurred in 2002. The 2012 MTEF aims to improve the cost-efficiency of public spending, in line with the medium-term strategic framework. In addition to complying with the Public Finance Management Act, the 2012 MTEF is driven by the activities and outputs set out in the delivery agreements, based on the medium-term strategic framework. The MTEF database has been reconfigured to reflect the new budgeting approach—that is, to capture the outcomes of service delivery.

The main aims of the MTEF were to forge a link between planning and budgeting, to move away from incremental budgeting, to involve parliament and civil society more in budget decision making, and to increase the output orientation of the budget. The National Treasury was the principal advocate, with widespread support at the top levels of government.

Design

The MTEF is a three-year rolling framework with indicative out-year ceilings. All central and provincial spending agencies and all categories of spending are covered. For central government, the MTEF and budget expenditure classifications are the same. Table G.15 provides a snapshot of an MTEF for the higher education subsector in South Africa.

Expenditure ceilings can be exceeded only with the approval of parliament or provincial legislatures, in line with the adjustments budget. The 2012 MTEF exercise takes place within a much constrained fiscal space; therefore, departments are encouraged to identify funds, including funds for underperforming programs, that can be reprioritized to programs that can achieve identified outcomes in contrast to activities that do not deliver services, such as advertising, vehicle hire, and travel.

Implementation

The National Treasury is in the lead and publishes guidelines on the MTEF, but the MTEF is based on consensus building via consultation between the National Treasury and spending agencies. Numerous bodies are involved in the process: a central government ministers' committee on the budget and provincial budget forums oversee budgets, a Budget Council recommends revenue distributions to provinces, and central and provincial medium-term expenditure committees focus on spending.

The National Treasury proposes initial ceilings based on an assessment of previous performance in the execution of expenditure by spending

Table G.15 Higher Education and Training in South Africa, 2012–14

R, millions

Indicator	Audited outcome			Adjusted appropriation, 2010–11	Revised estimate, 2010–11	Medium-term expenditure estimate		
	2007–08	2008–09	2009–10			2011–12	2012–13	2013–14
Program								
Administration	68.7	84.6	103.3	122.7	122.7	161.6	174.7	185.8
Human resource development, planning, and coordination	27.1	27.1	29.4	26.7	26.7	33.8	35.2	37.2
University education	13,241.0	15,413.0	17,152.8	19,540.3	19,540.3	23,429.5	26,076.5	27,844.5
Vocational and continuing education and training	2,545.3	3,112.5	3,261.4	3,933.3	3,933.3	4,475.4	4,889.2	5,462.9
Skills development	117.1	130.5	137.5	153.2	134.2	128.3	142.9	157.7
Subtotal	15,999.1	18,767.8	20,684.4	23,776.2	23,757.2	28,228.6	31,318.5	33,688.2
Direct charge against the National Revenue Fund	6,284.3	7,234.1	7,815.6	8,424.2	8,424.2	9,148.7	9,606.1	10,134.5
Sector education and training authorities	5,027.4	5,787.3	6,252.4	6,739.4	6,739.4	7,319.0	7,684.9	8,107.6
National Skills Fund	1,256.9	1,446.8	1,563.1	1,684.8	1,684.8	1,829.7	1,921.2	2,026.9
Total	22,283.4	26,001.9	28,500.0	32,200.4	32,181.4	37,377.3	40,924.6	43,822.7
Change to 2010 budget estimate				55.5	36.5	2,124.0	3,462.3	4,300.0
Economic classification								
Current payments	273.9	318.7	332.7	403.2	388.7	455.8	514.4	554.5
Employee compensation	146.2	174.8	201.8	251.6	249.6	301.5	334.1	359.7
Goods and services	127.6	143.9	130.9	151.6	139.1	154.3	180.3	194.8

(continued next page)

227

Table G.15 *(continued)*

Indicator	Audited outcome			Adjusted appropriation, 2010–11	Revised estimate, 2010–11	Medium-term expenditure estimate		
	2007–08	2008–09	2009–10			2011–12	2012–13	2013–14
Computer services	23.3	20.0	16.7	21.7	20.4	27.4	28.9	29.9
Lease payments	12.8	4.2	7.6	2.6	2.6	9.0	10.4	11.2
Property payments	1.8	10.6	10.9	26.9	26.9	45.1	49.6	53.2
Travel and subsistence	31.5	35.8	28.3	39.6	38.6	33.0	41.8	44.6
Transfers and subsidies	21,988.3	25,678.1	28,146.5	31,786.1	31,786.1	36,913.4	40,402.2	43,261.2
Provinces and municipalities	2,435.3	3,005.8	3,155.3	3,804.0	3,804.0	4,326.0	4,705.1	5,262.4
Departmental agencies and accounts	7,606.9	8,872.3	9,690.0	10,462.8	10,462.8	13,232.2	14,941.7	16,057.3
Universities and technical colleges	11,941.5	13,797.4	15,297.2	17,516.7	17,516.7	19,352.7	20,752.9	21,938.8
Foreign governments and international organizations	2.1	2.3	2.2	2.3	2.3	2.4	2.6	2.7
Households	2.5	0.3	1.8	0.3	0.3	—	—	—
Payments for capital assets	4.9	4.9	20.7	11.1	6.6	8.1	8.0	6.9
Buildings and other fixed structures	—	0.6	1.9	—	—	—	—	—
Machinery and equipment	4.8	4.1	14.9	11.0	6.5	8.1	8.0	6.9
Software and other intangible assets	0.1	0.2	4.0	0.1	0.1	—	—	—
Payments for financial assets	16.4	0.1	0.1	—	—	—	—	—
Total	22,283.4	26,001.9	28,500.0	32,200.4	32,181.4	37,377.3	40,924.6	43,822.7

Source: South Africa, National Treasury 2011.
Note: — = not available. South Africa's currency is the rand.

agencies. These ceilings are negotiated with spending agencies based on their sector strategies, and finalized ceilings are reviewed by parliament. The ceiling for the budget year is approved by parliament as part of the budget. Spending agency strategies are revised to reflect approved ceilings. The MTEF is reported to parliament in a medium-term budget policy statement.

The National Treasury takes the lead in revenue forecasting and macro-fiscal modeling. The accuracy of revenue forecasts has improved, with PEFA results as follows: revenue overperformance of 11 percent in 2005–06, 8 percent in 2006–07, and less than 1 percent in 2011–12.

All central and provincial government agencies have been required to produce three-year strategic plans since 2002. These are reviewed by parliament. However, some are no more than pro forma compliance efforts. New initiatives are supposed to be costed, with details provided to central or provincial medium-term expenditure committees. It is unclear how stakeholders can influence the MTEF, other than through parliamentary review. Funding for large and mega infrastructure projects is evaluated by the capital budgets committee.

Spending agencies produce many performance indicators, but these are a mixture of input, output, and outcome indicators and are not used systematically to inform budget decisions.

The National Treasury reviews expenditure bids from both central and provincial spending agencies in light of their sector strategies. Guidance is also provided on health, education, and social development spending by sector committees. While provinces have their own budget process, a uniform budget program classification applies if concurrent functions would be implemented by both the provincial and national governments. In such a case, the national department is responsible for tracking outcomes and expenditure for specific programs across the nine provinces. Otherwise a collaborative sectorwide exercise is applied, led by the National Treasury, in which the provincial budget program classification differs from that of national government.

Impact

MTEF was introduced in the context of high debt, but with a steadily improving fiscal balance. The introduction of the MTEF coincided with a continuing improvement in the country's fiscal position, which contributed to credit-rating upgrades based on a sound macroeconomic situation and strong institutions. Significant expenditure restructuring took place under the Reconstruction and Development Programme.

Underspending by the central government and overspending by provincial governments were long-standing problems. Under- and overspending were both reduced following introduction of the MTEF, although restrictions on carryover limit the former and demanding approval procedures limit the latter.

Influences

Macroeconomic stabilization has been the priority, and while the economy has grown, unemployment and poverty remain high. On the fiscal side, the aim has been to address large fiscal imbalances, poor service delivery, and lack of transparency and accountability.

The post-apartheid government was committed to wide-ranging political, economic, and social change, including budget reforms to support the Reconstruction and Development Programme. In the current economic and political climate, the MTEF facilitates more efficient use of resources but also allows tracking of service delivery targets.

The budget system had many weaknesses, and the MTEF was intended to be the centerpiece of comprehensive budget reform. The payoff is evident in perfect PEFA scores for budget credibility, although overall PEFA scores suggest lingering weaknesses elsewhere. The leadership of the National Treasury and commitment to a collaborative approach have contributed significantly to the success of the MTEF.

Some experience with medium-term budgeting in the 1980s, albeit unsuccessful, meant that the merits of the approach were apparent, as was the fact that industrial countries with Westminster-based budget systems were moving in this direction.

A well-functioning civil service has resulted in the MTEF working well at the central government level, at least at the technical level. The provinces still lag somewhat. Neither parliament nor provincial legislatures make full use of the information provided by the MTEF. Technical capacity is high at the central level, especially at the National Treasury, but relatively low at the provincial level.

The MTEF was largely a South African initiative, informed by good practice elsewhere.

The emphasis was on the adoption of good practices from the outset. The move to use information on performance, which has been unsuccessful, was too early. The Presidency is working on an outcomes-based performance management system, which will focus on targeted strategic outcomes as set out in the medium-term strategic framework. Measurable outputs linked to each outcome will be identified and will guide agreements on priority areas of work.

Uganda

Table G.16 summarizes the case study of Uganda.

Origins

Uganda's MTEF and associated budget framework paper were introduced in 1992. The intention was to improve budgetary allocations within a hard budget constraint, while maintaining macroeconomic stability. The MTEF was developed gradually, starting with aggregate ceilings for broad economic categories of expenditure as part of the response to the macroeconomic and fiscal crisis of the early 1990s. Since 1997, the framework has aimed to provide transparent sector allocations aligned with national development priorities, guided initially by the Poverty Eradication Action Plan (PEAP) and recently by the National Development Plan.

The MTEF was introduced to strengthen fiscal discipline by ensuring that budget allocations are planned within an MTFF consistent with macroeconomic stability. Driven by the objective of maintaining strict control over domestic borrowing, the initial focus was on fiscal aggregates rather than details of expenditure. However, with sustained macro-fiscal stability and growth, the main thrust of public policy shifted toward poverty reduction in 1997. The concern was that sustained economic growth may not deliver a commensurate improvement in the welfare of the poor. The MTEF was then adopted as a mechanism for translating PEAP priorities into resource allocations within a coherent medium-term macro-fiscal framework. The formulation of the MTEF became an integral part of the annual budget preparation process.

The introduction of the MTEF, though originally resisted, was reinforced by a political commitment to fiscal discipline. The political buy-in, particularly from the president, was central to its success. A critical mass of reform-minded politicians and technocrats, as well as donors, was instrumental in sustaining the MTEF. The merger of the finance and planning ministries to form the Ministry of Finance, Planning, and Economic Development (MoFPED) in 1998 was critical in establishing fiscal discipline, while building links between policy formulation, planning, and budgeting.

Table G.16   Summary of Case Study of Uganda

Issue	Details
Implementation	An MTFF was introduced in 1992. A pilot MTBF followed in 1995, with full implementation in 1997.
Basic features	The three-year rolling framework has fixed expenditure ceilings. All central government agencies and spending are covered, although government wages are not subject to MTEF scrutiny. The process of extending the MTEF to local governments began in 2000. A contingency reserve is built into the MTEF.
Macro-fiscal framework	Macroeconomic and fiscal forecasts and projections are coordinated with the International Monetary Fund. Overestimates of tax revenue and donor support have resulted in budget deviations. While tax revenue forecasts have improved, donor support remains unpredictable.
Strategic objectives	Initial emphasis was on achieving macroeconomic stability. Since 1997, allocations have been guided by the Poverty Eradication Action Plan and, more recently, by the National Development Plan. The MTEF is also consistent with the Public Investment Plan.
Link to budget	The MTEF is the centerpiece of a budget framework paper that guides preparation of the annual budget.
Participants and support	The Ministry of Finance is in the lead, aided by strong political support. Spending agencies have become increasingly engaged. Sector working groups play a central role in ensuring that policy priorities are funded and responsive to domestic stakeholder and donor views.
Institutional capacity	Merging the finance and planning ministries allowed for strong leadership and effective management of technical assistance. Implementation capacity at the local level is an issue.
Performance focus	Output-based budgeting was initiated in 2008 with a view to monitoring budget performance. Only a few sectors have made progress with this.
Quality of budgeting	The MTEF has been hailed a success across many dimensions of budgeting. Budget predictability has improved. However, MTEF updates mimic incremental budgeting, and powerful ministries ignore ceilings.
Other issues	Despite success, there are major areas for improvement, including the need to integrate donor financing and projects fully into the MTEF.

Note: MTBF = medium-term budgetary framework; MTEF = medium-term expenditure framework; MTPF = medium-term performance framework.

Design

Uganda's MTEF is a rolling framework covering a three-year period. Allocations serve as hard budget constraints for prioritization and resource use at the sector level. However, out-year ceilings, especially for sectors such as security and public administration and beneficiaries of project aid, are often an unreliable guide to final ceilings.

The MoFPED sets indicative ceilings for sector allocations. Sector working groups then propose changes within the overall sector resource ceiling that are consistent with policy priorities and strategies. Resources can be switched between domestic development and nonwage recurrent categories, but not from personnel (wage) expenditure. The Ministry of Public Service determines wage bill allocations.

All government agencies are covered by the MTEF and categorized by sector. The framework captures all expenditure by central government agencies, excluding arrears payments. Central government projections include fiscal transfers to local governments. The MTEF provides indicative allocations broken down by sector, institution, and priority programs. Table G.17 illustrates an MTEF for the Ministry of Education. The allocations are further divided into wage, nonwage recurrent, domestic development, and donor development expenditures. Aggregates are then consolidated at two levels of funding, Government of Uganda and Government of Uganda plus donor-funded projects. The Government of Uganda budget is funded by domestic revenue, domestic borrowing, and donor budget support, while donor projects are funded by project aid. A multipronged approach—using both a financial programming model and the cost implications of agreed priorities (allocations to local governments are guided by a fiscal decentralization strategy)—is adopted to formulate forward projections. Local governments are covered as votes or as agencies funded under the respective votes and under respective sectors in the MTEF.

The launch of the MTEF was an integral part of a planning and budgeting process promoting a link between policy analysis, planning, and budgeting. Initially, the PEAP and then the National Development Plan served as a national planning framework for the formulation of medium-term sector strategic plans and investment programs produced by the sector working groups. Sector strategic plans are designed to implement sector policy objectives of the PEAP and, in turn, to guide resource allocation within the MTEF. Strategic guidance influences decisions on the following: (a) policy priorities, (b) expenditure prioritization, (c) priority development or capital programs that would constitute the Public Investment Plan, and (d) resource allocations for each sector, program, and the respective institutions.

The MTEF provides indicative sector ceilings for Government of Uganda funding at the start of the budget preparation process in October. The framework also contains information on projected donor aid for projects. A contingency reserve is built into the MTEF to cover new

Table G.17 Past Expenditures and Medium-Term Projections of Education Expenditures in Uganda, by Vote Function

Vote and sector	2007–08 out-turn	2008–09 Approved budget	2008–09 Half one out-turn	MTEF budget projections 2009–10	MTEF budget projections 2010–11	MTEF budget projections 2011–12
Vote: 013 Ministry of Education and Sports						
0701 Preprimary and primary education	—	26.23	—	16.22	14.81	19.02
0702 Secondary education	—	138.52	—	233.00	235.71	262.03
0703 Special needs education, guidance, and counseling	0.50	0.72	0.29	0.82	0.82	1.07
0704 Higher education	6.33	3.70	1.53	10.70	9.70	6.90
0705 Skills development	—	40.39	—	43.04	28.62	45.37
0706 Quality and standards	10.66	17.96	7.34	39.70	40.25	44.89
0707 Physical education and sports	0.96	1.79	0.80	1.79	2.89	3.14
0749 Policy, planning, and support services	10.27	9.58	4.94	7.56	8.06	9.88
Total for vote	—	238.9	—	352.8	340.9	392.3
Vote: 111 Busitema University						
0751 Delivery of tertiary education and research	0.00	8.33	3.70	5.95	6.02	7.22
Total for vote	0.00	8.3	3.7	6.0	6.0	7.2
Vote: 132 Education Service Commission						
0752 Education personnel policy and management	2.73	3.17	1.40	3.17	3.20	3.82
Total for vote	2.7	3.2	1.4	3.2	3.2	3.8
Vote: 136 Makerere University						
0751 Delivery of tertiary education	—	59.25	—	58.47	56.18	64.06
Total for vote	—	59.3	—	58.5	56.2	64.1

Vote: 137 Mbarara University						
0751 Delivery of tertiary education	—	7.55	3.58	11.42	11.39	13.56
Total for vote	—	7.6	3.6	11.4	11.4	13.6
Vote: 138 Makerere University Business School						
0751 Delivery of tertiary education	6.01	6.05	2.56	6.05	6.19	7.33
Total for vote	6.0	6.0	2.6	6.0	6.2	7.3
Vote: 139 Kyambogo University						
0751 Delivery of tertiary education	15.61	15.63	7.60	16.69	19.53	22.85
Total for vote	15.6	15.6	7.6	16.7	19.5	22.8
Vote: 140 Uganda Management Institute						
0751 Delivery of tertiary education	0.41	0.43	0.21	0.43	0.43	0.51
Total for vote	0.4	0.4	0.2	0.4	0.4	0.5
Vote: 149 Gulu University						
0751 Delivery of tertiary education and research	5.62	6.94	—	7.98	10.35	11.88
Total for vote	5.6	6.9	—	8.0	10.4	11.9
Vote: 500>501–850 Local governments						
0781 Preprimary and primary education	388.85	417.03	197.16	417.04	434.75	504.18
0782 Secondary education	103.03	117.70	54.96	117.70	123.59	142.12
0783 Skills development	15. 52	18.35	7.70	18.35	19.17	22.15
0784 Education and sports management and inspection	—	—	—	0.00	0.00	0.00
Total for vote	507.4	553.1	259.8	553.1	577.5	668.5
Total for sector	—	899.3	—	1,016.1	1,031.7	1,192.0

Source: Uganda, Ministry of Finance, Planning, and Economic Development 2009.
Note: — = not available.

priorities or pressing needs endorsed by the cabinet during the budget preparation process.

In principle, the sector working groups are mandated to review and propose changes within the overall Government of Uganda ceilings for the sectors, with clear instructions issued by the MoFPED to prevent underbudgeting for priority and critical expenditures. Further adjustments to the ceilings could be made during negotiations conducted at various levels: (a) budget consultation with sectors led by the MoFPED, (b) discussion of the draft budget framework paper by the cabinet, (c) legislative review of the preliminary MTFF and indicative revenue and expenditure projections by parliament, undertaken before tabling the budget proposals, (d) consultations on salary increments and wage bill allocations led by the Ministry of Public Service, and (e) confirmation of external funding and future-year commitments with donors.

According to the existing legislative framework, unused funds are frozen at the end of the fiscal year. In-year adjustments to appropriations of the budget year are reconciled during rollover of the MTEF.

Implementation

The MoFPED takes the lead in MTEF preparation, allowing both top-down and bottom-up processes for budget preparation. As indicated, the MoFPED prepares the indicative MTEF ceilings that are issued at the start of budget preparation to facilitate the bottom-up process. The reconciliation of bottom-up budget requests with top-down ceilings is handled during (a) sector working group discussions, (b) interministerial budget meetings chaired by the MoFPED, as well as (c) review of the budget framework paper by the cabinet and parliament. Sector working group discussions, chaired by the lead line ministry, provide an opportunity to review previous expenditure performance and to discuss and build consensus on expenditure prioritization and resource allocations for sectors within the MTEF ceilings and results indicators linked to resource allocations. During the interministerial budget meetings, discussion focuses on funding priorities that could not be accommodated within sector ceilings. The recommendations resulting from the consultations, together with the sector submissions, are consolidated into a national budget framework paper, which is forwarded to the cabinet and later parliament. Guidance from both is incorporated into the final MTEF published with the annual budget documentation.

Preparation of the MTEF and budget decisions are guided by an annual budget calendar spelled out in the current legislative framework.

The process starts in September to October with a cabinet retreat to guide macro-fiscal framework and new expenditure priorities for the medium term. The first set of budget guidelines is issued in November to initiate the work of the sector working groups and preparation of the sector budget framework papers, which are integrated into a national budget framework paper in January for consideration by the cabinet and onward submission to parliament by the end of April, as required by the Budget Act 2001. The revised MTEF, guided by decisions from both the cabinet and parliament, together with the second set of budget guidelines are circulated in May to facilitate the preparation of budget estimates. Parliament does not approve medium-term ceilings but does provide strategic guidance on the overall sector priorities and expenditure projections for future years. MTEF ceilings are published in the relevant budget documents—background to the budget, budget speech, and national budget framework paper.

Forward projections are based on a financial programming model. The model provides a coherent framework that links relevant variables (for example, import revenues linked to level of imports). The model treats economic growth as an exogenous variable. The MoFPED and the Government of Uganda collaborate on running the model, with the framework being constantly updated. The macroeconomic and fiscal forecasts and projections are coordinated with the IMF. The MoFPED and the Government of Uganda have taken the lead during the last two to three years. The MTEF adopts more conservative forecasts than the IMF, which has tended to overestimate revenues and budgetary support. The MoFPED's Macroeconomic Department prepares the macro-fiscal framework and sets the resource envelope.

As discussed, sector working groups prepare sector strategic plans and sector budget framework papers. The policy documents are of mixed quality. The strategic plans, if well costed and aligned with priority areas, provide clear programs and reliable indicative recurrent and capital expenditures for the medium term. In practice, however, with the exception of education; health; roads; and justice, law, and order, most sectors do not have realistic strategic plans, and this undermines the prioritization and associated resource allocations within the MTEF. The medium-term projections for some sectors are set primarily on an incremental basis and are not necessarily linked to any assessment of the unit costs of providing a particular level of public service. The sector working groups normally meet twice a year to conduct periodic performance reviews and plan for the expenditure projections and financing. Selected subcommittees meet on a quarterly basis to monitor performance against budget releases and expenditure.

The MTEF accepts the prioritization of projects in the Public Investment Plan, and the budget and plan are fully aligned. However, revisions to the plan are not coordinated with those of the MTEF, and so differences can emerge for out-years.

The MTEF recently reinforced outputs and performance as the main thrust of budgeting, evolving from output-focused budgeting to output-based budgeting. Prior to 2008, sector working groups were mandated to formulate priority programs as well as performance indicators and targets that would demonstrate expected results of the planned expenditures without necessarily directly linking resources and outputs. In 2008, the government launched output-based budgeting with clear objectives: (a) to promote a link between resource allocation and expected outputs or results, (b) to initiate performance-based cash releases, and (c) to facilitate output-based monitoring of budget performance.

The MTEF was extended to local governments in 2000 with the introduction of local government budget framework papers, whose preparation is integrated into the preparation of local government annual budgets and harmonized with central government initiatives. The national MTEF indicates projected aggregate fiscal transfers over the medium term. Central ministries, working closely with the Local Government Finance Commission, use the approved resource allocation criteria to allocate aggregate transfers or grants for each local government. Local governments use information on medium-term transfers or grants to plan and budget for sector allocations in line with national and their own priorities.

Impact

Uganda's decade of implementing the MTEF has greatly improved the quality of budgeting by shifting from the traditional line item budgeting to policy-based budgeting with an increasing focus on outputs and outcomes. The MTEF is judged successful in three important respects. First, it reinforced the formulation of sound fiscal policy at the aggregate level by ensuring that medium-term budgets are planned within a robust macro-fiscal framework fully consistent with macroeconomic policy objectives. Second, it improved alignment of the intersectoral budget allocations with strategic priorities in the PEAP and enhanced predictability of funding necessary for their implementation in the medium term. Third, the formation and effective operation of sector working groups improved prioritization and budget planning at the sector and institutional levels.

As with any budgeting tool, several constraints have limited the efficacy of the framework. Some critical aspects of the framework—for instance, integrating project aid into the ceilings—have proved difficult to implement. Experience demonstrates that the MTEF cannot solve many deep-rooted problems in budgeting. Tackling these problems is essential if the MTEF is to be a more effective tool of budgetary resource allocation.

The MTEF has provided greater certainty to the budget process and simplified budget preparation and negotiation. However, there are doubts about the transparency of decisions with regard to sector resource ceilings, since these are decided by the MoFPED at the start of the budget process (often based on projected revenue), with little discussion. Budget deviations have also continued, mainly due to overestimates of tax revenue and donor support.

With the introduction of the MTEF, the predictability of the budget has improved significantly, allowing spending agencies to plan and manage their expenditures properly. Domestic revenue projections have improved over time, with shortfalls becoming smaller. However, variations between projections and actual disbursements of donor budget support remain mainly due to deficiencies of government systems, particularly procurement that delays disbursements, which distort proposed schedules. This causes severe disruptions to implementation of the budget. To minimize disruptions, the government has provided buffers and allowed domestic borrowing in response to shortfalls in budget support.

Expenditure allocations for priority programs have become more reliable, providing an incentive for better prioritization and planning of expenditure across sectors and programs. However, significant deviations between appropriated budgets and out-turns continue to occur for discretionary expenditures on nonpriority programs.

The MTEF and the budget process are well integrated. Uganda's MTEF has provided a mechanism for integrating the National Development Plan within the budget process, for linking expenditure planning at the central and local government levels, and for introducing medium-term budgeting to local governments. Nevertheless, there are problems: the strategic MTEF and budget framework paper stage is not separated sufficiently from the preparation of detailed budget estimates; routine updates of the MTEF through the year can mimic an incremental budgeting process; and the budget framework paper is presented to the cabinet in March before the budget has been finalized, with little opportunity to review strategic budget choices.

Influences

The MTEF was implemented after a period of war and economic crisis. Uganda started by establishing greater fiscal discipline and the macrofiscal framework for its MTEF. Focus then shifted toward sector resource allocations and broader stakeholder participation. Uganda's economic growth has provided the enabling environment for introduction of the MTEF (predictability for budget planners, increasing real levels of public sector resources, improvements in the performance of public services, and increased institutional capacities, albeit not linked to more realistic remuneration levels). The MTEF has been credited with contributing to sustained macroeconomic stability and facilitating the shift in expenditure composition toward policy priorities guided by the National Development Plan.

The MTEF received strong political support from the president (although the State House has been one of the worst transgressors in keeping its budget within the MTEF ceiling). Line ministries and ministers have become increasingly engaged in the MTEF process. The MoFPED initiated the MTEF in Uganda; it was not prompted by donors. Since 1997, the MTEF has been used as a tool for broadening stakeholder involvement and for engaging donor agencies in the budget.

The budget framework paper has been presented in the form of a cabinet memorandum with very limited circulation, which has undermined the transparency of the MTEF process. Other issues have also affected the quality of public financial management: (a) the rollout of the integrated financial management information system, intended to improve monitoring of budget performance, has been slow; (b) the role of the budget framework paper in the budget cycle needs to be clarified; (c) the MoFPED lacks a mechanism for projecting expenditure at the project and sector level; (d) expenditure planning needs to be less fragmented to allow the sector working groups to consider trade-offs between categories of public expenditure; (e) recurrent and development expenditures are not integrated within a single budget; (f) information on donor-financed projects remains insufficiently integrated into the budget planning process; and (g) the ability to scrutinize performance results is low, with in-depth assessment left to budget monitoring and accountability reports that focus on one or two sectors per quarter. Reflecting these issues, Uganda's PEFA scores for budget credibility are quite low; it is surprising that neither the 1999 nor the 2003 ROSC refers to the role of the MTEF.

Merging the finance and planning ministries has significantly facilitated MTEF introduction. The MoFPED has provided strong leadership and effectively managed technical assistance, which institutionalized the MTEF. However, public administration reform remains problematic. Spending on select areas of public administration that do not benefit the entire sector is crowding out spending in other sectors, and planned reductions in this spending may have been unrealistic. Lack of capacity has been a problem with MTEF implementation and decentralization.

The MTEF was used as an umbrella for a donor-supported PFM initiative. There has been a close relationship between MTEF and the Bank's PER exercise. Donors have played a supporting role with the provision of technical assistance, but without dedicated project assistance to support MTEF implementation. The MTEF is closely integrated with the PRSP process. Macroeconomic and fiscal forecasts and projections are coordinated with the IMF.

The MTEF does not adequately address trade-offs between expenditure on the wage bill and other categories at the sector level. External project financing is not yet fully integrated into the MTEF resource ceilings. Donor-financed investment allocations are separate from the MTEF process, which represents a potentially softer budget constraint for line ministries. Projections of external financing continue to be subject to significant variation both between MTEFs and in comparison with outturn figures. Finally, analysis of public expenditure priorities continues to focus on sectors and programs associated with the National Development Plan. There is a need to strengthen analysis and review of expenditure programs outside of the programs that are priorities under the National Development Plan.

References

Government of Armenia. 2011. "Medium-Term Public Expenditure Framework of the Republic of Armenia for 2001–2013." http://www.gov.am/files/docs/706.pdf.

Government of the Republic of Korea. 2010. "Korea National Fiscal Management Plan, 2010–14." Seoul.

Government of Nicaragua. 2011. "Marco presupuestario de mediano plazo, 2011–2014." Managua.

Holmes, M., and A. Evans. 2003. "A Review of Experience in Implementing Medium-Term Expenditure Frameworks in a PRSP Context: A Synthesis of Eight Country Studies." Overseas Development Institute, London.

Kraan, D.-J., D. Bergvall, I. Hawkesworth, V. Kostyleva, and M. Witt. 2008. "Budgeting in Russia." OECD *Journal on Budgeting* 8 (2): 1–58.

South Africa, National Treasury. 2011. "Estimates of National Expenditure 2011." Johannesburg, February 23.

Uganda, Ministry of Finance, Planning, and Economic Development. 2009. "National Budget Framework Paper FY 2009/10–FY 2013/2014." Kampala, March.

World Bank. 2011. "Performance Management (PM) in Russia." World Bank Policy Note prepared for the Ministry of Economic Development of the Russian Federation. World Bank, Washington, DC, January.

———. Forthcoming. "Public Finance Management." In *Public Administration in Russia: Analysis of a Decade of Reform*, draft chapter as of February 16, 2011. Washington, DC: World Bank.